"Clear, comprehensive, and brilliant; an indispensable resource for teachers, administrators, policymakers, and anyone interested in helping the next generation thrive. The sensible, practical strategies for inclusive education that the authors present in this marvellous book will support the wellbeing and scholastic success of every sort of young mind."

– Nick Walker, Professor of Psychology, California Institute of Integral Studies

"I love the whole book. It is such a nourishing and hopeful read. I think what has stood out to me most is that the book takes us forward. There is so much to complain about in education, but this put a fire in my belly."

– Kerry Murphy, Early Childhood Specialist

"This inspiring book offers practical, evidence-based strategies to help schools create environments where neurodivergent students feel they belong, can achieve, and will truly thrive. The UK government's desire to support all neurodivergent children makes this essential reading, but it is a powerful resource for everyone committed to inclusive education globally."

– Professor Mark Mon-Williams, University of Leeds and Bradford Institute for Health Research

"This is a brilliantly accessible book covering practical ways to implement neurodiversity-affirming approaches that will benefit all. Essential reading for practitioners."

– Victoria Honeybourne, Neurodiversity Specialist and Author

"A much-needed book that offers excellent insight into what changes and adaptations neurodivergent children deserve at school. Powerful writing and powerful advocacy."

– Pete Wharmby, autistic Author and Speaker

"If this book were a food it would fulfil three vital requirements: incredibly delicious, utterly nutritious, and easy to digest. I would recommend it to anyone with an appetite for learning about neurodivergent-affirming practice within education. A brilliant read."

– Dr Luke Beardon, The Autism Centre, Sheffield Hallam University

"The book is packed with valuable insights. I only wish something like this had been available when my son needed it. The range of perspectives brings real depth, with something for everyone to take away. I know some of the contributors personally, and they are well-deserving of being included, their voices add authenticity and meaning. Every institution should have a copy."

– Dr Venessa Swaby, Autistic Speaker, Founder A2ndvoice CIC and AT Autism Associate

It Takes All Kinds of Minds

It Takes All Kinds of Minds provides an inspiring and accessible introduction to neurodiversity in educational settings, informed by research and real-world experience.

Drawing upon core principles that underpin the neurodiversity paradigm, the book offers a carefully curated collection of chapters exploring many different kinds of minds and how they can best learn and flourish at school. The book is divided into three main parts: "Environments," "Practice and Pedagogy," and "Relationships in and around School," with each chapter underpinned by values of care, inclusion, celebration of difference, and the collective power of diverse minds. Pioneering contributions help to realise a vision of environments, relational systems, and pedagogical practices that are designed for all minds, learners, and educators.

Placing a focus on amplifying neurodivergent voices and having a direct impact on practice, this book is essential reading for practitioners at all stages of teacher education and professional development, as well as clinicians and outside agencies that work in partnership with schools.

Rachael Davis is a lecturer in Psychology and Education at Queen Margaret University, Edinburgh. Informed by her experiences as a teaching assistant, Rachel's current research prioritises neurodivergence voices to inform best practice in educational settings. She is a strong advocate of public engagement and community outreach, ensuring that research is accessible for everyone.

Claire O'Neill is an experienced teacher and teacher-educator, working in the areas of inclusion, neurodiversity, and wellbeing. She is also a writer and researcher, and shared her participatory autism research at the *It Takes All Kinds of Minds* conference in 2023. Claire's lived experience as a neurodivergent parent of two neurodivergent children informs both her professional work and research.

Sue Fletcher-Watson is a Professor of Developmental Psychology at the University of Edinburgh and was Co-Chair of the *It Takes All Kinds of Minds* conference in March 2023. Her recent research has focused on investigations of the Double Empathy Problem in cross-neurotype interactions, and on the application of the neurodiversity paradigm to methods of school support. Sue uses co-production methods in all her work and is an advocate for neurodivergent leadership in research. She is also a parent of two neurodivergent children.

It Takes All Kinds of Minds

Fostering Neurodivergent Thriving at School

Edited by Rachael Davis,
Claire O'Neill and
Sue Fletcher-Watson

LONDON AND NEW YORK

Designed cover image: *Maclean Creative, Edinburgh, copyright and reproduced with kind permission from Salvesen Mindroom Centre, Edinburgh*

First published 2026
by Routledge
4 Park Square, Milton Park, Abingdon, Oxon OX14 4RN

and by Routledge
605 Third Avenue, New York, NY 10158

Routledge is an imprint of the Taylor & Francis Group, an informa business

© 2026 selection and editorial matter, Rachael Davis, Claire O'Neill and Sue Fletcher-Watson; individual chapters, the contributors

The right of Rachael Davis, Claire O'Neill and Sue Fletcher-Watson to be identified as the authors of the editorial material, and of the authors for their individual chapters, has been asserted in accordance with sections 77 and 78 of the Copyright, Designs and Patents Act 1988.

All rights reserved. No part of this book may be reprinted or reproduced or utilised in any form or by any electronic, mechanical, or other means, now known or hereafter invented, including photocopying and recording, or in any information storage or retrieval system, without permission in writing from the publishers.

For Product Safety Concerns and Information please contact our EU representative GPSR@taylorandfrancis.com. Taylor & Francis Verlag GmbH, Kaufingerstraße 24, 80331 München, Germany.

Trademark notice: Product or corporate names may be trademarks or registered trademarks, and are used only for identification and explanation without intent to infringe.

British Library Cataloguing-in-Publication Data
A catalogue record for this book is available from the British Library

ISBN: 9781032796215 (hbk)
ISBN: 9781032796222 (pbk)
ISBN: 9781003493044 (ebk)

DOI: 10.4324/9781003493044

Typeset in Optima
by Deanta Global Publishing Services, Chennai, India

Dedicated to the memory of Alastair Salvesen, visionary, philanthropist, and staunch supporter of the It Takes All Kinds of Minds conference.

Contents

Editor Biographies — xv
Contributors — xvii
Acknowledgements — xxiv
Preface — xxvi
Glossary — xxviii
Introduction — xxxi

Part I Introduction: Environments – Edited by Sue Fletcher-Watson — 1

1 Using Outdoor Spaces to Support Neurodiversity-Affirmative Playtime in Schools — 3
Catherine Watson

Introduction — 3
Strategies for Schools — 4
References — 16

2 Space to Be Myself: Getting Play and Breaktimes Right for Neurodivergent Pupils — 20
Jenny Gibson and Samantha Friedman

The Importance of Play for Children's Development and Education — 20
Overview of Breaktimes — 22
Neurodiversity and School Breaktimes — 23
Neurodiversity-Affirmative Play for Education beyond Breaktimes – the Example of Forest School — 27
Practicalities of Creating an Inclusive Play Culture — 29
Summary — 30
Acknowledgements — 31
References — 31

Contents

3 Understanding and Meeting the Sensory Needs of Neurodivergent Learners: Implementing and Evaluating the Use of Flexible Seating in an Inclusive Primary School   **35**
Heba Al-Jayoosi and Laura Crane

Understanding and Meeting the Sensory Needs of Neurodivergent Learners	35
The Context: Mayflower Primary School	37
About Flexible Seating	39
Implementing and Evaluating Flexible Seating: A Partnership Approach	40
Introducing the Project to Staff and Pupils	43
Pupil Voice	45
Staff Voice	47
Acknowledgements	50
References	50

4 Harris Trust SPaRKs Music Project: Informing Creative Learning and Skills for Neurodivergent Teenagers   **52**
Jane Macdonell, Sam Johnston, Devin Casson, and David Calver

Introduction	52
How SPaRKs Began	53
SPaRKs in 2023–4	55
Developing the Programme for 2024–5	63
Acknowledgements	66

Part II Introduction: Practice and Pedagogy – Edited by Claire O'Neill   **67**

5 Creating Inclusive Learning Spaces: A Personal Journey, 30 Years in the Making   **71**
Gareth D. Morewood

Introduction	71
The Foundations	72
Five Core Elements	73
Models That Use the Five Core Elements	79
Conclusion	82
References	84

6 Embracing Monotropism and Flow — 86
Fergus Murray and Helen Edgar

What Is Monotropism?	86
The Power of Framing	88
Can't Not Won't	89
Radical Inclusion	90
Meeting Needs through Flow	92
Trust and Belonging	94
Recommendations for the Classroom	94
Conclusion	96
References	99

7 Embedding a Humanising, Compassionate Pedagogy for Collaborative Learning in the Neurodiverse Classroom — 102
Elaine McGreevy

Introduction	102
A Strained, Inequitable Education System	102
The Double Empathy Problem in the Classroom	105
Towards a Socially Just, Neuro-Inclusive, Compassionate Pedagogy	107
Bridging the Double Empathy Gap	108
Applying Self-Determination Theory to Collaborative Learning	110
References	114

8 Informing Educational Practice by Supporting, Listening to, and Acting upon the Voices of Neurodivergent Learners — 119
Craig Goodall

Introduction	119
Pitfalls to Avoid	121
Authentically Garnering the Voices of Neurodivergent Learners	123
Other Practical Approaches	129
References	132

9 ITAKOM and Intersectionality — 134
Frances Akinde

Background and Positionality	134
Introduction: The Personal Experiences of Educators Matter	135

Intersectionality	138
Supporting the Intersectional Learner	139
Intersectionality, Neurodivergent Staff, and Inclusive Schools	143
Conclusion	144
References	146

10 Character Strengths: Changing the Language to Change Expectations — 148
Clara O'Byrne

Introduction	148
Positive Psychology and Positive Education	148
Character Strengths	151
Language, Character Strengths, and the Neurodiversity Paradigm	153
The Struggle to Implement Changes	155
Classroom Applications	159
Recommended Reading	160
References	160

11 Universal Design for Learning in a Neurodiverse World — 164
Margaret Flood

Thinking about Neurodiversity and Variability in Education	164
What Is UDL?	166
Multiple Means of Engagement	167
Conclusion	177
References	177

Part III Introduction: Relationships in and around School – Edited by Rachael Davis — 179

12 The Learning About Neurodiversity at School Programme in the Context of Neurodiversity-Affirmative Practice — 183
Alyssa M. Alcorn, Amy Nic Thaidhg, and Alun Flynn

Introduction	183
Background: The LEANS Programme	184
Neurodiversity Teaching as a Situated Undertaking	186
LEANS and Neurodiversity-Affirmative Practice	190
A Conversation on LEANS and Practice	191

	Conclusion	195
	References	198
13	**Empowering Neurodivergent Young People: Insights from a School-Based Peer Support Initiative**	**199**
	Francesca Fotheringham, Katie Barrowman, and Justine Young	
	Neurodivergent Young People in Mainstream Schools	199
	Support for Neurodivergent Young People	201
	Peer Support	203
	The NEST Project	204
	Piloting the NEST Handbook	207
	Challenges to Consider from the Pilot Schools	209
	Success Stories from the Pilot Schools	211
	Acknowledgements	213
	References	213
14	**Islands of Safety: The Importance of Non-Teacher-Educators in Curating Felt Safety for Autistic Children and Young People**	**216**
	Kieran Rose	
	Into the Storm	216
	Drowning at Sea: Experiences of Autistic Children and Young People in School	217
	Offering a New Lens to Explore Difference	219
	A Temporary Life Preserver: What Is an Island of Safety?	224
	Swimming against the Tide: Becoming and Curating an Island of Safety	226
	Returning to the Storm	229
	References	232
15	**The LISTEN Framework: Fostering a Values-Led Neurodiversity-Affirmative Climate in Schools**	**234**
	Paula Prendeville	
	What Is the LISTEN Meta-Framework, and Who Is It For?	234
	L: Leadership and Language	235
	I: Integrity and Intersectionality	239
	S: Systems, Space, and Sensory Sensitivities	242
	T: Trauma-Informed Practice, Transitions, Trust, and Time	248

　　　　E: Empathy, Equity, and Ethical Practice　　　　　　　　254
　　　　N: Neurodiversity-Affirmative Needs-Based Planning　　257
　　　　Reference　　　　　　　　　　　　　　　　　　　　　　258

16　Conclusion: A Shared Journey Forward　　　　　　　259

　　　　Navigating the Path: Acknowledging Challenges and
　　　　　　Embracing Possibilities　　　　　　　　　　　　　259
　　　　Core Understandings That Support Neurodiversity-Affirmative
　　　　　　Practice　　　　　　　　　　　　　　　　　　　　260
　　　　Charting Your Course: Practical Steps for Embracing Change　261
　　　　A Final Invitation　　　　　　　　　　　　　　　　　　263

　　　　Index　　　　　　　　　　　　　　　　　　　　　　　265

Editor Biographies

Rachael Davis

I am a lecturer in Psychology and Education at Queen Margaret University, Edinburgh. Most of my research has focused on neurodivergence, identity, cognition, and education. Informed by my experiences as a teaching assistant, my current research prioritises neurodivergence voices to inform best practice in educational settings (including young people and adult learners). I am also a strong advocate of public engagement and community outreach, ensuring that research is accessible for everyone.

Claire O'Neill

I am a teacher and teacher-educator, working in the areas of inclusion, neurodiversity, and wellbeing. I like to write and research, and shared my participatory autism research at the *It Takes All Kinds of Minds* (*ITAKOM*) conference in March 2023. I am continually exploring the use of creative and innovative methods in my teaching and research. I am a neurodivergent parent of two neurodivergent children, and this lived experience informs my professional work and research.

Editor Biographies

Sue Fletcher-Watson

I am a neurotypical (or thereabouts) parent of neurodivergent children. I am also a Professor of Developmental Psychology at the University of Edinburgh, and I was Co-Chair of the *It Takes All Kinds Of Minds* (*ITAKOM*) conference in March 2023 in Edinburgh. My recent research has focused on investigations of the Double Empathy Problem in cross-neurotype interactions, and on the application of the neurodiversity paradigm to methods of school support. I use co-production methods in all my work and I am an advocate for neurodivergent leadership in research.

Contributors

Frances Akinde is a former headteacher, experienced Special Educational Needs and Disabilities (SEND) advisor, and author of *Be an Ally, Not a Bystander*. With over 20 years' experience in education, she has worked across mainstream, special, and alternative provision, as well as local authority settings. Frances is neurodivergent, has a hearing impairment, and uses her lived experience to champion inclusion, equity, and anti-racism in schools and workplaces. She is a certified Workplace Adjustments Assessor, co-founder of the BAMEed SEND hub, and a national speaker on allyship and intersectionality. Her work focuses on empowering others to create environments where every learner and adult feels seen, heard, and safe.

Alyssa M. Alcorn is a lecturer in the School of Psychological Science at the University of Bristol. Her main research interests focus on using the neurodiversity paradigm and participatory methods to develop evidence-based interventions that facilitate children's and young people's educational inclusion and wellbeing. Previously, she was based at the University of Edinburgh Division of Psychiatry as the research and impact lead for the Learning About Neurodiversity at School project. She has also worked at the Centre for Research in Autism and Education at the University College London Institute of Education, and the University of Edinburgh School of Informatics, UK.

Heba Al-Jayoosi is a Churchill Fellow and Assistant Headteacher and Inclusion Leader at Mayflower Primary School, an outstanding and highly inclusive primary school in the heart of the East End of London. She is also seconded as a deputy regional lead at Whole School SEND (a consortium hosted by the National Association for Special Educational Needs). Heba is undertaking a PhD at University College London's Institute of Education, exploring ways to improve family–school partnership for caregivers of autistic pupils from culturally and linguistically diverse backgrounds.

Contributors

Katie Barrowman is an education officer for inclusion with a local authority, and previously ran a provision for young people with additional support needs in a city school. She is passionate about inclusion and lifelong learning, and loves working with like-minded colleagues to make schools the best they can be for our learners.

David Calver relocated from East Anglia to the Scottish Borders in 2022 after 18 years in the education sector as a senior leader specialising in curriculum and leadership development. Having led and developed numerous change management programmes and teams within the education sector, David believes passionately in the merits of embedding a supportive coaching and mentoring culture within organisations to develop leaders at all levels and to prioritise staff health and wellbeing. As Chief Officer at YouthBorders, David's vision is of a collaborative, well-connected, and supportive sector whose members champion and encourage each other's successes. He aims to develop a systems-thinking approach to leadership within the youth sector which places equity of opportunity and wellbeing of young people at the core of every leader's decision making.

Devin Casson is a young singer-songwriter and solo musician based in the Scottish Borders. He is an emerging talent in Scotland's live music scene, and a tutor for school students at the Harris Trust's SPaRKs Project.

Laura Crane is Professor of Autism Studies at the University of Birmingham, UK, where she is Director of the Autism Centre for Education and Research (ACER) and Director of Research for the School of Education. The goal of Laura's work is to conduct research on topics that matter to autistic people and their allies through working in collaboration with them. Laura has a particular interest in improving the educational experiences of autistic children and young people through research-informed practice and practice-informed research.

Helen Edgar is late-identified autistic and a parent to two neurodivergent children. Helen worked for over 20 years as an early years/primary teacher, specialising in supporting children with profound and multiple learning disabilities in SEND settings near Birmingham, UK. In 2022, Helen founded Autistic Realms, a platform dedicated to advocating for neurodiversity-affirmative education and training, and providing accessible community resources.

Helen has a deep interest in how the theory of monotropism can help make sense of autistic experiences, particularly in relation to flow states, burnout, and supporting wellbeing.

Margaret Flood is an Assistant Professor in Inclusive and Special Education at Maynooth University, Ireland. With a background in special education teaching, curriculum and policy development, and teacher professional learning, Margaret is passionate about Universal Design for Learning (UDL) and inclusive education. She has led inclusive curriculum initiatives and supported professional development nationally and internationally at local, institution, and government agency level. As a Fulbright Scholar, she collaborated with the Centre for Applied Special Technology (CAST) on the UDL Guidelines 3.0. Margaret also hosts the podcast *Talking about All Things Inclusion*.

Alun Flynn is an experienced Health and Care Professions Council-registered Educational Psychologist, most recently Principal in Powys, mid-Wales, UK for 27 years. During this time he chaired the National Association of Professional Educational Psychologists in Wales/Cymru. He is currently a locum for the Jersey Government. An Aberdeen University Psychology graduate, Alun completed a PGCE at Cambridge, UK before teaching in a special school for children with complex needs. He also completed an educational psychology MSc at University College London before working in roles including Senior Educational Psychologist with Service Children's Education in Germany, and Associate Lecturer with the Open University in the UK. He holds a professional doctorate from the University of East London. He has published on various themes.

Francesca Fotheringham was the research lead for the Neurodiversity Peer Support Toolkit project, as outlined in Chapter 13. Francesca is currently a trainee educational psychologist studying for a Doctorate in Educational, Child & Adolescent Psychology at Queen's University Belfast, with a background in both research and practice. Francesca has worked in multiple pupil support roles across primary, secondary, and tertiary education as well as in additional support needs specialist provisions. She has also completed a PhD in children's emotional development and led research projects in student wellbeing and neurodiversity.

Contributors

Samantha Friedman is a Lecturer in Applied Psychology at the University of Edinburgh, UK, where she is a member of the Developmental Psychology in Education Research Group within Moray House School of Education and Sport. Samantha's research focuses on critical perspectives on autism, nature, wellbeing, and the intersection of these topics. She is particularly interested in supporting autistic and otherwise neurodivergent young people through nature-based learning and play.

Jenny Gibson is Professor of Neurodiversity and Developmental Psychology at the Faculty of Education, University of Cambridge, UK, where she leads the Play and Communication Lab research group and is also Co-Director the centre for research on Play in Education, Development and Learning (PEDAL), and Co-Director of the Centre for Human-Inspired Artificial Intelligence (CHIA). Jenny has long been fascinated by the connections between linguistic and social aspects of child development. Most of her research investigates this link, usually with neurodivergence, play, and mental health as key topics. Jenny is also a qualified speech and language therapist, specialising in autism and developmental language disorder.

Craig Goodall is currently an Advisory Teacher for the Autism Advisory and Intervention Service in the Education Authority Northern Ireland, having previously spent 13 years teaching young people in an Education Other Than At School (EOTAS) provision in that region, working extensively with autistic students whose needs were not met by mainstream education. He serves as an Associate Lecturer (Autism) and MEd dissertation supervisor at St Mary's University College, Belfast, Northern Ireland, and has been an MEd Autism dissertation supervisor at Dublin City University, Ireland. Craig has published widely, including his book *Understanding the Voices and Educational Experiences of Autistic Young People: From Research to Practice*.

Sonny Hallett is a counsellor, writer, and illustrator based in Edinburgh. They are trans, mixed race, and autistic. Their work is mostly focused on neurodiversity, queerness, and other intersecting experiences of difference, as well as on how therapy might work better for minoritised populations. They hope that their writing and illustration might help others broaden their understanding and imaginations around different ways of being and experiencing the world.

Samuel Johnston is the Creator and Lead Tutor for the Harris Trust's SPaRKs Project. Sam's passion for music stems from his love for creativity and diverse thinking. After performing as a live artist and songwriter since 2018 and finishing his BA Hons in Music and Sound through the University of West London, Sam wanted to give young people the opportunity to immerse themselves in the early stages of being part of the music industry. Sam is a live musician and songwriter whose work can be found in the Scottish Borders-based band Three Out Of Four. He has since moved on to theatrical projects and has been involved in numerous productions, both as a performer in shows such as *American Idiot* and *Rent* at the *Edinburgh Fringe Festival*, and *School of Rock* at the Theatre Royal in Glasgow, UK with Shine Productions. In 2025, Sam was accepted into the Royal Conservatoire of Scotland for a Post-Graduate Diploma Course in Musical Theatre Directing.

Jane Macdonell is the founder of the Scottish Borders-based charity the Harris Trust. She created the trust in 2021 after the death of her son Harris. The aims of the Harris Trust are to provide music, sport, and outdoor learning opportunities for children and young people with a particular emphasis around supporting mental wellbeing and embracing neurodiversity. Jane previously worked for the National Health Service as a Consultant Paediatrician.

Elaine McGreevy is a neurodivergent speech and language therapist, trainer and author. She works with autistic children and young people in an independent neurodiversity-affirmative practice. Prior to this, she worked for 25 years in Autism and Child Development Services in the National Health Service, providing support to neurodivergent children in their homes, schools, and early years settings, She is co-founder of Divergent Perspectives, and offers training to support practitioners to transform their practice to align with the principles of the neurodiversity paradigm.

Gareth Morewood has been involved in education for over 30 years. For the last six years he has been the Educational Advisor for Studio III (www.studio3.org), previously having worked for 25 years in UK schools, during 17 of which he led specialist provision in a large, inclusive secondary school in the North of England. Gareth has extensive front-line experience supporting schools and families, and working directly with young people in the UK and abroad, notably in Chile, Dubai, Portugal, Ireland, Gibraltar, and across Scandinavia. With Andy McDonnell, Gareth developed the LASER Approach, which fuses his critically acclaimed Saturation Model (Morewood, Humphrey & Symes, 2011) with Low Arousal approaches (McDonnell & Deveau, 2018) as part of a system-led model of inclusive practice.

Fergus Murray is an autistic writer, science tutor, and community organiser. They co-founded the Autistic Mutual Aid Society Edinburgh, UK, with their partner Sonny Hallett and others in 2017, and started Weird Pride Day (on 4 March) in 2021. Fergus is especially interested in the role of flow states in autistic learning and wellbeing, and also in the flowing movement of water, which often occupies their attention completely. Fergus writes about neurodiversity, science, and politics on their Medium page, and runs monotropism.org with help from co-author Helen Edgar.

Amy Nic Thaidhg is a primary school teacher with experience of teaching in Ireland, Scotland, Switzerland, and the USA. She initially specialised in Special Educational Needs, and has masters degrees in Education and Psychology. As a Fulbright Fellow in New York, her final project addressed how to successfully support educators to meet the needs of learners with dyslexia. She is a panel member for Dyslexia Scotland's General Teaching Council for Scotland recognition programme, and mentors colleagues across Scotland regarding dyslexia provision. Amy was a member of the design team that developed the Learning About Neurodiversity at School project, and has completed research in the areas of neurodiversity, e-learning, and learning for sustainability.

Clara O'Byrne is a Chartered Psychologist with over 25 years' experience of working in special education and disability advocacy. A former National Council for Special Education advisor and special school teacher, she runs a private practice in West Cork, Ireland. Clara has published research on disability and stigma in peer-reviewed journals. Her interests include supporting schools and parents to work in partnership to centre neurodiversity-affirmative approaches and post-diagnosis/identification support for neurodivergent teens and adults. Clara is a neurodivergent person and parent to multiply neurodivergent children, and combines her personal experience with her professional knowledge.

Paula Prendeville is a Chartered Educational Psychologist and Associate Fellow of the British Psychological Society and holds a PhD from University

College Dublin. She has engaged in education and disability practices in roles as a teacher, psychologist, ethicist, teacher-educator, policy analyst, and researcher. She has published research at the intersection of education, disability, health and policy. Paula has informed special education and disability policy both nationally and internationally, including prior roles as a national practice and policy advisor in inclusive education in Ireland, as national coordinator for Ireland at the European Agency for Special Needs and Inclusive Education, and as a consultant at the World Bank.

Kieran Rose has a background in education and is an autistic parent to three autistic children. Through consultancy and supervision he supports organisations and professionals worldwide to critically reflect, challenge stigma, and reframe autistic experience through an intersectional lens. Kieran is an academic researcher focusing on masking, identity, stigma, trauma, and care practice, and delivers training across health, education, and social care, including for the National Health Service and Health and Social Care Northern Ireland, and teaches on five teaching streams at the Anna Freud Centre in London. Kieran is faculty member at the Science & Technology Applied Research Institute in the USA and Universidad de Castilla-La Mancha in Spain, and is co-author of the highly acclaimed book *Autistic Masking: Understanding Identity Management and the Role of Stigma*.

Catherine Watson is an educator and researcher, currently working at Middletown Centre for Autism (NI/ROI). Her research focuses on the role of outdoor play and outdoor play environments in supporting the wellbeing of children and young people. Catherine has presented her research internationally and has worked with local schools to effect meaningful change in outdoor play practices by centering the voice of neurodivergent pupils.

Justine Young trained as a teacher of Art and Design and became actively involved with pupils who have additional learning needs, taking great care to ensure that all learners are given a meaningful experience. Justine became part of the school's Pupil Support department, and has since been working with an array of learning and emotional needs, developing targeted interventions that give learners the opportunity to succeed.

Acknowledgements

Rachael

First, thank you to the brilliant contributors to this book. Your chapters are thoughtful, generous, and full of insight – it's been a real privilege to work with you. Thanks to fellow editor Claire for your unwavering enthusiasm and incredible insight. This book is so much better for your involvement, and I've been lucky to work alongside you. Thanks to Sue for your constant support – a brilliant friend, colleague, and a generous mentor. You've shaped the way I think about research and the world, and I'm endlessly grateful for your time, care, and encouragement.

Thank you to Laura Crane and Gilly Forrester for showing me how to navigate the world of academia with empathy and confidence. Your support and guidance have been invaluable.

To friends, colleagues, and collaborators who've shared writing time, read drafts, and talked ideas through – Anthony Schrag, Charlie Whelan, Caryll Jack, Rosie Arthur, and Bérengère Digard – thank you.

Thank you to Robert and Angela Davis for your encouragement, support, and belief from the beginning. Thank you to James Swatton for your unwavering championing, kindness, and empowerment, always.

Claire

My first thank you goes to my co-editors, Rachael and Sue, for inviting me to join the editing team and for being such wonderful collaborators.

This book would not exist without our contributing authors; thank you for the generous sharing of your wisdom and for your patience throughout the editorial process. My gratitude also extends to Sonny, whose gorgeous illustrations capture the essence of the book parts so well. To Clare, Molly, and the entire team at Routledge, thank you for your expert guidance in bringing this project to fruition.

I am also deeply grateful to the colleagues, learners, and school communities who have shaped my work over the years. You have taught me how to appreciate, support, and encourage all kinds of minds in the classroom and beyond.

Lastly, to my family, Eamonn, Cuan, and Aifric, *céad míle buíochas* for your unwavering love and support.

Sue

First and foremost, I am deeply grateful to everyone who made the *It Takes All Kinds of Minds* conference happen. Sophie Dow for her towering vision and absolute determination, Robin Dow for his rigorous planning, Alan Thornburrow for his commitment and passion, and everyone at Mindroom for their compassionate and dedicated approach to supporting neurodivergent people and their families. Thank you too to Alastair Salvesen, who brought us together in the first place and never flagged as a champion of neurodivergent people. I must also thank our dozens of speakers and hundreds of delegates – you all made the conference a huge success, and without that we would not have been invited to create the wonderful book you are reading now. Thank you also to my colleagues who supported me to take a sabbatical, during which a lot of the work for this book got done. Thank you to my beloved husband and children for tolerating the rather porous boundaries I set up between work and home. And a final thanks most of all to everyone who contributed to this book, and especially to Claire and Rachael – I couldn't have wished for a more thoughtful and insightful pair of co-editors.

Preface

The *It Takes All Kinds of Minds* (ITAKOM) conference aimed to promote a better understanding of neurodiversity and neurodivergence. Through this vision, we hoped to accelerate progress towards a society where all kinds of minds are welcomed and celebrated for the contributions they bring to our schools, workplaces, communities, and society overall.

The conference took place in March 2023 at the Edinburgh International Conference Centre (EICC). It was co-chaired by me, Sue Fletcher-Watson, and Sophie Dow, founder of Mindroom. Sophie and I had long worked together – in fact, we first met when I attended the first ever Mindroom conference also held at the EICC in 2003. At the time I was a student on a masters degree at Durham University, and the conference had a profound effect on my future research plans and career. There is every reason to hope the 2023 *ITAKOM* conference did the same for others. We welcomed 1,000 delegates from 24 countries to an event that later won an award for inclusive practice and received glowing delegate feedback, such as: "Attending the conference in person was an amazing experience, the most affirming and hopeful space I have ever had the pleasure to be in as a neurodivergent health professional."

One of the challenges of a one-off conference like *ITAKOM* is how to ensure the event has a legacy beyond the event itself. We were therefore delighted to be approached by Routledge to explore the possibility of an edited volume inspired by the sections of the programme devoted to neurodiversity in education. In this book, we have tried to replicate many of the principles of the conference – which aimed to give equal space to science and reality – especially those most applauded by delegates. First and foremost, a progressive neurodiversity-affirmative approach is taken in every chapter we present here. Those chapters represent a broad range of perspectives: "From researchers, to educators, professionals and those with lived experience: fantastic to have such a broad range of voices and backgrounds." Importantly, many of the authors – perhaps even a majority (though we haven't taken a head count!) also bring lived experience to their writing, as well as professional knowledge: "It was refreshing to attend a conference which gave equal floor space to people with lived experience and professionals working within the field." We hope the resulting volume inspires you and gives you hope for the future. "I wish I could've taken everyone I know to this conference, just so that they could get a better insight into the world of neurodivergence."

We agree – let's make sure no mind is left behind!

Sue Fletcher-Watson

Glossary

- **Ableism:** "A system of assigning value to people's bodies and minds based on societally constructed ideas of normalcy, productivity, desirability, intelligence, excellence, and fitness." (Talila Lewis, 2022 – https://www.talilalewis.com/blog/working-definition-of-ableism-january-2022-update)
- **Alexithymia**: People who have alexithymia may have have trouble identifying, understanding, and describing emotions. They may also struggle to show or feel emotions that are seen as socially appropriate. (Autistica – https://www.autistica.org.uk/what-is-autism/anxiety-and-autism-hub/alexithymia)
- **Co-production**: A type of participatory method which involves researchers with members of communities affected by the research. Co-production acknowledges that people with "lived experience" are often best placed to advise on what changes or support will make a positive difference to their lives. (NHS England – https://www.england.nhs.uk/always-events/co-production/)
- **Hermeneutical injustice**: When someone is unfairly prevented from making sense of their own experiences, identity, or circumstances and/or talking about them. Edlich, A., & Archer, A., 2024. Rejecting Identities: Stigma and Hermeneutical Injustice. *Social Epistemology*, 1–13. https://doi.org/10.1080/02691728.2024.2407646
- **Interoception**: A sensory system within the body that allows individuals to consciously or unconsciously detect, interpret, and react to their physical and emotional conditions. National Autistic Society – https://www.autism.org.uk/advice-and-guidance/professional-practice/interoception-wellbeing
- **Intersectionality:** The cumulative way in which the effects of multiple forms of discrimination (such as racism, sexism, and classism) combine

and overlap, especially in the experiences of marginalised individuals or groups. *Merriam-Webster Dictionary* – https://www.merriam-webster.com/dictionary/intersectionality
- **Minority stress:** Psychological and physiological effects that arise from discrimination faced by individuals belonging to marginalised and/or stigmatised social groups. *APA Dictionary of Psychology* – https://dictionary.apa.org/minority-stress
- **Neuroconstructivism:** A theory of cognitive development that emphasises how development is shaped by dynamic interactions between genetics, brain activity, and the environment. It views learning as a gradual, and context-dependent process where neural systems change and adapt over time. Westermann, G., Mareschal, D., Johnson, M. H., Sirois, S., Spratling, M. W., & Thomas, M. S., 2007. Neuroconstructivism. *Developmental science, 10*(1), 75–83. https://doi.org/10.1111/j.1467-7687.2007.00567.x
- **Neurodivergent intersubjectivity:** The process of how neurodivergent people connect, communicate, and relate with other neurodivergent people to create understanding. Heasman, B., & Gillespie, A., 2019. Neurodivergent Intersubjectivity: Distinctive Features of How Autistic People Create Shared Understanding. *Autism: The International Journal of Research and Practice, 23*(4), 910–921. https://doi.org/10.1177/1362361318785172
- **Neurominority:** "[A] population of neurodivergent people [who] all … share a similar form of neurodivergence, … the form of neurodivergence they share is one of those forms that is largely innate and that is inseparable from who they are, … and the form of neurodivergence they share is one to which the neurotypical majority tends to respond with some degree of prejudice, misunderstanding, discrimination, and/or oppression." Nick Walker – https://neuroqueer.com/neurodiversity-terms-and-definitions/
- **Participatory sense-making:** A process through which individuals co-create meaning during social interactions. It highlights how understanding and meaning emerge not just within individuals, but through their engagement with others. Hanne De Jaegher – https://hannedejaegher.net/research/participatory-sense-making/
- **Poly-victimisation:** Exposure to multiple types of victimisation, whereby someone is directly or indirectly harmed or deprived of protection from harm by the actions of others. Finkelhor, D., Ormrod, R. K., & Turner, H. A. (2007). Poly-victimization: A Neglected Component in Child

Victimization. *Child Abuse & Neglect, 31*(1), 7–26. https://doi.org/10.1016/j.chiabu.2006.06.008
- **Rhizomatically:** This term comes from the concept of the rhizome, and describes a way of thinking or understanding that explores interconnected, changing ideas that don't follow a linear path. The idea of thoughts as root-like structures are often used – as opposed to branch-and-trunk-like structures that have more linear directions. Young, E. B., 2013. *The Deleuze and Guattari Dictionary.* A&C Black.
- **Working memory**: "Short-term maintenance and use of information necessary for performing complex cognitive tasks such as learning, reasoning, and comprehension." (*APA Dictionary of Psychology* – https://dictionary.apa.org/working-memory

Introduction

A paradigm shift towards neurodiversity is underway in UK research and practice, across health, social care, and education, and gaining momentum in many other countries. However, this shift is still in its early phases, and while increasing numbers of people have heard of neurodiversity, few feel confident with the terminology, let alone what it means for practice "on the ground."

This book aims to fill that knowledge gap for educators, providing accounts of how the neurodiversity paradigm can be applied in a range of school contexts. We will examine what neurodiversity means for classroom management and pedagogy, for environments outside of the classroom, such as the playground and canteen, and for various kinds of staff roles. But first, we want to set the scene with some clear definitions of the underlying concepts that motivated this book.

Setting the Scene: What Is Neurodiversity?

Neurodiversity itself can be defined as the variation between humans, which means we all take in, process, and respond to information in different ways, giving each of us our own experience of the world. Neurodiversity is another dimension of diversity between people, along with diversity in gender, sexuality, ethnicity, and culture. While every individual is unique with respect to how they process information, we can also usefully and somewhat meaningfully group people who have broadly similar processing styles. These styles can be called *neurotypes*, and we often give these groups labels. The group that we presume is the biggest is referred to as *neurotypical*. We don't know for sure that this is literally the biggest group, and indeed the boundaries of "neurotypical" are poorly defined. But particularly in education, this is a useful descriptor for a group of people who tend to find that their preferred processing style is a good match for what is expected in school. For example,

Introduction

they might find it easiest to concentrate when things are quiet, and they might find written text a really effective way to take in new information. These things are not true for everyone!

Attention deficit hyperactivity disorder (ADHD) autism, dyslexia, and dyscalculia are all examples of neurotypes that are minorities and associated with specific clinical or learning diagnoses. People with these neurotypes can be described as *neurodivergent*, or members of *neuro-minorities*. Other neurotypes probably exist that don't currently have a clinical label – for example, we know that working memory problems are common and have a big impact on school learning, but there is no established label for people who experience this challenge. "Neurodivergent" is a useful umbrella term which can be used to describe collectively people who have both diagnosed and undiagnosed profiles that seem to reflect an atypical or minority processing style. When there is a mixed group of people from multiple neurotypes, this group can be described as *neurodiverse*. Unless you are sure, it's fair to assume that any group of more than about six people is neurodiverse!

People of the same neurotype are not identical to each other, but they may have some degree of shared experience and common processing style. This means that something that works for one pupil with dyslexia is worth trying with another, and that an autistic teacher might have useful tips to share with an autistic student. Our classifying and labelling systems are far from perfect – something which is increasingly supported by transdiagnostic scientific discovery – meaning we shouldn't rely too much on these labels to indicate a given individual's abilities or needs. Nonetheless, the prevalence of labelling by diagnosis, and the benefits people derive from these labels in terms of identity, shared community, and resource signposting, mean that it is currently sensible to think about neurodiversity in terms of how it intersects with existing categorical definitions.

A *paradigm* is defined by the *Oxford English Dictionary* as "A conceptual or methodological model underlying the theories and practices of a science or discipline at a particular time; [hence] a generally accepted world view." The *neurodiversity paradigm* is a set of concepts that can underpin the theories and practices of a range of disciplines, at this time most prominently in psychiatry, psychology, and education. For many, including the editors of this book, neurodiversity provides a world view when it comes to their interactions and behaviours too.

The set of concepts that form the neurodiversity paradigm have been variously defined, but one influential list comes from the writing of Nick Walker

(2021) – the following fundamental principles are paraphrased from her writing and elaborated slightly by us in terms of their educational implications.

1. Neurodiversity is a natural and valuable form of human diversity that happens "by itself."

This means that every school and classroom should expect neurodiversity among their class and in the staffroom and adopt strategies that accommodate this inevitable feature of humanity. The inclusion of neurodivergent people should recognise the inherent value that comes from the differences between us, celebrating that diversity and working to find a place for each person to thrive on their own terms.

2. There is no "normal" or "correct" neurotype.

The dominant way of understanding neurocognitive difference is that certain groups of people can be meaningfully categorised as impaired in comparison to an ideal "normal brain." This way of understanding also suggests that what is normal (prevalent) is also *normative*, and good. In turn, this presents advantages for those categorised as such, because a system made by neurotypical people will tend to work best for other neurotypical people, for example. The neurodiversity paradigm explicitly rejects this categorisation. Rather than trying to "fix" people, we must work to recognise inequities between neurotypes and overcome those, so that everyone can flourish.

3. The experience of neuro-minorities is heavily dictated by social forces.

Like other types of minoritised or marginalised people, discrimination, stereotyping, stigma, and prejudice have a huge influence on the lives of neuro-minorities. Recognising and combating these negative influences is a key part of applying the neurodiversity paradigm in practice and delivering justice for neurodivergent people.

Neurodiversity-Affirmative Practice in Education

It is worth taking a moment to explicitly describe what the neurodiversity paradigm shift is moving away from and what we are moving towards.

Introduction

Historically, and today in most settings, neurodivergence is pathologised, and models of support tend to be structured around the identification of deficits, and amelioration of them, often at the individual level. To give a concrete example, a pupil who finds it hard to sit still (among other things) might end up with an ADHD diagnosis. Often a next step might be to provide training and incentives designed to encourage the child to learn to sit still for longer and longer periods of time. They might have a reward chart or be given cognitive strategies designed to combat their natural inclinations. All of these steps send the very strong message that sitting still is desirable, and if they fail to do this, they need to devote time and effort to changing to fit in with what other children are doing fairly effortlessly. This practice is largely defined by the *normalcy paradigm* – in brief, this is a world view that implies that it is desirable to be "normal" (meaning average, or part of the majority) and that falling outside the normal range means something is wrong with you.

What is the alternative? Drawing on the principles of the neurodiversity paradigm, this pupil might instead have their need to move recognised and embraced. They might be allowed to take movement breaks and be seated in an area of the class that permits this with minimum disruption to others. They might be provided a wobble cushion to sit on, allowing them to discreetly move while seated and working. They might be supported to identify what work they can do while moving (e.g., listening to the teacher at the start of the lesson is easier while moving, than when working on a maths problem in your workbook) and encouraged to move at those times to still be able to access learning.

This scenario provides a nice example of the concept of *met and unmet needs* which we find a really helpful framing for talking about individual pupil profiles. Rather than defining needs as "special" or "additional," this terminology reminds us that every pupil has needs in terms of accessing learning. Many of these needs are easily met by the standard provision in a mainstream school – for example, the need for a desk and a chair, the need for regular breaktimes throughout the day, and the need for information to be repeated and practised before it is learned. Other needs are not part of the standard package and are therefore frequently unmet – they must be identified, and a suitable solution put in place. In our scenario, the need for a wobble cushion to sit on is a clear example of this. An important question for any educator to ask themselves is *which of my pupil's needs are/are not being met, and why?* This element also reminds us that while the neurodiversity paradigm encourages us to celebrate diversity, this doesn't mean pretending that everyone needs the same thing or ignoring the challenges faced by neurodivergent people of all ages.

The concept of met and unmet needs is highly relevant to the *social model of disability*. This disability rights-led model emphasises that the degree of disability experienced by an individual is largely dictated by their environment, rather than disability being defined by an impairment that resides within the individual. For example, someone with reduced mobility will be disabled by the cost of a high-quality wheelchair, narrow doorways, step-only access, and small toilets. All of these will make spaces inaccessible and limit independence. By providing disability aids like wheelchairs and making environments accessible, we can reduce disability and maximise autonomy and power. The social model of disability shares many features with the neurodiversity paradigm, including the emphasis on the rejection of any notion of "normal" or "correct" ways of being, and recognising the social forces that lead to disadvantage.

If we can understand and apply these principles of the paradigm in education, we will be delivering *neurodiversity-affirmative practice* – a form of practice that is informed by, and delivers on, the principles of the neurodiversity paradigm. This includes schools focusing on changing the environment to improve the school experience for all pupils and avoiding the promotion of supports that attempt to "normalise" differences in children. Instead, an aim should be to increase understanding, awareness, and acceptance of diversity in all children. Pupils and staff in a school that adopts neurodiversity-affirmative practice should feel not just accepted, but welcome, celebrated, and supported, no matter what their neurotype or profile of needs.

Neurodiversity-Lite

One issue to guard against when adopting a neurodiversity-affirmative stance is what we call *neurodiversity-lite*. This is a watered-down version of neurodiversity often characterised by the adoption of neurodiversity terminology, with no change in the underlying structures or provision. In some cases, practitioners may be trying to make improvements but fail to reflect deeply on what is involved in delivering those improvements. In others, schools may adopt neurodiversity language to keep pace with an evolving climate, but with no intention of deeper change. A classic form of neurodiversity-lite is apparent in some forms of *strengths-based practice*. To be clear, we consider the identification and celebration of individual pupils' strengths to be an inherently positive concept. It can help pupils with their self-esteem, to facilitate informed choices as their education progresses, and to find their niche in the world. However, neurodiversity is not limited to strengths-based practice, and the idea that an individual only has value to the extent that they have an identifiable strength or talent is profoundly anti-neurodiversity.

Neurodiversity-lite is deeply problematic. Adopting language may give a false impression that change has already taken place, thus actively hindering further improvement. Neurodivergent people in organisations that use neurodiversity language without deeper engagement will not only miss out on the intended benefits of the approach but may actively reject a movement that, if properly applied, should be liberatory. This isn't to deny room for critique or improvement beyond the ideas shared here – but any such improvement needs to start from an informed position, not from a set of false assumptions.

Need for and Scope of This Edited Volume

What is the point of all this change? There is ample evidence that current efforts at inclusion in school are not working. Traditional conceptualisations in educational settings position children and young people in neuro-minorities as having a deficit or impairment. As a result, supports and practices have, until recently, been rooted in a model that exacerbates negative educational experiences as they attempt to change the child rather than dismantle the environmental barriers around them. Consequently, neurodivergent children and young people are more likely to be excluded from school and to participate less when they are in class. Their relationships are affected, and their sense of belonging in school is limited. Young people report higher levels of bullying or victimisation, and a lack of understanding from peers and teachers. Mental ill-health is very common among neurodivergent young people, with many not attending school at all due to extreme anxiety. Neurodivergent teachers are likewise subject to high rates of stress, mental ill-health, and burnout, and of course, these issues ripple out to affect family members too. Here we do not explore these negative consequences in detail – other volumes comprehensively describe the challenges experienced by neurodivergent young people. Instead, we adopt the position that a neurodiversity-affirmative approach is a key way to avoid these catastrophic outcomes. It can provide a new way to understand and address the varying needs of the school community, giving each individual an equitable opportunity to fulfil their potential and enjoy their school years.

This book, inspired by the pioneering *It Takes All Kinds of Minds* conference in Edinburgh, offers a carefully curated collection of chapters exploring many different types of minds and how they can best learn and flourish at school. The authors bring diverse experiences and disciplines, but nonetheless create a cohesive message that is impactful, accessible, and accurate. Despite our efforts to be as inclusive as possible in the authorship and topics of chapters presented here, we have necessarily had to limit our scope in order to provide a manageable volume. The book contains content relevant to all educational settings, but will probably have the most obvious implications for mainstream primary and secondary schools. That said, if you are an early years practitioner, further or higher education professional, or work in a specialist base or separate special school, we hope you will find useful lessons here on topics such as outdoor spaces, Universal Design and values-led change.

We have also been constrained by the reach of our own knowledge and networks, which means this volume represents experiences in UK classrooms above all. Although the insights shared here may be applicable worldwide, we recognise the lack of global perspectives as a limitation and hope authors and editors who can fill that space will approach publishers, encouraged by this model.

The example of the wobble cushion provided above is a very minimal case of how a classroom might take a step towards embracing neurodiversity – by meeting a need rather than expecting the child to learn to compensate or hide that need. However, it is doubtless also the case that profound and radical change to the system will be required to cultivate deeply neurodiversity-affirmative practice. Despite remaining committed to this kind of liberatory change, this volume on the whole aims to provide theoretical, experiential, and research-based insights that have pragmatic applicability within schools here and now.

What to Expect as a Reader

This book is organised into three main parts: "Environments," "Practice and Pedagogy," and "Relationships in and around School." In each part we present a handful of chapters written by authors who frequently combine experience as practitioners, researchers, and from their own lives. The chapters vary widely in their content, but each describes a specific context or process – understanding of these can be used to drive neurodiversity-affirmative practice in schools, boosting inclusion, and promoting a depathologising stance. Each chapter starts with an introduction to the topic, and ends with practical recommendations in the form of Reflective Activities and Key Takeaways. The book is not a how-to manual, and often presents intellectually challenging and theoretically complex ideas. However, we hope these practical sections provide ways for interested readers to think about how to implement what they have learned in their own practice.

The book's theoretical lens combines neurodiversity-affirmative practice and the social model of disability. These movements, while relatively new in education, are highly relevant and are being acknowledged by governmental bodies and organisations. Neurodiversity is starting to be recognised more widely, yet there is very little that is currently offered to educators to better understand the importance of neurodiversity in inclusive practice, and how to apply these ideas. This book will provide a concise and accessible introduction to neurodiversity, informed by research and real-world experience, written with and for practitioners, to directly impact educational settings. We anticipate that these will in time become the standard for good practice and will remain up-to-date and relevant for practitioners in the long term.

Reference

Walker, N. *Neuroqueer Heresies: Notes on the neurodiversity paradigm, autistic empowerment, and postnormal possibilities*. Fort Worth, TX: Autonomous Press, 2021

Part I Introduction: Environments
Edited by Sue Fletcher-Watson

School consists of a lot more than what happens at the front of the classroom. For many pupils, breaktimes, lunch, and after-school clubs provide a much-needed respite from the rigours of lessons. They can be the highlight of the school day – a chance to spend time with friends, move your body, and be silly. Some children for whom classroom learning is effortful may find that in the playground they can excel, climbing higher or running faster than others of their age.

However, for other pupils these times in the school day are among the most stressful. The lack of structure and explicit rules during playtime and lunch can be intimidating. Playground spaces and games may be a new opportunity to feel like an outlier – everyone else can balance on the see-saw, everyone else just "gets" what they're supposed to do. Social spaces at school can be a sensory nightmare – echoey corridors, crowded cafeterias with hundreds of clashing cutlery and plates. Of course, when bullying happens at school it is most present in these contexts too, where supervision is minimal and cruelty can be hidden from adult view.

In this part of the book we explore how schools can shift their environment to apply the neurodiversity paradigm beyond a focus on pedagogy and learning. Across four chapters we examine classroom seating, playground design, breaktime expectations, and creative activities as contexts in which neurodivergent children may often be disadvantaged – but could be flourishing. Authors draw on research evidence and their own practice to show what choices schools can make when thinking about inclusion across the entire school day and environment.

1

Using Outdoor Spaces to Support Neurodiversity-Affirmative Playtime in Schools

Catherine Watson

Introduction

The benefits of play are well understood, but less discussion has been devoted to the role of the environment in supporting quality outdoor play. We will therefore begin by considering the importance of the outdoor play space and how this can specifically impact neurodivergent children and young people.

The Importance of Outdoor Play Spaces

Children are not spending as much time outdoors as previous generations; the effects of this are reflected in increasingly poor health and wellbeing outcomes (Dodd et al., 2023; Loebach et al., 2021). It is important that when children have the opportunity to play outside, they can do so in supportive environments which are designed to include, gently challenge, and engage all children. Research illustrates that traditional playgrounds which are designed around predetermined activities based on motor play generally have limited usability and low play value, and offer little opportunity for social interaction for neurodivergent children (Czalczynska-Podolska, 2024). It is therefore essential that we move towards inclusive playground design which can meet a much wider variety of needs.

The principles of Universal Design (UD) have increasingly been applied to playgrounds and can serve as a useful guide for designing neurodiversity-affirmative outdoor play spaces that enable children to engage in play at their own developmental level (NSW Government, 2023). An early definition by North Carolina State University describes UD in outdoor spaces as the "design of products and environments to be usable by all people, to the greatest extent possible, without the need for adaptation and specialised design" (Mace, 1996). Core features of UD playgrounds include accessibility within the play space, simple and intuitive design, a range of sensory stimuli, resting and gathering areas, and a choice and variety of play features to provide high play value. Research shows that playgrounds designed with inclusivity in mind provide more opportunities for children to actively engage in play in their own way and have higher levels of use among all children (Hurst et al., 2023). By adopting a UD approach, play providers can ensure that the right to authentic play is protected and promoted for all children.

> **A person's environment has a huge impact on the experience and extent of disability. Inaccessible environments create disability by creating barriers to participation and inclusion.**
> **(World Health Organization, 2022)**

For many children, the majority of their outdoor play takes place in school, where up to a quarter of the day is spent in the playground. This has implications for the quality of play and the play opportunities afforded due to the availability and organisation of outdoor space. Teachers can acknowledge and support the infinite possibilities of play by re-evaluating the playground and associated attitudes towards play through a neurodiversity lens which welcomes the strengths, interests, differences, and needs of all children.

Strategies for Schools

In the following sections, we discuss considerations across the several areas mentioned above relating to the playground that may be helpful when evaluating outdoor play provision in school settings.

(1) Structuring the Outdoor Environment – Layout and Design

Layout and design are important factors in ensuring that the playground is both accessible to and usable by as many pupils as possible. A large, open space which offers a clear view of pupils is typically favoured by schools for safety and supervision purposes – however, playgrounds designed in this way tend to be dominated by certain groups and activities (typically "boys' football"), relegating other pupils to the margins (Graham et al., 2022; Ndhlovu & Varea, 2018). This limits other forms of play; particularly those favoured by neurodivergent children whose play needs, preferences, and behaviours often differ from neurotypical children as they perceive and interact with the world around them in different ways. With limited opportunities for play and respite, children may struggle to occupy themselves, resulting in increased reports of behavioural incidents at lunchtime when children become aimless and bored (Pearson & Howe, 2017). Neurodivergent children in particular may find it difficult to navigate expectations when faced with nothing but an open concrete space, particularly after transitioning from the highly structured classroom environment. An unpredictable playground environment can cause anxiety for children who thrive off routine, while noise and crowding can lead to sensory overwhelm.

The following is an introduction to several strategies that can benefit play spaces in your educational environment.

Strategy 1: Zoning

A helpful strategy to include all children in the play space is zoning. By dividing the open space into smaller, contained areas, schools can relieve the stress and uncertainty experienced by many neurodivergent pupils by offering a variety of activities to engage with within their own structured settings. Organising the playground in this way provides a sense of predictability, allowing the child to feel in control of the space. To maximise play value, the space should incorporate a variety of play types with a suitable range of challenges, such that pupils of all abilities can play together, rest, socialise, and move freely between zones. Structuring the outdoor space in this way acknowledges the importance of choice and autonomy for the child while enabling as many children as possible to engage in their preferred play activities in their own way.

Teachers can ensure that the playground is carefully mapped to consider the flow of students and the placement of zones within the space to help avoid overstimulation (e.g., keeping active games away from the quiet sensory play area). There should be a clear boundary denoting where each zone begins and ends, with larger, physical network games (e.g., football) in particular well contained. This can be done for little to no cost, using resources at the school's disposal. For instance, pre-existing playground features such as walls, fences, ground markings, and paths can be used to create visual boundaries between activity zones, and items such as cones, planters, bunting, or markers of different colours and textures can be used to divide the space depending on resources available.

Strategy 2: Transitional Spaces

Transitioning to and from the playground can be a source of anxiety, and neurodivergent pupils have identified that being able to safely access the play space is particularly important to their engagement and enjoyment of outdoor breaktimes (McAllister & Sloan, 2017). Providing designated access points to make the transition between the indoor and outdoor school environments can empower pupils to access the playground at their own pace, offering a safe place until they are ready to join in. These transitional areas can be designed to offer shelter and calming sensory input, such as planters with different colours, scents and textures, shaded canopies, or soft fairy lights. Including a map of the site at key transition points can assist students in making choices about their play and planning their route before entering the main play space. Creating an orientation path around the perimeter of the playground can provide a safe zone, enabling children to observe the space and assess the level of physical or social contact they might expect before engaging in play. It is important that the orientation path is smooth, even, and accessible, and wide enough that all users have the space needed to comfortably navigate the area. The boundary between the path and play area should be made clear so that children can easily leave the play space if they are feeling overwhelmed and re-enter when they feel ready.

Strategy 3: Creating Green Spaces

Incorporating greenery into the design of the space can be an effective means of promoting wellbeing in the outdoor space, particularly in built-up areas where children may otherwise lack access to nature. Exposure to nature is calming, with the potential to reduce stress and anxiety, restoring balance, and alleviating the effects of mental fatigue (Meredith et al., 2020). Covering playground railings with a variety of plants, shrubs, and foliage not only looks appealing, but also can reduce noise filtering in from busy nearby roads, improve the air quality, and provide shade on sunny days. Children tend to gravitate towards green spaces, and creating tranquil, nature-rich areas within the playground affords opportunities for rest, relaxation, and gentle socialising in a calmer, less crowded environment.

Reflective Activity – Reimagining Your Play Space

Start with a blank template and redesign your play space with the needs of your pupils in mind. You might consider:

- Accessibility – Ensure the environment is accessible to children with motor differences and wheelchair users, including ramps, pathways, and surfacing materials. Consider the height of play structures for children of varying abilities.
- Diverse play opportunities – Incorporate a range of play equipment that caters to different abilities.
- Safety features – Use soft, impact-absorbing surfaces and ensure that the space is securely enclosed, and equipment meets safety standards for all children.
- Sensory elements – Include sensory-rich features like textured surfaces, musical instruments, water play, and interactive elements to engage children with sensory processing differences.
- Social opportunities – Design spaces that encourage cooperative play but allow for flexibility so children can engage at their own comfort level.
- Comfort – Provide sheltered, shaded areas and accessible seating for children to rest and unwind.
- Quiet zones – Designate quiet spaces where children can retreat to calm down when feeling overwhelmed.

- Structured layout – Create clear pathways and distinct areas for different types of play, such as active play, quiet zone, and exploratory spaces, accommodating various interests and abilities.
- Visual supports – Use clear, simple signage, visual aids, and tactile maps to help children understand how to use equipment and navigate the playground independently.

(2) Play Materials and Resources

> Every child has the right to play in an appropriate, inclusive environment. However, children's play needs and requirements can differ greatly. A neurodiversity-friendly setting supports children to play together through the provision of inclusive equipment and play cues, with materials and resources chosen to benefit children of all abilities; ensuring that no child feels left out. This approach fosters social inclusion, encourages sensory exploration, promotes independence, and enhances physical and cognitive development (Harris et al., 2024; James et al., 2022).
>
> **The following suggestions provide a starting point for thinking about play materials and resources in your setting.**

Strategy 4: Choosing Play Equipment

An inclusive playground will consist of a range of quality equipment comprising both fixed and moveable elements. Investment in thoughtfully chosen equipment which appropriately challenges and engages users of all capabilities can yield long-term benefits by supporting students to make choices according to their own needs and preferences. Fixed elements add predictability to the play space, which can be comforting to neurodivergent children and young people. For this reason, it is a good idea to have a selection of items that don't change. This might include intuitive, easy-to-use play equipment which offers sensory input, such as swings, slides, wheelchair-inclusive roundabouts, in-ground trampolines, fixed activity panels, or a seating area for relaxed socialising.

Keeping these items within designated activity zones adds further consistency for playground users who may prefer to engage with the same items and routines in their play. For children who seek it, challenge can be gradually built up by introducing moveable elements in the vicinity of the fixed equipment to maintain a sense of security while inviting engagement with other potential objects of interest. Arranging any loose materials and resources so that the pupils can see them and make choices for themselves can support autonomy in play. It helps to store items in a designated area with clear visual labels so that children can access them independently. The resources should reflect the pupils' interests and activities, with adjustments made over time and any changes communicated clearly to pupils in advance – for example, through visual supports.

Strategy 5: Play Prompts and Cues

Neurodivergent children may struggle with abstraction, so clear play cues and prompts must be provided to spark engagement throughout the playground. It may be unclear, for instance, that a wooden platform is a stage for performing on until dressing up materials, musical instruments, and other props are added. Play components shaped in recognisable designs such as a car, a house, or a pirate ship can facilitate creative and imaginative play without being overly prescriptive (Brown et al., 2021).

Additionally, playground markings offer opportunities for physical activity without the challenge of climbing or manoeuvring off the ground. Interactive games such as hopscotch, mirror-me, snakes and ladders, and bean bag toss invite social play and communication, while fitness circuits can be completed independently or with friends. Marking out areas for team games (e.g., rounders pitch, multi-sports area) or high-energy activities (e.g., shuttle runs, ball dribbling, skipping) provides visual context for the activities which pupils can expect in these spaces. To support children to engage with these features, it is helpful for staff to be fully trained in the use of playground markings, and for visual cues and props made available where appropriate (e.g., rules of the game; spinners, balls, bean bags for throwing).

(3) Sensory Play

> Many neurodivergent children and young people experience differences in how they process and respond to sensory input from the environment. Participation in outdoor play offers a range of input across all of the senses, specifically the three "power systems" – vestibular (movement and balance), proprioceptive (body awareness), and tactile (touch). The materials and resources in each play zone should afford the students a choice of sensory play opportunities exploring textures, sound, movement, visuals, smells, and taste. These activities should be thoughtfully arranged to help reduce overstimulation through clear boundaries denoting the specific areas where particular activities are to occur.
>
> **The following strategies can be used as useful starting points when considering sensory play in your education environment.**

Strategy 6: Motor Activities

Outdoor activities which involve motor planning help children develop core strength and coordination skills while helping regulate their nervous system. This can be supported by building an appropriate degree of challenge and accessible motor opportunities into the play space, for example, obstacles to navigate (logs, rocks, tyres, boulders), stepping stones, low balance beams, and a variety of surfaces and textures for walking on. Other areas can incorporate more challenging environmental obstacles where appropriate, such as uneven and multi-level surfaces that physically challenge and require problem-solving skills.

Strategy 7: Loose Parts

Maintaining an engaging outdoor play space that stimulates the senses does not need to be costly. Recyclable loose parts materials such as crates, pallets, tyres, nets, logs, fabrics, sand, water, and stones can be sourced cheaply or for free and hold high play value due to their open-ended and sensory nature. One of the benefits of loose-parts materials is their lack of prescribed function, which can spark imagination and be manipulated in potentially limitless ways by children in play. This can easily be adapted for children who prefer a bit more guidance in their play by incorporating loose parts elements into structured play settings. For example, adding loose parts to the creative play zone with a visual of how to build a rocket ship; providing a dressing-up box of fabrics, materials, and props in the imaginative play area; augmenting sand play with a variety of shovels and containers, seashells, sticks, or pebbles; or filling tyres with soil to use as planters for sensory gardening.

Strategy 8: Using the Elements

The natural elements can also be embraced to enhance sensory play. Keeping designated provisions for rainy, windy, sunny and snowy days along with wellies, waterproof jackets, sun cream, hats, etc. can enable children to play outside in all types of weather. Items to stimulate play might include windmills, chimes, streamers, kites, bubbles, funnels, containers for collecting rainfall, buckets and spades, and even sleds!

Create sensory profiles for individual pupils that may benefit from this support, detailing their responses to various sensory stimuli in order to tailor play activities to their needs.

If possible, staff should avail themselves of training on sensory processing and how to support children's sensory needs during play.

(4) Developing an Outdoor Play Policy

> Play is enhanced when there is a clear and shared vision for the outdoor environment, its possibilities, and the opportunities it provides for students. It can be helpful for your setting to clarify and communicate its position on outdoor play in the form of a designated policy. The outdoor play policy serves to ensure the protection and fulfilment of every child's right to play (Article 31) and inclusion (Article 23) under the United Nations Convention on the Rights of the Child by ensuring a consistent approach towards outdoor play and recognition of its value throughout the whole school setting. Its function is to enable every child to avail of the benefits of outdoor play in an enriching and supportive environment.
>
> **The following steps can be used as a guide to help produce your own outdoor play policy for your setting.**

Strategy 9: Consult with Key Stakeholders

Children and young people have the right to express their views, feelings and wishes in all matters affecting them, and to have their views considered and taken seriously (Article 12). As key stakeholders in play, it is considered best practice to involve children in the formulation of the play policy. There are several engaging methods which can support neurodivergent children to share their ideas, including talking mats, photovoice, drawing, focus groups, diamond ranking, or writing, all of which can be adapted to suit individual needs and communication preferences (Bloom et al., 2020; Lewis-Dagnell et al., 2023). Pupil voice should be given due weight and woven throughout the policy (Play Midlothian & Play Scotland, n.d.).

As well as input from pupils, it is recommended to consult with school staff, parents and carers to gain additional perspectives into the play needs and preferences of their children and discuss issues which may need tackling together (e.g., the provision of suitable outdoor clothing). It can be helpful to share research on the benefits of outdoor play and make connections to how this underpins play practice in the setting to ensure that everyone is on the same page (Early Childhood Ireland, 2016).

Strategy 10: Identify the Vision for Outdoor Play in Your School

Once you have established the play needs within your school, you can begin to think about how your outdoor environment can be used to support neurodiversity-affirmative play. Outline a series of aims that reflect the school's vision for outdoor play.

Aims might be to:

- Ensure that all children are given the opportunity for daily outdoor play, fresh air and exercise.
- Fulfil the child's right to play and inclusion via an enriching outdoor environment that meets the diverse needs of children in the setting.
- Provide opportunities for a range of play types including sensory, motor, social and imaginative.
- Enable children to have ownership of the play that happens in the outdoor environment.
- Support children to become confident in taking risks and developing their skills and independence.

Outline the Key Considerations

The policy should then outline how play and development will be supported in the outdoor environment for all ages and abilities.

Questions to Consider

- Play opportunities – Are there clearly defined activity zones and a range of resources offering choices reflective of children's interests and abilities?
- Staff roles and responsibilities – How will staff support and extend children's play and learning outdoors? It may be helpful to briefly outline roles and responsibilities, for example, maintenance of equipment, health and safety checks.
- Equality and inclusion – Can the outdoor space be accessed, used, and enjoyed by children of all ages and abilities?
- Approach to risk and challenge – Does the outdoor environment allow for and promote developmentally appropriate risk?
- Health and safety – What are the procedures for risk assessment, accident protocols, supporting safety, and positive behaviour strategies?
- Weather – How will the setting respond to different weather conditions? Do children have access to suitable outdoor clothing that allows them to access the outdoors in all weathers?

(5) Post-primary Play Spaces

> The need for play does not stop in childhood. Global trends show that physical activity tends to decrease between childhood and adolescence, which can have negative implications for physical and mental health (Marques et al., 2020), and research has underlined the continued importance of outdoor play for social connectedness, supporting mental wellbeing, getting regular exercise and boosting physical confidence and competence (Biddle et al., 2019; Zhang et al., 2020). Outdoor breaks provide an ideal opportunity for teens to practice physical skills, and stimulating playgrounds suited to the needs and interests of adolescents can offer subtle and engaging ways of developing physical literacy, including balance, coordination, agility, throwing, catching, and gripping. Despite this, there are typically much fewer resources in the playground at the secondary level, and it has been found that introducing more facilities can boost physical

activity by up to three times for this age group (Haug et al., 2010). Research with secondary school pupils found that swings – specifically large 360° swings – were the feature most desired by adolescents visiting outdoor play environments, with other notable features including sports courts, playgrounds, paths, grassy open space, seating, fitness equipment/jungle gyms, and nature (Rivera et al., 2021).

The following information offers several prompts that can be useful when designing play spaces for adolescents.

Strategy 11: Designing Play Spaces for Adolescents

Planning the space around designated activity zones which appeal to the target age group can once again create a more inclusive play space by giving a sense of consistency, space, and autonomy to all pupils. When designing outdoor play areas for adolescents in secondary schools, Learning Through Landscapes – a leading UK charity dedicated to outdoor learning and play – recommends breaking the space up into smaller discreet but not hidden areas, providing shelter and seating in varied locations and styles, a wider choice of activities and open-ended use structures, walking paths and routes for pleasure, significant variety in topography, colours and materials used, and planting more trees, shrubs, and flowers for interest and shelter (Robinson, 2014).

School ground greening has been linked to adolescent wellbeing through improved opportunities for physical activity, socialising, and mental restoration, with positive implications for school achievement (Chawla et al., 2014; Kelz et al., 2015). Replacing traditional asphalt schoolyards with grass and other green features is found to increase equity and remove hierarchies in the play space by providing novel opportunities for engagement in non-sport activities, appealing to more social and collaborative play and reducing sedentary behaviours for all children (Raney et al., 2019).

Adolescent girls in particular are less likely to have their needs met by outdoor play spaces. The needs of girls can be built into the environment through the provision of high vantage points which enable girls to feel safer, and dividing the space up across varying levels to prevent the domination of space by any particular group (Make Space for Girls, n.d.). Notably, outdoor facilities for adolescents tend to focus on sport rather than play, despite girls voicing a preference for non-competitive, more social forms of active play tailored towards their age, with features including swings, trampolines, obstacle courses and gymnastic equipment, and unfixed equipment such as skipping ropes, speakers for music, and chalk (Pawlowski et al., 2019; Walker & Clark, 2023). Including social play and exercise areas with equipment arranged so that users can face each other and talk at the same time or simply engage in parallel physical activity with friends creates opportunities for more relaxed and low-demand forms of play.

Key Takeaways

This chapter outlines several strategies for making outdoor play spaces neurodiversity-affirmative. Whether you are designing a space from scratch or updating your existing provision, careful and considered design can make the playground more inclusive in a way that benefits all pupils. Key recommendations to consider include:

- A structured and carefully organised play environment, including transitional, rest, and orientation spaces
- Clear physical and visual boundaries
- Gentle "play cues" which contribute to the generation of play ideas and autonomous play
- The use of loose parts in structured areas to provide unstructured play within a structured environment
- Easily accessible motor planning activities built into the design
- A dedicated policy and shared vision for outdoor play throughout the school
- Planning for play which meets the needs of all children up to age 18

Reflective Activities

Exercise 1 – Complete an audit of your existing outdoor provision from a neurodiversity-affirmative perspective. A template produced by Middletown Centre for Autism can be found online at https://outdoor-play.middletownautism.com/.

Observing play and adhering to best practice recommendations is an excellent starting point, but ultimately, the best way to design a space that reflects the needs of children in your setting is to ask the children themselves. This can be done in a way that is appropriate to the communication needs of your group and includes parents' and caregivers' perspectives. Any changes made to the play environment are to support all pupils to engage in play in their own way and should encourage authentic play as chosen by the child.

Exercise 2 – Consult with the children and young people in your setting to understand the outdoor space from their perspective. Create specific action points and add these to your school development plan. Topics to explore might include: Enjoyment, Favourite Activities, Equipment, Accessibility, Sensory Experiences, Safety, Social Interaction, New Ideas, and Suggestions for Improvement.

References

Armitage, M. (2005). The influence of school architecture and design on the outdoor play experience within the primary school. *Paedagogica Historica, 41*, 535–553. https://doi.org/10.1080/00309230500165734

Biddle, S., Ciaccioni, S., Thomas, G., & Vergeer, I. (2019). Physical activity and mental health in children and adolescents: An updated review of reviews and an analysis of causality. *Psychology of Sport and Exercise, 42*, 146–155. https://doi.org/10.1016/j.psychsport.2018.08.011

Bloom, A., Critten, S., Johnson, H., & Wood, C. (2020). A critical review of methods for eliciting voice from children with speech, language and communication needs. *JORSEN, 20*(4), 308–320.

Brown, D. M. Y., Ross, T., Leo, J., Buliung, R., Shirazipour, C. H., Latimer-Cheung, A. E., & Arbour-Nicitopoulos, K. P. (2021). A scoping review of evidence-informed recommendations for designing inclusive playgrounds. *Frontiers in Rehabilitation Science, 2*. https://doi.org/10.3389/fresc.2021.664595

Chawla, L., Keena, K., Pevec, I., & Stanley, E. (2014). Green schoolyards as havens from stress and resources for resilience in childhood and adolescence. *Health Place, 28,* 1–13. https://doi.org/10.1016/j.healthplace.2014.03.001

Czalczynska-Podolska, M. (2024). Therapeutic playground: Typology of solutions and analysis of selected public playgrounds as places with therapeutic potential. *Sustainability, 16,* 6414. https://doi.org/10.3390/su16156414

Dodd, H. F., Nesbit, R. J., & Fitzgibbon, L. (2023). Child's play: Examining the association between time spent playing and child mental health. *Child Psychiatry & Human Development, 54,* 1678–1686. https://doi.org/10.1007/s10578-022-01363-2

Early Childhood Ireland. (2016). Outdoor play policy. https://test.earlychildhoodireland.ie/wp-content/uploads/2021/03/outdoor-play-policy.pdf

Graham, M., Dixon, K., Azevedo, L. B., Wright, M., & Innerd, A. (2022). A socio-ecological examination of the primary school playground: Primary school pupil and staff perceived barriers and facilitators to a physically active playground during break and lunch-times. *PLoS ONE, 17*(2), e0261812. https://doi.org/10.1371/journal.pone.0261812

Harris, K., Rosinski, P., Wood-Nartker, J., & Hill Renirie, R. (2024). Developing inclusive playgrounds that welcome all children—Including those with autism. *Review Journal of Autism and Developmental Disorders, 11,* 433–441. https://doi.org/10.1007/s40489-022-00345-3

Haug, E., Torsheim, T., Sallis, J. F., & Samdal, O. (2010). The characteristics of the outdoor school environment associated with physical activity. *Health Education Research, 25*(2), 248–256. https://doi.org/10.1093/her/cyn050

Hurst, K., Lee, C., & Ndubisi, F. (2023). Universal Design in playground environments: A place-based evaluation of amenities, use, and physical activity. *Landscape Journal, 42*(2), 55. https://doi.org/10.3368/lj.42.2.55

James, M. E., Jianopoulos, E., Ross, T., Buliung, R., & Arbour-Nicitopoulos, K. P. (2022). Children's usage of inclusive playgrounds: A naturalistic observation study of play. *International Journal of Environmental Research and Public Health, 19*(20), 13648. https://doi.org/10.3390/ijerph192013648

Kelz, C., Evans, G. W., & Röderer, K. (2015). The restorative effects of redesigning the schoolyard. *Environment and Behavior, 47,* 119–139. https://doi.org/10.1177/001391651351052

Lewis-Dagnell, S., Parsons, S., & Kovshoff, H. (2023). Creative methods developed to facilitate the voices of children and young people with complex needs about their education: A systematic review and conceptual analysis of voice. *Educational Research Review, 39.* https://doi.org/10.1016/j.edurev.2023.100529

Loebach, J., Sanches, M., Jaffe, J., & Elton-Marshall, T. (2021). Paving the way for outdoor play: Examining socio-environmental barriers to community-based outdoor play. *International Journal of Environmental Research and Public Health, 18*(7), 3617. https://doi.org/10.3390/ijerph18073617

Make Space for Girls. (n.d.). Better design suggestions for parks. https://cdn.prod.website-files.com/6398afa2ae5518732f04f791/63ef55119a91ac83137151c9_Better%20Ideas.pdf

Mace, R. L., Hardie, G. J., & Place, J. P. (1996). *Accessible environments: Toward universal design.* Raleigh: North Carolina State University. https://www.universaldesignresource.com/accessibleenvironments/

Marques, A., Henriques-Neto, D., Peralta, M., Martins, J., Demetriou, Y., Schönbach, D. M. I., & De Matos, M. G. (2020). Prevalence of physical activity among adolescents from 105 low, middle, and high-income countries. *International Journal of Environmental Research and Public Health, 17,* 3145. https://doi.org/10.3390/ijerph17093145

McAllister, K., & Sloan, S. (2017). Designed by the pupils, for the pupils: An autism-friendly school. *BJSE, 43*(4), 330–357. https://doi.org/10.1111/1467-8578.12160

Meredith, G. R., Rakow, D. A., Eldermire, E. R. B., Madsen, C. G., Shelley, S. P., & Sachs, N. A. (2020). Minimum time dose in nature to positively impact the mental health of college-aged students, and how to measure it: A scoping review. *Frontiers in Psychology.* https://doi.org/10.3389/fpsyg.2019.02942

Ndhlovu, S., & Varea, V. (2018). Primary school playgrounds as spaces of inclusion/exclusion in New South Wales, Australia. *Education 3–13, 46*(5), 494–505. https://doi.org/10.1080/03004279.2016.1273251

NSW Government. (2023). Everyone can play – A guideline to creating inclusive play spaces. https://www.planning.nsw.gov.au/sites/default/files/2023-03/everyone-can-play-a-guideline-to-inclusive-playspaces.pdf

Pawlowski, C. S., Veitch, J., Andersen, H. B., & Ridgers, N. D. (2019). Designing activating schoolyards: Seen from the girls' viewpoint. *International Journal of Environmental Research and Public Health, 16*(19), 3508. https://doi.org/10.3390/ijerph16193508

Pearson, R., & Howe, J. (2017). Pupil participation and playground design: Listening and responding to children's views. *Educational Psychology in Practice, 33*(4), 356–370. https://doi.org/10.1080/02667363.2017.1326375

Play Midlothian & Play Scotland. (n.d.). Writing a play policy. https://www.playscotland.org/resources/print/Writing-a-Play-Policy.pdf?plsctml_id=20555

Raney, M. A., Hendry, C. F., & Yee, S. A. (2019). Physical activity and social behaviors of urban children in green playgrounds. *American Journal of Preventive Medicine, 56,* 522–529. https://doi.org/10.1016/j.amepre.2018.11.004

Rivera, E., Timperio, A., Loh, V. H. Y., Deforche, B., & Veitch, J. (2021). Important park features for encouraging park visitation, physical activity and social interaction among adolescents: A conjoint analysis. *Health and Place, 70.* https://doi.org/10.1016/j.healthplace.2021.102617

Robinson, M. (2014). Grounds for learning 11-18 secondary school play inspiration and ideas. https://ltl.org.uk/wp-content/uploads/woocommerce_uploads/2019/05/play-in-secondary-schools-ideas-and-inspiration.pdf

World Health Organization. (2022, December 2). Global report on health equity for persons with disabilities (ISBN 978-92-4-006360-0). https://iris.who.int/handle/10665/364834

World Health Organization. (n.d.). Disability. https://www.who.int/health-topics/disability#tab=tab_1

Walker, S., & Clark, I. (2023). Make space for girls – The research background 2023. https://www.makespaceforgirls.co.uk/resources/research-report-2023

Zhang, Y., Mavoa, S., Zhao, J., Raphael, D., & Smith, M. (2020). The association between green space and adolescents' mental well-being: A systematic review. *International Journal of Environmental Research and Public Health, 17,* 6640. https://doi.org/10.3390/ijerph17186640

2

Space to Be Myself
Getting Play and Breaktimes Right for Neurodivergent Pupils
Jenny Gibson and Samantha Friedman

The Importance of Play for Children's Development and Education

Opportunities for play and relaxation are an important part of school life for children and young people, providing them with opportunities to learn more about the world around them, to develop interests and competencies, to build social relationships, and to regulate their emotions and behaviour. The essence of play is that it is intrinsically motivated; in other words, play is fun in its own right and something that a child chooses to do because they enjoy it. Play can also act as an important way for children to explore difficult feelings and to "let off steam" when experiencing distress, anger, or frustration. There is a recuperative function of play too; for example, play can be a restorative experience after a demanding lesson. Studies that follow groups of children over several years have found that play is positively linked with later mental health, wellbeing, and academic achievement (Gibson et al., 2021; Toseeb et al., 2020; Zhao & Gibson, 2023). Neurodivergent children often play differently, and these differences have not always been validated by teachers and parents. Additionally, play often occurs during breaktimes at school, which can present additional affordances and challenges, especially for neurodivergent children. In this chapter we explore how these important opportunities offered by play and relaxation can be made accessible to all pupils, with emphasis on including neurodivergent children, and the role of school breaktimes in supporting play.

Our approach is founded upon the neurodiversity perspective set out in the Introduction; however, before we explore the topic of neurodiversity and play at school in detail, we will introduce some of the other ideas that have influenced our thinking and practice about play and breaktimes. Let us start with a perspective drawn from human rights. We are inspired by the United Nations Convention on the Rights of the Child (UNCRC), a statement which sets out the civil, political, economic, social and cultural rights that all children should enjoy (UN General Assembly, 1989). The statements of rights set out in the UNCRC (known as "articles") are all equally important; however, there are some that are especially relevant to our conversation about play and breaktimes for neurodivergent children. Article 31 protects the child's right to play and relax, while Article 23 sets out that disabled children have a right to full participation and engagement in their communities, and Article 29 sets out the importance of an education that builds each child's own talents and abilities to the full. Putting these things together, the child rights perspective provokes us to consider how schools can ensure play, relaxation, and learning through play opportunities are created, and how equality of access is supported for neurodivergent children.

We are also influenced by ideas from developmental psychology, particularly a framework called neuroconstructivism that emphasises how each child's developmental pathway is unique, changes over time, and is influenced by a combination of factors, from the child's own biology through to the influences of wider society (Karmiloff-Smith, 1998, 2009). An important lens neuroconstructivism brings to the study of play is the idea of mutual influences at work as children mature. For example, a child's self-regulation skills will be influenced by the opportunities to play and recuperate at school, and the play opportunities a teacher decides to offer may be influenced by their knowledge of the child and their development.

Putting together these different perspectives, we argue that:

- Adults should provide individually differentiated, inclusive play opportunities within schools, to honour children's rights and to meet their developmental needs.
- School breaktimes are a natural place to provide opportunities for children to enjoy their rights to play and relaxation.
- School breaktime also supports children's development and wellbeing.

Let us dig a bit deeper into the idea of breaktimes, how they work, and what can be done to improve access for neurodivergent pupils.

Overview of Breaktimes

In British schools, breaktimes are usually periods of unstructured time provided to pupils at one or more times in the school day during which they might play, go outdoors if the weather permits, socialise, and experience respite from structured learning activities. Elsewhere in the world, these breaks are often referred to as "recess," but the purpose is broadly the same. Some schools provide structured activities such as organised games, or provide objects designed to stimulate play (sometimes called "loose parts play") or fixed play structures such as climbing frames or swings. While breaktimes are typically supervised, especially at the primary level, pupils are usually further away from adults compared to classroom time. In England, children in primary schools receive, on average, over 20 more minutes of breaktime than secondary school pupils, and the amount of breaktime pupils are given in schools has decreased over the last 25 years across all levels of schooling (Baines & Blatchford, 2023).

Breaktimes offer pupils the opportunity to play, to engage socially with others, and to act more autonomously than is typically allowed in classroom settings. Additionally, there is some evidence that children are more able to sustain attention on academic tasks after breaktime, and that breaktimes help increase physical activity levels among children (Hodges et al., 2022). Research also suggests that breaktimes spent in green spaces compared to built environments might be more effective for facilitating improvements in attention (Amicone et al., 2018). Breaktimes, particularly those spent outdoors, also provide important opportunities for pupils to engage in a range of forms of play, including independent and imaginary play and games with rules (Baines et al., 2020)

However, breaktimes can bring along a range of downsides too. Being further away from adult supervision can allow opportunity for bullying and aggression to occur more frequently (Forsberg et al., 2022). The lack of curricular focus of breaktimes means that some teachers believe it to be "wasted" time. Reflecting this view that breaktimes are not as valuable as classroom instruction time, some teachers, and even school policies, restrict breaktimes as a punishment for perceived poor behaviour in the classroom or as a reaction to attendance difficulties (Baines & Blatchford, 2023).

The experience of breaktime therefore depends to a large extent on how a given school community values it, and the resources and attention devoted to curating a suitable physical and social environment. When adults have not embraced their role in ensuring children's play needs can be met at school, neurodivergent young people can find things particularly difficult. Instead of experiencing joy, relaxation, and opportunities for informal learning, neurodivergent children may experience sensory distress, high levels of stress, loneliness, and risk of engagement with bullying and victimisation.

In the next sections we will discuss some of the considerations that educators and other members of school communities should be aware of when planning to create positive play experiences for neurodivergent young people. Much of the evidence we will discuss relates to autism, as it is perhaps the most researched and discussed neurotype; however, the principles of inclusive differentiation will apply to many different neurotypes, and we hope that the ideas and insights will be used to guide individualised practice.

Neurodiversity and School Breaktimes

Our key message is to **celebrate and accommodate diversity in play** styles and preferences. For too long, neurodivergent, especially autistic, play has been characterised using a deficit model. It is still common to see reports assessing children as having a "limited play repertoire" or individual education goals that aim to restrict play activities, such as spinning, at all times. From testimony and research evidence produced by autistic people and allies, it is clear that these deficit-focused narratives are harmful and false (Alexander, 2024). Engaging in "stimming," repeated iteration of the same activity, or withdrawing from group activities completely can provide recuperation and joy for autistic pupils (Conn, 2015). For those with ADHD, breaktimes can provide essential outlets for physical activity and promote self-regulation and attention in subsequent lessons (Ridgway et al., 2003). The best playtime provision allows for this variety of preference and need.

> *I need space to myself; I am a loner. Breaktimes in the library reading [Lord of the Rings] are the best!*
> **Neurodivergent student**

Our neuroconstructivist perspective also prompts us to consider how the interactions in the social environment at breaktime contribute to development and wellbeing. Breaktimes provide valuable opportunities for neurodivergent pupils to connect socially on their own terms. In class, pupils are often told which activities to complete, which topics to focus on, and with whom to interact. This leaves little room for following personal interests and can increase difficulties for neurodivergent young people if they have to interact in ways or with people that make them uncomfortable. It is a misconception that autistic people do not desire social connections, with loneliness being a significant risk factor in development of mental health conditions (Kasari & Sterling, 2013; Locke et al., 2010). In contrast, connection with *like-minded* others is important for neurodivergent wellbeing (Watts et al., 2024) and cited as significant in autistic play experiences (Pritchard-Rowe et al., 2023).

Studies of autistic playground behaviour have found that autistic children spend greater amounts of playtime in solitary play and less time in reciprocal interactions when compared to non-autistic peers (Calder et al., 2012; Gibson et al., 2011; Locke et al., 2016). More recently, however, acknowledgement that social interactions can look different for different neurotypes has led to the understanding that parallel socialisation, playing, or engaging in similar activities alongside a peer without necessarily actively collaborating can be an enjoyable and meaningful way to socialise (Francis et al., 2019; Pritchard-Rowe et al., 2023). Thus, during breaktimes, neurodivergent pupils might enjoy opportunities to make or build upon connections with other neurodivergent young people and those with similar interests with whom social interaction might feel less effortful (e.g., Crompton et al., 2020; Watts et al., 2024). Conversely, breaktimes which allow for free play and choice of activity might allow for neurodivergent young people to engage in mixed-neurotype interaction on their own terms and in a setting with less pressure than in traditional classrooms, which often value and uphold normative social standards. For those children who want to engage but might find it difficult – for example, those with developmental language disorder – supported initiation strategies can be helpful (Lloyd-Esenkaya, 2022).

> Here is an example from the authors' experience: Jayden (pseudonym), a 7-year-old child with developmental language disorder, was desperate to join in with football at playtime, but he was often the last out of the classroom and the game usually started without him. His strategy for joining the game was to run in and pick up the ball – which frustrated those already playing, leading to conflict and exclusion from the game. To address this, the school changed the way footballs

were accessed by the children. Each breaktime, children who wanted to play football would wait in a group, and a different child each day was given the job of carrying out the football to the designated area, setting up the teams, and kicking off the match. This helped all the children to build a routine that supported play initiation skills. Jayden had some practice sessions with the teaching assistant to build his skills in setting up the game, and he also benefited from peer modelling as well as the calmer, more inclusive way of setting up the game. Most importantly, the changes helped Jayden to join in and have fun.

Relatedly, breaktimes can be used to **support pupil agency and autonomy** regarding what they do (or don't do) and with whom they engage (or not). Agency and autonomy are considered essential to children's thriving and learning at school. Unfortunately, neurodivergent young people are often denied autonomy, sometimes because of misconceptions that they cannot make their own choices or because their choices are perceived to go against social "norms" and therefore in need of "correction" (Alexander, 2024). Reduction in breaktimes as a punishment is therefore inappropriate, both because it infringes children's right to play and relax and because it diminishes autonomy in the school setting, where free choice is already difficult to come by.

What this means, practically, is that adults should pay close attention to the preferred play of neurodivergent children and young people, communicating with them (or their advocates) about how best to set up breaktimes that enable them to do what they enjoy. It is important, however, to take a holistic view. If a student with sensory processing disorder wants to spend breaktimes in a quiet corner of the library because they love reading and want some time out in a space with fewer sensory demands – fantastic, work with the librarian to make it happen! If they are retreating to the library to avoid bullies and would otherwise rather join in skipping games outdoors, however, a different approach is needed.

Structure at breaktime is also a significant consideration. At first thought, it may seem that structure is the antithesis of play, however this is not the case. Play is not simply chaos; even what we think of as "free play" is typically constrained by external factors (e.g., the railings around the playground or the availability of play equipment) or by factors within the play itself, such as made-up or established rules (e.g., roles assigned during pretend play, football rules). In a school breaktime context, adults set up (by design or by accident) many of the structures that provide these constraints. Getting the structure right is essential for inclusion of neurodivergent pupils.

On the one hand, filling breaktimes with highly structured activities limits pupils' ability to exercise autonomy (Baines & Blatchford, 2023). Many neurodivergent individuals struggle with "organised fun," which is often not designed with their needs and preferences in mind and is in fact not fun for them at all. This can contribute to feelings of alienation and stress and hinder them from accessing their right to play and relaxation. On the other hand, some neurodivergent pupils might struggle with a lack of structure, particularly when contrasted against the highly structured nature of the rest of the school day. For many neurodivergent pupils, breaktimes might be optimally restorative when they know what to expect – for example, clarity around procedures, where they can go, and what they can do – but are given room to choose within those boundaries. A lack of structure and oversight at breaktime can contribute to increased conflict among peers and opportunities for bullying (Forsberg et al., 2022), placing neurodivergent students at risk of bullying and disability discrimination.

Both the social and the spatial aspects of breaktime structure therefore need to be considered when finding solutions for creating neurodiversity-positive structures – for example, educators should be addressing questions such as: *Are breaktime staff appropriately trained? How can the available space be used to create a variety of play affordances? Where can pupils let off steam? Where can pupils take some quiet time out?*

Finally, we encourage educators to **"think sensory"** at breaktimes. Many neurodivergent pupils have sensory needs which require them to seek out or avoid certain stimuli. These sensory needs are not fixed; an individual's ability to cope with sensory stimuli or seek out stimuli can change rapidly. Unmet sensory needs are a common cause of school attendance difficulties related to emotional distress for neurodivergent young people (Connolly et al., 2023). For young people who are sensitive to various sensory stimuli, school common areas (e.g., canteens, corridors, halls) and times of day when many young people are gathered together might be particularly difficult. This is due to the increased sensory stimuli that results from having many young people in the same space, with the noise of multiple overlapping conversations, the smell of food or body sprays, and the potential for unwanted touch due to spaces being crowded, among other possible stimuli.

[I experienced] sensory overload due to yelling, shouting, and many visual stimuli in motion, which were exacerbated by the experience of the cafeteria (even more chaotic and stressful due to the obligation to eat food I considered distasteful).
Neurodivergent adult, reflecting on breaktime at school

Thus, paying attention to the sensory environment during breaktimes is important in creating neurodiversity-affirmative school settings. While spending breaktime outdoors might provide for an easier sensory experience for some neurodivergent young people (Finnigan, 2024; Friedman et al., 2024; MacLennan et al., 2023), this will not always be possible. Additionally, not all neurodivergent young people find the outdoors to be a preferable sensory environment, particularly at times when playgrounds or other outdoor play spaces are crowded (Birkett et al., 2022). Many schools implement the use of a sensory or soft play space that pupils are able to access at breaktimes or, for some schools, as needed throughout the day. Though widely used, sensory-adaptive environments lack compelling evidence to support their implementation (Williams et al., 2024) and are often created without the input of the children for whom they are designed. However, for some young people, sensory rooms can provide a welcome respite and opportunity to attune to sensory needs during breaktimes.

Neurodiversity-Affirmative Play for Education beyond Breaktimes – the Example of Forest School

Play is also significant for learning and development in educational contexts other than breaktimes. Play-based pedagogies can tap into the intrinsic motivation and agency that support independent learning in ways that are beneficial for all, but are especially relevant for neurodivergent pupils, for whom mainstream class settings are too often unmotivating or exclusionary (Bailey & Baker, 2020). This is often recognised in early years education settings (Gibson & McNally, 2024; Murphy, n.d.), but we encourage all readers of this chapter to consider how radically embracing the links between education and play can lead to a more truly inclusive perspective on education.

Here we present a short example relating to forest school practices to show the power of play in learning contexts that support agency and autonomy, recognise and adapt for neurodivergent learner differences, provide appropriate levels of structure, and consider that the sensory environment can be applied to many aspects of pedagogy and curriculum – not just at breaktime.

Forest school is a form of nature-based learning that is child-led and holistic (Knight, 2011). The ethos of forest school centres on the need to provide learners with autonomy to engage in properly assessed risks, decide what they would like to do, and build trust with the environment and the people in it on their own terms. Forest schools are commonly used as alternative provisions or home education activities for young people who struggle to attend school, many of whom are neurodivergent. Although it is a new research area, forest school seems to be beneficial for neurodivergent young people's wellbeing, perhaps particularly because of the opportunities to promote autonomy (e.g., Friedman et al., 2022). Crucially, though, opportunities to exercise autonomy at forest school exist within structure, which could help neurodivergent pupils access the benefits. For instance, activities at forest school sometimes involve an inherent level of risk that must be assessed. Supporting children to assess this risk and to make adjustments for their own safety can be seen as autonomy-promoting, rather than autonomy-hindering, if facilitated in a child-centred way (Arvanitis et al., 2024).

Typical forest school routines, which can also be seen as rituals, can be considered elements of structure that help neurodivergent pupils know what to expect so they are able to exercise autonomy more comfortably. For example, forest school sessions might be structured around a brief chat at the fire circle at the start and end of the session. This routine helps children know what to expect during their transition into and out of the forest school space, which can reduce some anxiety and promote learning. The playful interplay between autonomy and structure within the forest school ethos can provide inspiration for improving access to playful pedagogies at school for neurodivergent young people.

As we have established, both neuroconstructivist- and neurodiversity-informed approaches to understanding learning and development emphasise the critical nature of providing physical and social environments that are matched to psychological needs. Much like a forest school session, skilled educators can adapt lessons, bringing in agency to support pupils' interests, attune to their needs holistically, and provide a reasonable balance of autonomy and structure.

Practicalities of Creating an Inclusive Play Culture

Together, the factors we have discussed represent essential aspects of creating an inclusive play culture in schools. Two principles are key to practical implementation:

1. Breaktimes require careful planning and curation on the part of adults responsible for children's learning and wellbeing, deserving the same attention as classrooms and lessons
2. Educators require deep knowledge of each neurodivergent pupil's unique play and recuperation needs to implement appropriate play opportunities

When putting the first principle into practice, the concept of Universal Design (Rose & Meyer, 2002) is helpful. This is the idea that everyone can benefit from simple changes applied to the way things are done in order to promote inclusion. For example, rather than giving ear defenders to a child with auditory sensitivity one minute before the school bell rings for breaktime, schools could opt instead to use in-class electronic alarms, allowing different tones to be selected for each class, or turned to silent mode if needed. It will also mean considering staff training needs alongside pupil needs.

> *Create a culture where the staff are actively engaging in the breaktime too (i.e., not standing around in groups with cups of coffee). It is important for young people to have autonomy and independence, but quite often they need support to initiate games or activities, and without this might just stand around being bored.*
> **Practitioner advice**

While Universal Design principles are a fantastic starting point, however, we often need inclusive design principles to complement them in order to facilitate genuine inclusion, and this will support the implementation of the second principle (Rosa, 2023). Inclusive design recognises that differentiation is essential to move us from a "one size fits a few" to "many sizes fits all" approach. In the context of breaktimes, this might mean designing the playtime offer with specific neurodivergent pupils in mind, and building in flexibility to adapt as they change and grow. It is important to consider intersectionality too: neurodivergent individuals will have other characteristics, for example language, ethnicity or gender, that interact with their environment to contribute to their unique play needs. We therefore recommend regular consultation with neurodivergent pupils to ensure that their play needs are fully understood.

> *Personal experiences lead me to emphasise the role of school culture in the quality of recess. In particular, teachers' efforts in fostering collaborative peer relationships during school time positively influenced breaktime. Another key factor was the flexibility of the environment and the absence of rigid rules.*
>
> **Neurodivergent adult**

Summary

In this chapter we have discussed the important role that play can have in supporting neurodivergent pupils to thrive at school (see Key Takeaways). We put children's right to play and relaxation at the centre of our discussions, as well as considering how play can act as an important catalyst for learning and development in multiple domains. Breaktimes are a natural starting place to ensure the right to play is embedded in schools in a way that is inclusive of neurodivergent students. We used the example of forest school to demonstrate that play-based pedagogies can be implemented more radically in education, providing a unique opportunity to celebrate and accommodate diversity.

Key Takeaways

- Neurodivergent children have rights to education, play, and relaxation.
- Play is important because it is fun, it promotes learning, and it supports recuperation and wellbeing.
- Breaktimes need careful planning to ensure they meet neurodivergent children's needs and preferences.
- Neurodivergent play can look different to expectations – and that's OK.
- Withholding playtime infringes children's rights and may be harmful to some neurodivergent children.
- Play can be used to support new approaches to pedagogy that may suit neurodivergent children.

Reflective Activities

These prompts are designed to get you thinking about what this means in practice in your own school or education setting:

- According to what I have learned here, what does my school do well when it comes to breaktimes?
- How can we adapt our procedures and practices around breaktimes to better respond to the sensory needs of our neurodivergent pupils?
- What can I do to celebrate neurodivergent play, in all its forms?

Acknowledgements

Thanks to the autistic and play/forest school community colleagues who provided feedback and quotations for this chapter. These include anonymous contributors and Felicity Cooper.

References

Alexander, M. (2024). 'Shut your face!'; Prioritising, valuing and enabling autistic children's autonomy. *Play Radical.* https://playradical.com/2024/02/08/shut-your-face-prioritising-valuing-and-enabling-autistic-childrens-autonomy/

Amicone, G., Petruccelli, I., De Dominicis, S., Gherardini, A., Costantino, V., Perucchini, P., & Bonaiuto, M. (2018). Green Breaks: The restorative effect of the school environment's green areas on children's cognitive performance. *Frontiers in Psychology, 9*(OCT), 301023. https://doi.org/10.3389/FPSYG.2018.01579/BIBTEX

Arvanitis, A., Barrable, A., & Touloumakos, A. (2024). The relationship between autonomy support and structure in early childhood nature-based settings: Practices and challenges. *Learning Environments Research, 27*(1), 101–119. https://doi.org/10.1007/s10984-023-09470-0

Bailey, J., & Baker, S. T. (2020). A synthesis of the quantitative literature on autistic pupils' experience of barriers to inclusion in mainstream schools. *Journal of Research in Special Educational Needs, 20*(4), 291–307. https://doi.org/10.1111/1471-3802.12490

Baines, E., & Blatchford, P. (2023). The decline in breaktimes and lunchtimes in primary and secondary schools in England: Results from three national surveys spanning 25 years. *British Educational Research Journal, 49*(5), 925–946. https://doi.org/10.1002/BERJ.3874

Baines, E., Blatchford, P., & Golding, K. (2020). Recess, breaktimes, and supervision. *The Encyclopedia of Child and Adolescent Development*, 1–11. https://doi.org/10.1002/9781119171492.WECAD268

Birkett, L., McGrath, L., & Tucker, I. (2022). Muting, filtering and transforming space: Autistic children's sensory 'tactics' for navigating mainstream school space following transition to secondary school. *Emotion, Space and Society, 42*, 100872. https://doi.org/10.1016/J.EMOSPA.2022.100872

Calder, L., Hill, V., & Pellicano, E. (2012). 'Sometimes I want to play by myself': Understanding what friendship means to children with autism in mainstream primary schools. *Autism: The International Journal of Research and Practice, 17*(3), 296–316. https://doi.org/10.1177/1362361312467866

Conn, C. (2015). 'Sensory highs', 'vivid rememberings' and 'interactive stimming': Children's play cultures and experiences of friendship in autistic autobiographies. *Disability & Society, 30*(8), 1192–1206. https://doi.org/10.1080/09687599.2015.1081094

Connolly, S. E., Constable, H. L., & Mullally, S. L. (2023). School distress and the school attendance crisis: A story dominated by neurodivergence and unmet need. *Frontiers in Psychiatry, 14*, 1237052. https://doi.org/10.3389/FPSYT.2023.1237052/BIBTEX

Crompton, C. J., Sharp, M., Axbey, H., Fletcher-Watson, S., Flynn, E. G., & Ropar, D. (2020). Neurotype-matching, but not being autistic, influences self and observer ratings of interpersonal rapport. *Frontiers in Psychology, 11*. https://doi.org/10.3389/FPSYG.2020.586171/FULL

Finnigan, K. A. (2024). Sensory responsive environments: A qualitative study on perceived relationships between outdoor built environments and sensory sensitivities. *Land, 13*(5), 636. https://doi.org/10.3390/LAND13050636/S1

Forsberg, C., Hammar Chiriac, E., & Thornberg, R. (2022). 'I think we have a good time if there are no disputes': Pupils' dynamic perspectives on being on breaktime. *Educational Studies*. https://doi.org/10.1080/03055698.2022.2120763

Francis, G. A., Farr, W., Mareva, S., & Gibson, J. L. (2019). Do Tangible User Interfaces promote social behaviour during free play? A comparison of autistic and typically-developing children playing with passive and digital construction toys. *Research in Autism Spectrum Disorders, 58*. https://doi.org/10.1016/j.rasd.2018.08.005

Friedman, S., Gibson, J. L., Jones, C., & Hughes, C. (2022). 'A new adventure': A case study of autistic children at Forest School. *Journal of Adventure Education and Outdoor Learning, 24*(2), 202–218. https://doi.org/10.1080/14729679.2022.2115522

Friedman, S., Noble, R., Archer, S., Gibson, J., & Hughes, C. (2024). 'It helps make the fuzzy go away': Autistic adults' perspectives on nature's relationship with well-being through the life course. https://doi.org/10.1089/AUT.2023.0009

Gibson, J. L., & McNally, S. (2024). Play in the education and care of young autistic children. In *Resilience and wellbeing in young children, their families and communities* (pp. 147–158). Routledge.

Gibson, J. L., Hussain, J., Holsgrove, S., Adams, C., & Green, J. (2011). Quantifying peer interactions for research and clinical use: The Manchester Inventory for Playground Observation. *Research in Developmental Disabilities, 32*(6), 2458–2466.

Gibson, J. L., Newbury, D. F., Durkin, K., Pickles, A., Conti-Ramsden, G., & Toseeb, U. (2021). Pathways from the early language and communication environment to literacy outcomes at the end of primary school; the roles of language development and social development. *Oxford Review of Education, 47*(2), 260–283. https://doi.org/10.1080/03054985.2020.1824902

Hodges, V. C., Centeio, E. E., & Morgan, C. F. (2022). The benefits of school recess: A systematic review. *Journal of School Health, 92*(10), 959–967. https://doi.org/10.1111/JOSH.13230

Karmiloff-Smith, A. (1998). Development itself is the key to understanding developmental disorders. In *Trends in cognitive sciences*. https://doi.org/10.1016/S1364-6613(98)01230-3

Karmiloff-Smith, A. (2009). Nativism versus neuroconstructivism: Rethinking the study of developmental disorders. *Developmental Psychology*. https://doi.org/10.1037/a0014506

Kasari, C., & Sterling, L. (2013). Loneliness and social isolation in children with autism spectrum disorders. *The Handbook of Solitude: Psychological Perspectives on Social Isolation, Social Withdrawal, and Being Alone*, 409–426. https://doi.org/10.1002/9781118427378.CH23

Knight, S. (2011). *Forest school for all*. Sage. https://uk.sagepub.com/en-gb/eur/forest-school-for-all/book235112

Lloyd-Esenkaya, V. (2022). *Zedie and Zoola's playful universe: A practical guide to supporting children with different communication styles at playtime*. Speechmark.

Locke, J., Ishijima, E. H., Kasari, C., & London, N. (2010). Loneliness, friendship quality and the social networks of adolescents with high-functioning autism in an inclusive school setting. *Journal of Research in Special Educational Needs, 10*(2), 74–81. https://doi.org/10.1111/J.1471-3802.2010.01148.X

Locke, J., Shih, W., Kretzmann, M., & Kasari, C. (2016). Examining playground engagement between elementary school children with and without autism spectrum disorder. *Autism, 20*(6 SRC-GoogleScholar FG-0), 653–662. https://doi.org/10.1177/1362361315599468

MacLennan, K., Woolley, C., Andsensory, E., Heasman, B., Starns, J., George, B., & Manning, C. (2023). 'It Is a big spider web of things': Sensory experiences of autistic adults in public spaces. *5*(4), 411–422. https://doi.org/10.1089/AUT.2022.0024

Murphy, K. (n.d.). *Self-directed neurodivergent play | Beginner's guides | Tapestry*. 2023. Retrieved July 26, 2024, from https://tapestry.info/self-directed-neurodivergent-play/

Pritchard-Rowe, E., de Lemos, C., Howard, K., & Gibson, J. L. (2023). Diversity in autistic play: Autistic adults' experiences. *Autism in Adulthood*. https://doi.org/10.1089/aut.2023.0008

Ridgway, A., Northup, J., Pellegrin, A., LaRue, R., & Hightshoe, A. (2003). Effects of recess on the classroom behavior of children with and without attention-deficit hyperactivity disorder. *School Psychology Quarterly, 18*(3), 253–268. https://doi.org/10.1521/scpq.18.3.253.22578

Rosa, M. (2023). *Universal and inclusive co-design of the built environment and the transportation systems - Engineering Professors Council*. Engineering Professors Council. https://epc.ac.uk/toolkit/universal-and-inclusive-co-design-of-the-built-environment-and-the-transportation-systems/

Rose, D. H., & Meyer, A. (2002). *Teaching every student in the digital age: Universal design for learning*. Association for Supervision and Curriculum Development.

Toseeb, U., Gibson, J. L., Newbury, D. F., Orlik, W., Durkin, K., Pickles, A., & Conti-Ramsden, G. (2020). Play and prosociality are associated with fewer externalizing problems in children with developmental language disorder: The role of early language and communication environment. *International Journal of Language & Communication Disorders*, 1460–6984.12541. https://doi.org/10.1111/1460-6984.12541

UN General Assembly. (1989). Convention on the rights of a child. *United Nations, Treaty Series, 1577*, 3.

Watts, G., Crompton, C., Grainger, C., Long, J., Botha, M., Somerville, M., & Cage, E. (2024). 'A certain magic' – Autistic adults' experiences of interacting with other autistic people and its relation to quality of life: A systematic review and thematic meta-synthesis. *Autism*. https://doi.org/10.1177/13623613241255811/ASSET/IMAGES/LARGE/10.1177_13623613241255811-FIG3.JPEG

Williams, K. L., Dumont, R. L., Schiano, N. R., Lawlor, K. F., Greaney, K., Kim, R., Duryea, E., Rios-Vega, Lady, Simms, K. D., & Schaaf, R. C. (2024). Use of sensory adaptive environments with autistic children: A scoping review. *Research in Autism Spectrum Disorders, 114*, 102362. https://doi.org/10.1016/J.RASD.2024.102362

Zhao, Y. V., & Gibson, J. L. (2023). Evidence for protective effects of peer play in the early years: Better peer play ability at age 3 years predicts lower risks of externalising and internalising problems at age 7 years in a longitudinal cohort analysis. *Child Psychiatry and Human Development, 54*(6), 1807–1822. https://doi.org/10.1007/S10578-022-01368-X/TABLES/4

3

Understanding and Meeting the Sensory Needs of Neurodivergent Learners

Implementing and Evaluating the Use of Flexible Seating in an Inclusive Primary School

Heba Al-Jayoosi and Laura Crane

Understanding and Meeting the Sensory Needs of Neurodivergent Learners

The sensory needs of neurodivergent learners are diverse and varied. In Table 3.1, we provide a summary of some of the broad range of sensory needs that staff may observe in a mainstream primary school, acknowledging that there is likely to be overlap in sensory needs across different diagnostic categories.

There are two schools of thought around how best to support the sensory needs of neurodivergent learners. One suggestion is to encourage children to learn how to suppress "undesirable" sensory behaviours. For example, staff may encourage children to have "quiet hands" and to focus on "nice sitting." An alternative – neurodiversity-affirmative – suggestion is to embrace the unique ways different children interact with the sensory environment, recognising that sensory behaviours (e.g., hand flapping) may serve important social and self-regulatory functions for neurodivergent children (e.g., Conn, 2015; Veerasamy, 2024).

In recent years, there has been an abundance of approaches implemented in schools to meet the sensory needs of neurodivergent learners. These approaches range from providing children with sensory supports such as

Table 3.1 Examples of the Sensory Needs That May Be Experienced by Neurodivergent Learners

Dawud is 7 years old and has a diagnosis of developmental coordination disorder, often referred to as dyspraxia. Dawud often: • Has difficulties focusing on information shared on a big screen • Struggles with using scissors and with lengthy writing tasks • Finds it challenging to be in the lunch queue	Liyana is 11 years old and has a diagnosis of attention deficit hyperactivity disorder. Liyana: • Can find it hard to attend to a task assigned by their teacher • Constantly seeks movement during lessons • Needs to fidget with her hands
Adam is 5 years old and has a diagnosis of autism. Adam finds that: • The physical proximity of other children is challenging and he prefers to have his own space • It is difficult to filter out sounds, with loud sounds proving to be quite distressing • Cold surfaces feel painful to touch	Alexandra is 8 years old and has a diagnosis of developmental language disorder. Alexandra may: • Need space for practical activities to embed her learning • Struggle with maintaining attention on lengthy teacher demonstrations, especially when the delivery is primarily verbal

fidget toys and ear defenders through to more extensive adaptations to the school environment such as the implementation of quiet zones or sensory rooms. The research underpinning such approaches is fairly limited, meaning that school staff often rely on well-marketed but non-evidence-based sensory interventions to support their learners (Dynia et al., 2023). Such initiatives may come at a huge cost to the school. For instance, schools may need to invest their limited budgets in buying equipment; they may need to source space to house equipment; they may have to ensure that there are sufficient staff available to supervise children accessing sensory supports; and they may need to devote time to overseeing practical issues (e.g., timetabling for the use of sensory supports and associated staffing; monitoring the state of equipment and fixing any damage).

Practical and economic issues aside, a crucially important question is whether sensory support used in schools should be reserved for neurodivergent children, who arguably show the highest levels of sensory need. There are several reasons why we believe this should not be the case. First, international policy and legislation emphasise the need for inclusive educational practices (e.g., United Nations, 2006; UNESCO, 1994). While theoretical and practical definitions of inclusion vary (Pellicano et al., 2018), it is often suggested that good inclusive practices benefit all learners – not just those who are neurodivergent. Second, while current legislation in England (Department for Education, 2014; Department for Education and Department for Health, 2015) calls for the provision of support to be based on need as opposed to a diagnostic label, in practice this is not always the case (Boesley & Crane, 2018). Yet there may be several reasons why neurodivergent children do not have a diagnostic label. For example, many neurodivergent children "fly under the radar" through "masking" or "camouflaging" their neurodivergent traits (e.g., Halsall et al., 2021). Further, others may face barriers to accessing a formal diagnosis, given that a range of inequalities (e.g., socio-economic status, ethnicity) exist for neurodivergent children and their families (Roman-Urrestarazu et al., 2021). Therefore, there is a risk associated with limiting support only to those with a formally diagnosed neurodivergence. Finally, making support available to all learners serves an important function in terms of reducing and combating stigma. Research has shown that neurodivergent students may experience discrimination from their peers at school (Zahir et al., 2024). As such, ensuring that all learners can access and make use of sensory supports could reduce the risk of neurodivergent children experiencing negative outcomes such as bullying, exclusion, and poor mental health (cf. Zahir et al., 2024). Overall, given the pressures on schools to spend resources wisely and the desire to meet the needs of pupils without being constrained by diagnosis, we decided to examine a whole-school approach to offering sensory support – flexible seating – within Mayflower Primary School.

The Context: Mayflower Primary School

Mayflower Primary School is a mainstream primary school (including a nursery) that caters for children aged 3–11 years. It is based in the London Borough of Tower Hamlets and at the time of writing has approximately 400 pupils on roll. Tower Hamlets is an inner London borough with a high proportion of its population coming from culturally and linguistically diverse backgrounds. It also has one of the highest percentages of pupils with special educational needs and disabilities (SEND) nationally. Mayflower School is in the Poplar area of Tower Hamlets, which has a high level of socio-economic deprivation and a very high proportion of pupils who speak English as an additional language.

Mayflower is a flagship storytelling school (Smith et al., 2020) with a creative approach to learning embedded at the heart of the curriculum. Mayflower also has an excellent reputation for inclusive practice, evidenced by the strong outcomes of pupils with a recognised SEND (which refers to around a fifth of the school's pupils). The school provides learning to pupils in mixed-ability groups, where pupils have agency over their own learning. The school also has a strong commitment to practice-informed research and research-informed practice.

One of the strengths of the school is harnessing the expertise of external professionals for the benefit of all pupils. One such example refers to how the school works with an occupational therapist (OT), who works holistically across the school to support the needs of all learners. For example, the OT implements "Sensory Circuits" for pupils aged 3–7 years, whereby short bursts of physical activities are used to alert, organise, and calm children so that they are ready to learn (for further details, see Griffin, 2023). However, the OT also works with individual children who have specific sensory needs and would benefit from specialist support. One of the recommendations the OT made for this latter group of children was to implement alternative seating options. For example, they recommended that one child should be able to use a standing desk, and another should be able to use a rocking chair. Not long after these recommendations were implemented, the first author (the school's Assistant Head and Head of Inclusion) was awarded a Churchill Fellowship to visit schools that were part of the ASD Nest programme in New York City. The ASD Nest programme (for an overview, see Koenig et al., 2009) aims to facilitate inclusive education for autistic students through implementing a range of strategies and supports which are designed to meet a broad range of pupils' needs (including sensory needs). One of the initiatives implemented by ASD Nest schools was alternative seating options on a whole-class level, whereby any child could access and make use of an alternative seating option. Anecdotally, staff at ASD Nest schools reported that this approach was felt to benefit all pupils in the classes, not just those who were neurodivergent. Upon obtaining external funding via an Activate Grant from the Churchill Fellowship to purchase alternative seating options for use across the whole school, Mayflower set out to implement and evaluate the use of a "flexible seating" model as a whole-school adaptation to meet the sensory needs of all learners.

About Flexible Seating

Flexible seating involves providing a range of alternative seating options that pupils can choose from, alongside choices around where they engage with their learning. Complementing the classic chairs used in mainstream primary schools in the UK (typically chairs with hard plastic seats and backs, on four metal legs, which are stackable), seating options might include rocking chairs, ball chairs, standing desks, wobble stools, floor chairs, floor rockers, sensory cushions, and sketching desks (see Figure 3.1).

The evidence base behind flexible seating is fairly limited. From a theoretical perspective, we know that neurodivergent children may experience the sensory environment differently to their neurotypical peers, even from very early in development (e.g., Isaacs & Riordan, 2020; Pellicano, 2013). As such, adaptations such as flexible seating may serve an important role in ensuring a child is ready to learn. However, our review of the literature (for further information, see Giuliano et al., 2024) suggests that the existing research on the relative pros and cons of flexible seating yields fairly mixed results, both in relation to neurotypical and neurodivergent learners. Further, we identified several limitations with the existing literature. For example, research did not often consider the impact of flexible seating on *all* learners in a school (e.g., children of different neurotypes and of different ages); research tended to evaluate the use of specific seating options rather than providing learners with a broad range of options to engage with and choose from; and research did not always integrate the views of all staff in a school (e.g., teachers, teaching assistants) alongside the views of all pupils (whether neurotypical or neurodivergent). We therefore sought to address these gaps in knowledge through our work.

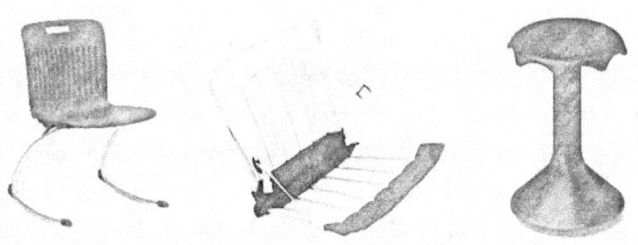

Figure 3.1 Examples of Flexible Seating Options (Rocking Chair, Floor Chair, Wobble Stool)

Implementing and Evaluating Flexible Seating: A Partnership Approach

Our Team

Our project was highly collaborative in nature, co-led by the two authors of this chapter – Heba Al-Jayoosi and Laura Crane. Heba is Assistant Head at Mayflower Primary School, where she is also Head of Inclusion. Heba is passionate about ensuring that all children thrive at school, particularly neurodivergent children. Laura is a Professor of Autism Studies at the University of Birmingham, where she specialises in autism education research. Laura is committed to undertaking co-produced research that makes a genuine difference to research and practice. Together, we assembled a team of collaborators with a range of relevant academic, professional, and lived experiences (categories were not mutually exclusive).

> *The partnership we had with academic researchers played a massive role in the success of our project. We do many things in schools that are really creative and extremely useful, but much of the evidence we gather is anecdotal and local to our contexts. The academic researchers we worked with introduced rigour and structure to the project in a way which we couldn't have done alone as school-based practitioners, and on a whole-school scale.*
>
> **Heba Al-Jayoosi, Assistant Head and Head of Inclusion**

The Chair Committee

Central to the project – and the broader ethos of Mayflower – was pupil voice. Pupils in each class were allowed to elect members of the chair committee, in the same way they elected school ambassadors or lunchtime ambassadors, so they were familiar with this approach. The committee consisted of 20 pupils, two from each class, from Years 2 to 6 (i.e., children aged 7–11 years). The chair committee were tasked with taking feedback from their peers about the different seating options and communicating this to the Assistant Head during scheduled meeting times, but also whenever there was something they felt was important to talk about in relation to the project. As with all activities at Mayflower, it was crucial to have an open-door policy as well as a structured time for the pupils to provide feedback, with no judgement applied to their views. As one example of the role of the chair committee, their early feedback led to the ball chair being removed from the project. This decision was taken as pupils had fed back several issues: it did not fit under tables, it took up too much space, it was regularly punctured with pencils, and it was perceived to be "very annoying" when other children used it as a space hopper (i.e., when they bounced around the room on it) rather than as a seat.

What the chair committee said ...

"It was kind of nice because I felt important. I liked it because we all got to share our ideas." – Rabiul

"It was honestly amazing. I loved the experience and getting to trial everything. The meetings were really fun as I got to hear other people's thoughts and ideas." – Hafsa

"It was fun because we got to decide which chairs we got more of. It wasn't boring meetings and sometimes meetings were quite fun and silly – you do need some silly in your life." – Rebecca

"Being on the chair committee was amazing! The meetings were fun and we got to decide which chairs pupils get to use." – Joshua

Flexible Seating as a Whole-School Approach

When flexible seating was introduced as a whole-school initiative, some alternative seating options were already in use by individual pupils, including rocking chairs, wobble stools, and sensory cushions. As such, pupils were already familiar with what some of the alternate seating options looked like and may have used them at some point. However, these options would have typically been reserved for the pupils for whom they were prescribed. In introducing flexible seating on a wider scale, there were several issues that Mayflower considered, including:

- What would flexible seating look like on the ground?
- How much work would be involved for staff?

- Could/should we prioritise this initiative over and above other endeavours?
- How could we make implementation a whole-school collaborative effort – who gets to join, and in what capacity?
- Does seating really matter, and why?
- What changes might we expect to see as a result of introducing flexible seating?
- Does flexible seating fit into our ethos?
- Could we continue to fund this initiative in the future?
- IS IT FUN?!

After consulting with the OT and the chair committee, it was agreed that each classroom would start the academic year (in September) with 11 different kinds of seating options available to them (either in their classrooms or available to borrow from other classrooms). The seating options were assigned to classes based on class sizes, class layout, and the degree of desk-based versus carpet-based activities expected based on children's ages. The seating options used (in addition to regular classroom chairs) were as follows:

- Reception (ages 4–5 years): floor chair, sensory cushion and wobble cushion
- Year 1 (ages 5–6 years): floor chair, floor rocker, ball chair, wobble stool and rocking chair
- Year 2 (ages 6–7 years): floor rocker, wobble stool, rocking chair, floor desk and standing desk
- Years 3–6 (ages 7–10 years): rocking chair, wobble stool, floor desk and standing desk
- Year 6 (ages 10–11 years): rocking chair, wobble stool, floor desk, standing desk and sketching desk

The seating options were introduced gradually, with the aim of eventually (i.e., by the end of the evaluation) having 50 per cent of the total seats in each class designated as flexible seats, and the remaining 50 per cent as regular classroom chairs. To that end, a quarter of the flexible seating options were purchased by the end of the first school term (i.e., at the end of December), and an additional quarter of the seating options were purchased for each classroom by the middle of the academic year (i.e., by the following March, which is when the research project took place). It was agreed with the chair committee that the remaining 50 per cent of seating options would be purchased after considering the results from the research, and these were all purchased by the end of the academic year (i.e., by July).

Seating options were placed in different areas of the classrooms depending on the nature of the seat. For example, wobble cushions were placed on carpet areas, rocking chairs were tucked underneath tables, and standing desks were housed on top of tables. Pupils were able to move all the seating options, according to their needs, for each different lesson. For example, pupils could move rocking chairs if they wanted to work in a different part of the classroom, or they could use standing desks towards the front or back of the class (either on a table or on the carpet, as appropriate). It should be noted that the broader layout of classrooms restricted the use of some seating options. For instance, there was no carpeted area in some of the classrooms used by older pupils, so this led pupils to use seating options that could be more easily used alongside tables. Conversely, classrooms for the younger pupils were already purposefully designed to facilitate movement during learning, alongside structured carpet time. As such, these classrooms lent themselves better to the use of floor chairs or wobble cushions. Crucially, in all classrooms, children could choose where and when to use the seating options available to them. Staff were only given three rules about the seating options: (1) make them visible, (2) make them accessible, and (3) give minimal direction for using them.

Introducing the Project to Staff and Pupils

The whole-school evaluation of flexible seating gained leadership buy-in due to several factors. First, the school has a strong focus on inclusion and research-informed practice, with the Head of Inclusion holding additional responsibility for leading research in the school (e.g., in seeking research opportunities that could enhance provision in the school). Second, the evaluation was fully funded (via an external grant from the Churchill Fellowship), which meant that the school did not have to find additional funds to support the implementation of flexible seating. Third, the project did not require major adaptations to the school building, meaning it was relatively easy to implement (and reverse, if necessary!). Finally, and of crucial importance, the evaluation was conducted in partnership with academic researchers, meaning that the work would be rigorous and expertly informed, but also required relatively little from busy school staff in terms of data collection and analysis.

The evaluation was introduced to staff at a training day, allowing them plenty of time to ask questions. The project was also given a very high priority that academic year, and was listed in the school development plan, meaning that its implementation and outcomes were closely monitored. The rationale for the project was explained to staff, and their opinion was sought on the practicalities of introducing flexible seating. For example, staff emphasised the importance of introducing a few options at a time. Staff were informed that their views would be sought on the approach later in the academic year, with dedicated time being allocated for the staff to share their views as part of a mandatory staff training day (i.e., to avoid staff having to contribute their perspectives within or outside of their busy working days). Staff were welcoming of the fact that the project would be evaluated by a team of researchers working with the school, to reduce the burden on them. Indeed, great care was taken to ensure that involvement in the project would not be burdensome for staff.

The project was introduced to pupils in a whole-school assembly led by the Assistant Head, who explained that the school was involved in research to find out what would make Mayflower a better learning environment for everyone. It was explained that the focus of the research was on different kinds of seating options. Pupils were already familiar with the term "research" and the idea there were no right or wrong answers when it came to research findings. Time was spent reviewing the different kinds of seating options that were already in school, explaining that the school needed more options for everyone to try. Pupils were told that they would be working with their teachers, teaching assistants, and university researchers on this year-long project, and that results would be given to them as they were obtained. The children were told that their choices would inform future purchases of seating options, and that what they contributed could be important for other schools in the UK and beyond. The researchers who collected data for the project took care to get to know the pupils (e.g., through having lunch with them, and playing with them in the playground). Through embedding themselves in the school setting, the goal was for the researchers to really understand the school context, but also to ensure that pupils felt comfortable interacting with them during data collection.

> *It was so exciting to be part of such an innovative and forward thinking project! I honestly wasn't sure what the outcomes would be and there were no expectations for it to "work" or "be successful."*
>
> **Teresa Ward, English and Key Stage 1 Lead at Mayflower**

Pupil Voice

We wanted to elicit the voices of pupils in a way that would be fun and engaging for them, but also in a way that was in keeping with the activities they tended to engage with at school on a day-to-day basis. For example, when pupils were asked to complete surveys about the chairs that they liked or did not like, they were provided with "Word Banks" that they usually had access to during writing tasks, to support them in conveying their ideas. Further, as older children often engaged in collaborative group activities with their classmates, we designed a "Headteacher for the day" activity, whereby groups of pupils were tasked with planning the purchase of chairs for their future classrooms. Groups were only given two rules: (1) there was no limit on the amount of money they could spend, and (2) the chairs they planned to buy had to be chairs that were already part of the project. Once groups worked collaboratively to design their ideal classrooms, they each gave a presentation to their class to explain how and why they designed their classroom in the way they had.

Data collection was undertaken by the Assistant Head together with two research assistants. Conscious that the research assistants were unfamiliar to the children, we made sure that they spent time getting to know the school and the pupils before collecting any data. For example, the research assistants had lunch with the pupils, visited their classrooms, and spent time in the playground with them. One week before collecting data, the research assistants also visited each class to remind them of the research, explain the different activities they would be invited to take part in, and answer any questions the children had. These efforts were crucial to ensure that the pupils felt comfortable being involved in the research.

"Working in collaboration with Mayflower was extremely beneficial for the research process as it allowed for a greater understanding of the day-to-day priorities of the staff, pupils and school as a whole, and helped inform our research goals and the data collection process. Being able to develop a rapport with the pupils before their participation allowed for easier acceptance of the researchers during data collection. Children had also been prepped on the research aims and were therefore keen to help, but were also keen to learn about their

> *own needs via the research process and then express these needs to us via their enthusiastic participation."*
>
> *– Aaron Giuliano, Research Assistant*
>
> *"I think it was exciting and inclusive and all children wanted to join. If I could join a research project like this again I would!"*
>
> *– Kirsty Miah, Teaching Assistant at Mayflower*

A total of 315 pupils were involved in the research, sharing their views on what they thought about flexible seating in their school. Our key findings were:

- **Preferences varied for individual children**, so what was listed as a "favourite" chair for some children was considered a "least favourite" chair for others.
- **Pupils had clear preferences for some seating options over others** – for example, the rocking chairs were one of the most popular seating options.
- **Preferences were very similar across neurodivergent and neurotypical children**, suggesting that flexible seating might be a beneficial approach for all children.

We also asked children about why they liked or disliked certain seating options in their classrooms, and five categories of response were identified, providing an insight into their decision making:

- **Sensory considerations** – for example, "I like to wobble," "I don't like rocking."
- **Engagement** – for example, "Helps me to think and learn," "Helps me manage my distractions."
- **Emotion and comfort** – for example, "It is calming to rock," "It makes me relaxed."
- **Fun and novelty** – for example, "It's exciting to use," "It's fun."
- **Classroom considerations** – for example, "Can be used on the carpet or on your desk," "I can now rock safely."

Staff Voice

We felt that it was essential to complement pupil voice with staff voice; after all, even if pupils really loved flexible seating, if staff felt this approach meant they were unable to teach their learners, or that it posed insurmountable barriers to their practice, we would need to think carefully about whether it was the right approach for the school. A total of 33 staff (including teachers and teaching assistants) provided their views on flexible seating. Our results showed that staff were overwhelmingly positive about the approach in relation to its impact on both staff and pupils.

Key findings were:

- Staff stressed the importance of **flexible seating as a whole-school approach**, instead of solely being used with neurodivergent children.
- Most staff **would recommend flexible seating to other schools**.
- Like pupils, staff also had **clear preferences for some seats** (e.g., rocking chairs, folding floor seats) **over others** (e.g., ball chair, floor rocker).

Further analysis of staff views on the use of flexible seating identified three key aspects that they thought were critical to the implementation of flexible seating:

- **Happy bodies and happy minds**: While staff felt that the mindset needed for the implementation of flexible seating was initially "a challenge to get used to," they noted several positive outcomes in terms of the learning, mood, and concentration of their pupils. Staff felt that these outcomes linked to the additional movement flexible seating offered, which pupils were felt to really benefit from.
- **Attending to a diversity of need**: Staff explained that flexible seating benefited a diversity of learners – not just those who were neurodivergent – in lots of different ways. Yet, crucially, flexible seating was not seen as something that every neurodivergent child would want or need, and it certainly was not perceived to be a panacea for every sensory need within a class.
- **Choice, agency, and interdependence**: Staff spoke of how choice was crucial to the perceived success of flexible seating, and that pupils' choices were often thoughtful (e.g., based on how they were feeling or the subject they were studying at the time). This agency was felt to have broader positive benefits, giving pupils ownership over their learning. Staff added

that this process of exploration was not always spontaneous, with staff input being crucially important too (e.g., in encouraging conversations with pupils around their own needs and the needs of others). Having a strong culture of inclusion already embedded within the school was felt to support this process.

For full information on our results, see Giuliano et al. (2024).

Key Takeaways

In a climate where school leaders are continuously struggling to balance their budgets, Mayflower felt very fortunate to have secured funding to enable the implementation and evaluation of flexible seating. Importantly, some questions still remain unanswered, for instance whether our learning would be applicable to other school contexts (e.g., other primary schools or secondary schools). Despite this, our key takeaways from our project are:

- Flexible seating might be a helpful adaptation for schools to meet the sensory needs of a diverse range of learners. Importantly, flexible seating should not be targeted exclusively towards those who are neurodivergent, and we must not necessarily assume that those who are neurodivergent will benefit from flexible seating. We must take a whole school approach that respects the diversity of need among our pupils.
- Listening to the voices of staff and pupils enabled us to embed flexible seating in a way that was meaningful and beneficial to the school community as a whole. The inclusion of staff and pupil voice was not tokenistic, and extensive efforts were made to ensure that every stakeholder had the opportunity and the time to share their views.
- Even if schools are not able to invest in flexible seating as a whole school approach, our results provide clues around ways we can make the school environment more inclusive for their diverse

learners, such as finding ways to provide pupils with a sense of agency over their seating arrangements.
- Working collaboratively with a diverse team (including those with academic, professional, and lived experience, alongside the input of a chair committee) ensured that the research was rigorous and relevant to practice. This approach also maximised the chances of success in creating an approach that fitted with the ethos of the school and was deeply informed by staff and pupil voice.

Reflective Activities

Mayflower has learnt so much from the process of implementing and evaluating flexible seating that could now be embedded within other projects (in our school or other schools). For schools which are considering whether to implement and evaluate a new approach, our key recommendations are:

- Consider if this is the right time for your school to introduce change on a large scale: think long-term about what the costs for evaluation are (either financially or in kind), and whether this project can be prioritised.
- Think carefully about your school ethos and whether you can envision the change you are proposing being implemented on a wider scale.
- Think about what is already successful in your school that you can extend on a larger scale – remember that not all ideas have to be brand new!
- Give enough time to consider how you will involve key stakeholders meaningfully, and allow enough time to explain the project you are proposing to everyone involved.
- Always involve pupils however you can – they have the power to champion a project and, in fact, will be your biggest advocates if they are allowed to be!
- Think about working in partnership with academic researchers, through approaching them to see what might be possible. Busy

school practitioners do not always have the time to implement evaluations on such a scale and with such rigour, but the support of academic researchers can be invaluable in this regard.
- Always think about next steps following on from approaches that have already been trialled. For example, Mayflower is now modelling the evaluation of flexible seating in an evaluation of the use of ear defenders as a whole-school adaptation.

Acknowledgements

The authors would like to express their sincere thanks to their collaborators on this project: Aaron Giuliano, Thayla-Mae Bradley, Katy Unwin, Sarah O'Brien, Spencer Hayes, and Nicole Conradie. Very special thanks go to the school chair committee, and all participating staff and pupils. We would also like to thank the ASD Nest team for inspiring our whole-school evaluation of flexible seating. Finally, a huge thank you to the Churchill Fellowship for making our project possible through its generous funding.

References

Boesley, L., & Crane, L. (2018). 'Forget the health and care and just call them education plans': SENCOs' perspectives on education, health and care plans. *Journal of Research in Special Educational Needs, 18*, 36–47. https://doi.org/10.1111/1471-3802.12416

Conn, C. (2015). 'Sensory highs', 'vivid rememberings' and 'interactive stimming': Children's play cultures and experiences of friendship in autistic autobiographies. *Disability & Society, 30*(8), 1192–1206. https://doi.org/10.1080/09687599.2015.1081094

Department for Education. (2014). *Children and families act*. London: Department for Education.

Department for Education and Department of Health. (2015). *Special educational needs and disability code of practice: 0 to 25 years*. London: HMSO.

Dynia, J. M., Walton, K. M., Sagester, G. M., Schmidt, E. K., & Tanner, K. J. (2023). Addressing sensory needs for children with autism spectrum disorder in the classroom. *Intervention in School and Clinic, 58*(4), 257–263. https://doi.org/10.1177/10534512221093786

Giuliano, A., Al-Jayoosi, H., Bradley, T., Unwin, K., O'Brien, S., Hayes, S., & Crane, L. (in prep). Bouncy balls and rocking chairs...in school?! Staff and student views of flexible seating implementation within an inclusive primary-age setting.

Griffin, K. (2023). *Success with sensory supports: The ultimate guide to using sensory diets, movement breaks, and sensory circuits at school.* London: Jessica Kingsley Publishers.

Halsall, J., Clarke, C., & Crane, L. (2021). 'Camouflaging' by adolescent autistic girls who attend both mainstream and specialist resource classes: Perspectives of girls, their mothers and their educators. *Autism, 25*(7), 2074–2086. https://doi.org/10.1177/13623613211012819

Isaacs, D., & Riordan, H. (2020). Sensory hypersensitivity in Tourette syndrome: A review. *Brain & Development, 42*(9), 627–638. https://doi.org/10.1016/j.braindev.2020.06.003

Koenig, K. P., Bleiweiss, J., Brennan, S., Cohen, S., & Siegel, D. E. (2009). The ASD nest program: A model for inclusive public education for students with autism spectrum disorders. *TEACHING Exceptional Children, 42*(1), 6–13. https://doi.org/10.1177/004005990904200101

Pellicano, E. (2013), Sensory symptoms in autism: A blooming, buzzing confusion? *Child Development Perspectives, 7,* 143–148. https://doi.org/10.1111/cdep.12031

Pellicano, L., Bölte, S., & Stahmer, A. (2018). The current illusion of educational inclusion. *Autism, 22*(4), 386–387. https://doi.org/10.1177/1362361318766166

Roman-Urrestarazu, A., van Kessel, R., Allison, C., Matthews, F. E., Brayne, C., & Baron-Cohen, S. (2021). Association of race/ethnicity and social disadvantage with autism prevalence in 7 million school children in England. *JAMA Pediatrics, 175*(6), e210054. https://doi.org/10.1001/jamapediatrics.2021.0054

Smith, C., Guillain, A., & Barron, K. (2020). *The storytelling schools method - Handbook for teachers.* Heathfield: Twinberrow Publishing

UNESCO. (1994). *The Salamanca statement and framework for action on special needs education.* Paris: Unesco.

United Nations. (2006). *United Nations convention on the rights of persons with disabilities.* New York, NY: United Nations.

Veerasamy, S. (2024). Managing self-regulatory behaviour in young autistic children in the Western Cape, South Africa. *South African Journal of Childhood Education, 14*(1), a1352. https://doi.org/10.4102/sajce.v14i1.1352

Zahir, R., Alcorn, A. M., McGeown, S., Mandy, W., Aitken, D., Murray, F., & Fletcher-Watson, S. (2024). Short report: Evaluation of wider community support for a neurodiversity teaching programme designed using participatory methods. *Autism, 28*(6), 1582–1590. https://doi.org/10.1177/13623613231211046

4

Harris Trust SPaRKs Music Project

Informing Creative Learning and Skills for Neurodivergent Teenagers

Jane Macdonell, Sam Johnston, Devin Casson, and David Calver

Introduction

The Harris Trust is a small charity based in the Scottish Borders in the UK. It was started in March 2021 in memory of Harris Macdonell, who took his own life at the age of 19. Harris loved music, sport, and the outdoors, and received an autism diagnosis aged 16.

The charity aims to raise awareness and provide training around neurodiversity and mental health, to assist the provision of music, sports and outdoor activities, and peer support, and to promote respect, acceptance, and a sense of belonging for neurodivergent young people. Harris Trust continues to grow, and currently has several projects providing inclusive activities that seek to promote mental and physical wellbeing. The music projects – SPaRKs (Songwriting, Performance and Recording Kickstarter) and "Music with Erin" – take place in several Scottish Borders primary and secondary schools and are led by young adults with experience of neurodivergence. The mini rugby project based at Selkirk Rugby Football Club provides autism-friendly sessions for primary children run by young suitably trained coaches. The Harris Trust also funds forest and outdoor learning projects in Selkirkshire schools which cater for children and young people who experience more learning success when outdoors.

The SPaRKs Music Project in secondary schools is aimed at, but not exclusive to, creative students who are neurodivergent or who may be experiencing mental health problems. SPaRKs sessions provide an environment where young people can make connections with others who have a similar interest in music. Students are offered the opportunity to gain skills relevant to the music industry through workshop-based learning, and crucially, learning is student-centred, allowing them to make choices – for example, exploring different genres of music or creating their own setlists. Students are encouraged to take part in a live performance, but the focus is largely about increasing confidence and self-esteem.

This chapter first introduces the experience of starting up the SPaRKs Music Project in 2022, followed by its progression over the first two years and plans for future developments. We end with key takeaways and points for reflection and to support educators who would like to consider implementing similar projects in their schools.

How SPaRKs Began

SPaRKs was the brainchild of Sam Johnston, a 22-year-old music graduate with a diagnosis of Asperger's syndrome. Sam heard Jane talk about her son Harris on the radio and decided that he wanted to do something music-related with the Trust. He approached the Trust with the idea of setting up a contemporary music project that would meet its aims.

The idea was embraced by Jamie Bryson, Headteacher at Selkirk High School. Meetings were arranged with music and pastoral staff, and there was considerable discussion about which students could benefit most from the project. The aims of the project were to:

- Build confidence and self-esteem
- Provide a way to amplify student voices
- Encourage teamwork, collaboration skills, and creative thinking

The focus was on students who had an interest in music but needed an incentive to attend school more regularly. While a neurodevelopmental diagnosis was not required, several of these students were neurodivergent. This selection process took three or four weeks. After receiving a brief outline of the project, students were offered the opportunity to take part, and parents/carers were sent an introductory letter about SPaRKs.

An additional needs assistant was given time for the sessions to ensure students attended on time, to quietly supervise, and to facilitate communication between SPaRKs tutors and pastoral staff. A room in the music department adjacent to the Harris Trust-funded recording studio was available for all sessions. Staff identified the most suitable slot for the sessions to take place so that students were not missing out on critical classes. Six students started SPaRKs in September 2022. One student left school during the second term, but the other students completed the pilot project.

Sam Johnston managed the sessions on his own in the first term. It was challenging to get to know the group and encourage interaction. However, early in the project, Sam was fortunate to meet Billy Kennedy at a local gig. Sam described the project to Billy, who is a professional musician and member of the acclaimed band Frightened Rabbit. Billy is now a mental health practitioner and previously attended Selkirk High School. He was immediately interested in becoming involved, and volunteered to support Sam with the project. He regularly attended sessions, contributing to the practical instrument instruction and sharing his knowledge of the music industry. This collaboration was invaluable for Sam, particularly in helping him to be more flexible with the students' pace of learning.

The pilot took place over 12 weeks. Sam encouraged the students to consider performing at a Harris Trust fundraiser gig at the music venue MacArts in Galashiels in March 2022. Three of the students played their instruments for a set together with Sam and his band, and one student chose to assist with sound production. The event was well attended, and the students took great pride in their involvement.

> *The SPaRKs project reveals to students their creative potential. It's important and exciting for all of them but for some, I think it's life-changing because of the confidence and community that comes out of it.*
>
> **Jamie Bryson, Headteacher, Selkirk High School**

Feedback from the students was incredibly positive, and a short film was made of the progress throughout the year. This can be viewed on the Harris Trust website (www.harristrust.org).

SPaRKs Music Project

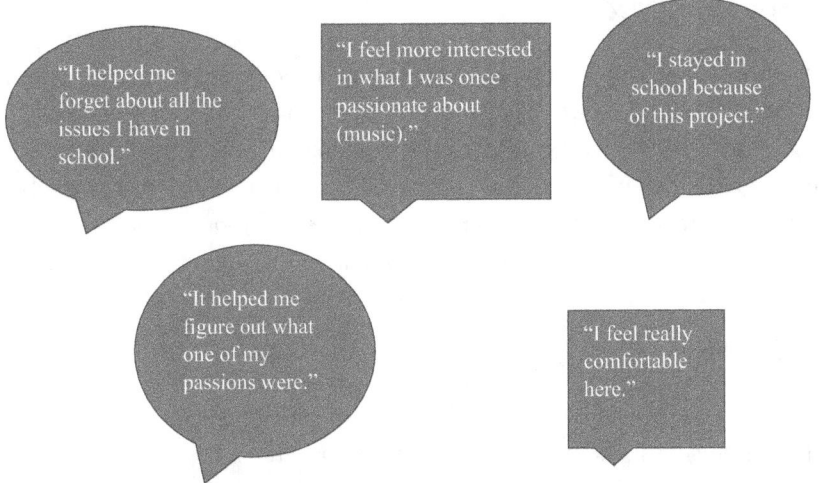

SPaRKs in 2023–4

Following positive feedback from staff and students at Selkirk High School, the Harris Trust met over the school summer holidays to reflect on the year. Staff from the MacArts music venue offered the opportunity of working in association and we developed a joint plan for 2023–4. This detailed the topics that would be covered and an extended number of sessions which included weekend workshops at MacArts. We decided to expand to other schools, and arranged meetings with pastoral and music staff at Earlston, Jedburgh, and Galashiels High Schools. We discussed the experience of the pilot and provided the new improved SPaRKs/MacArts programme, which included the following summary of the plan for the academic year.

September–December 2023

Performance and Production – a dive into the standard practices of live musicians including rehearsing a student-selected setlist of songs, preparing the songs for a live performance, and understanding the technical nature of live music and stage work. Students will learn how to organise a live setup including creating a set order and writing up a theoretical technical specification for a gig.

January–March 2024

Marketing and Management – give students a closer look into the methods of promotion used by industry professionals when promoting the image of an artist. Students will investigate different marketing methods and learn about the pros and cons of different social media platforms when used to market any music content. They will also learn about the different roles of the industry relating to artist management and publishing.

March–June

Songwriting and Recording – conclusion to the students' work as they take skills learned throughout the project and apply them to create their own portfolio-based work in the form of a recorded project. They will learn key fundamentals of effective songwriting and recording methods. They will also have the opportunity to showcase this material in a live performance.

All the schools agreed to join Selkirk on the project. As before, the process of selecting new students was made following discussions between music and pastoral staff. The students all had an interest in music but varying degrees of accomplishment. Some students were described as "high achievers" but would benefit from opportunities to increase confidence and self-esteem. Most students were neurodivergent. Eighteen students were selected across the four schools.

> *Before I took part in the SPaRKs project, I had already been an enthusiastic musician, and I was progressing in my instrument playing and theory knowledge at a steady pace. At the beginning of S6 [Sixth Year], I was offered to be a part of the SPaRKs project by my music teacher, so I decided to participate. Everything about music in the real world was completely new to me. Being able to learn these things has been a lot of fun, and to be able to participate in showcases with professional musicians was an experience that I will never forget. The SPaRKs project has helped me massively to progress as a musician by not only being taught new ideas that aren't taught in school but also in building up my confidence to perform to an audience.*
>
> **Nathan Mejer, Jedburgh Grammar Campus**

A significant bonus to the project was the addition of Devin Casson as a tutor in November 2023. Devin, a recent school leaver who was developing her solo music career, had first-hand experience of the difficulties faced by neurodivergent students. Sam and Devin attended the "Introduction to Youth Work" course provided by Youth Scotland. Over the year, alongside the delivery of the SPaRKs project, they accepted feedback on their skills as tutors from staff and later received mentorship from Youth Borders. Devin agreed to take responsibility for introducing Youth Scotland's Dynamic Youth Awards and engaged 12 students in this during the second term.

In addition to the weekly sessions in the four schools, two weekend workshops were offered at MacArts to provide an opportunity for students across the schools to socialise, as well as to learn about the following aspects of live performance:

- Stage planning – Learning how to plan the stage layout for a live performance
- Stage setup – Getting hands-on experience in setting up the stage and equipment for a show
- Sound checking – Understanding the technical aspects of sound checking and its crucial role in a live performance
- Live performance – Having the chance to showcase their skills by performing at least one song

All the students were then given the opportunity to perform at a live gig at MacArts in March 2024. This gig was open to the public, and each school group performed two of their songs from the year. A student who had been learning skills with the sound and lighting engineers at MacArts also participated, and Sam's band 3 Out of 4 and Devin and Billy Kennedy's new band Haiver played original material. The students played their versions of cover songs ranging from Kate Bush to Queen and Nirvana. The show was great fun and entertaining as well as musically impressive.

> *The SPaRKs project provides an opportunity some of our young people would not dream of, to be in a band and perform their own music, on stage in front of a large audience. It's amazing and transformative for their confidence.*
>
> **Laura Thomson, Deputy Headteacher, Pupil Support, Selkirk High School**

By the end of the second year, several factors contributed to the success of the project. The Harris Trust was able to fund tutors and obtain services and advice from the management group at MacArts. The tutors were dedicated and had support from specific staff in schools and from Billy Kennedy. A mentoring arrangement had been formed with Youth Borders, and Devin had successfully recruited students for Dynamic Youth Awards. Feedback showed that students' motivation was increased by creative activities that were hands-on and that they felt increased confidence and self-esteem. As a result of their year in SPaRKs, several students across the schools started a band together called SeekingSoundBand. Another student has started performing solo at MacArts "Incubator Sessions."

> *The SPaRKs project provides a platform for our neurodivergent students to blossom as performers and collaborators. Sam and his team help foster a creative environment where each student's ideas are valued and built upon. I have seen a massive change in their creativity and confidence in the classroom.*
>
> **Fraser Hewitt, Music Teacher, Selkirk High School**

The following is an interview with SPaRKs tutors Sam Johnston, and Devin Casson. In their own words, this provides an opportunity to explore in greater depth the impact of SPaRKs, the challenges, and successes, and to gain insights that can inform similar creative learning and skills working with neurodivergent teenagers.

What have you most enjoyed about leading the SPaRKs sessions?

Sam

"What I probably enjoyed most about the sessions was seeing the change in the students throughout the project. It was the same type of transformation that I had when I started getting into music from getting out of the typical school educational system and breaking into a flexible system. It was creative, allowed me to kind of speak my own voice and be in opportunities that I wouldn't have been in before. And that transformation has been very significant to me. So, to pass on that opportunity has been amazing."

Devin

"I've most enjoyed seeing students work towards and then actually achieve the goals that they've set themselves in every leg of the project. They've all set challenges, and you see their reactions and it's like, 'Oh my gosh, I did that,' especially with live performance. It's amazing to see them come out of their shells and develop not just their music skills, but their social skills with each other, and watch them meet people that have something in common with them. I never had anything like that when I was at school, so it's been amazing for me to see as well. I feel like I've kind of grown with them a wee bit."

What have been the most challenging aspects of SPaRKs for you, and how have you coped?

Sam

"The most challenging aspect for me personally has been the unpredictability of the project as it's gone on. We've had changes in timetables. We've had students who have had to drop in and out. We've had students who might not necessarily need the project, whether it be they have their own personal interests, or the project just doesn't gel with them. We have had to adapt to that, but at the same time, we've coped with it. The one thing we've always said is 'trust the process.' Because in the industry, from my experience, it's always been that things take time. They take time to settle in and to kind of work out. The people who want to be on the project and the people who benefit the most from the project are the ones who are going to stay throughout the whole thing. The way I cope is just trusting the process and making small adjustments. It might be how we deliver a certain task, or it might be how we approach working with a particular student in a particular area."

Devin

"I think one of the most challenging things for me was learning how to work in a group. I'm used to having full creative control of what I'm doing. So, coming in and being like, 'Oh my, there's three or four other people here and they all have a different view on this. How do we get everybody's ideas onto one thing?' That was a new situation for me to be in. But I just went with the flow a bit. Sometimes I just had to take a breath and think 'It's fine – remember, nothing's ever going to be absolutely perfect.' And yeah, shouldn't be, we shouldn't be striving for that. I think the other thing was learning how to help other people out – almost teaching people how to play instruments. When I'm by myself it's all down to me. I can just do what I want, but everybody else works in a totally different way, so it was adapting to people's different learning styles. We've had to really figure out what works best for the individual. And sometimes it's not always that easy. We're still learning all the time.

Some students at the start wouldn't say anything. They just sit there quietly, which is fine. But over the years they've started to really come out – there's a few that we've thought, 'Wow, they never used to be quite as confident as that.' They can see that what they contribute is there and everything's valid and that everybody has something awesome to put towards it."

Has SPaRKs changed your views or understanding of neurodiversity?

Devin

"I think it's still a new thing to me. So, I'm learning about myself and how I am.

The one thing I've felt is being surrounded by other people around my age as well because I had a lot of experience in the past with [neurodivergent] people who are either way older than me or way younger than me. So, because I'm around the same age of everybody at SPaRKs, it has made me feel slightly less alone in a lot of things. I'm not saying that I was totally negative beforehand, but it's quite nice to have other people that think like this and not be stressed out as much."

Sam

"I'll be honest, it's enhanced my understanding of neurodiversity. This might be from my background in both music and how I've kind of grown up and taken on neurodiversity. For me, neurodiversity is less of something that should be looked on as a hindrance, which a medical term would say it is. When people get diagnosed, 'Oh, you have this or that.' It's taken upon as a hindrance or something that people would think it's something wrong with them. But if you break it down to a different perspective of, 'No, it just means you're different,' then it puts on the perspective of, well, it's an opportunity. You know, either way, that the SPaRKs project has been an opportunity for the young people in a way, understanding their own mental health and how it impacts the way they work is an opportunity because it means that they are able to focus on the positive aspects. And it makes them far more unique. In an industry where it's all about being unique, that's a powerful asset. I would put money on the number of musicians that are on the various spectrums of ADHD, autism, and people just don't know it. But you could tell because of how unique their work is. I see that from doing SPaRKs, it's enhanced that belief that it's an opportunity that has room for development. And that's a very positive thing."

Can you give any examples of how SPaRKs has helped the students involved?

Devin

"We had a student come on later than everybody else. They were quiet to start with. There were only a few of them in the session anyway, so it was obvious that they were quiet, they had a guitar, and they told us they wrote songs. We didn't hear much from them until the showcase happened and they got up and they were singing and playing guitar. And then after that, they understood what a great feeling it is to be on stage and performing. So they've gone out and got gigs and started performing live. And I know they've had like two or three gigs in the last couple of weeks just since that showcase. So just to see that, 'Oh, this is something I want to do, possibly as a career, but even just as a hobby.'"

Sam

"I think the one that stands out for me was that there was a student from one of the schools who from observations and over the project, getting to know him from a mental health perspective and his background, it's clear he came from a background that was very linear in a way. There were a lot of religious undertones going on in his life and before being on SPaRKs, he never felt he was able to talk to people about that. He was never able to kind of express himself in a creative way. He's become keen to take part as much as possible. Even though he's progressing from high school, he's already made an intention to come back next year as a mentor for other students.

The students have built a network amongst themselves across the schools, and a group has even started their own band."

How do you find the interaction with school staff?

Sam

"Overall, it's been positive – every school is different. One school seems focused on academic success, another has felt very forward-thinking. One is in the centre of the Borders, right next door to MacArts, which has enabled a great collaboration. All four different schools with different students and staff, and that means we've had a different experience with all of them. Whilst I would say we would prioritise the students and what they want to do, it is still good to speak to the staff and find out what their perspective is and to keep that open dialogue going as well. Jedburgh was very open for us to collaborate with the school concerts that they had. Earlston students will be performing at their awards ceremony. Some students want to come back next year, and there are students who are now going out on their own and looking for these opportunities that may come their way. There are staff that I know encouraged that."

Devin

"I think for me as someone who was slightly apprehensive going back into school from a previous negative experience, it's been generally fine. I mean, I haven't had as much contact directly with teachers as Sam has, but we always give them a wee brief of what's happened in each session. We talk to them before and after sessions about everybody's progress and it's always positive. They're always really encouraging of the work that we're doing, the work you can see the students are up to."

How do you balance creativity with organisation/learning outcomes in a session?

Devin

"We have been aware that when we're sitting down for an hour, it's not going to work for most people because they get bored. So we always make sure we have that bit of like, 'OK, let's get up, let's just jam out a tune,' whatever. And I mean, especially with this, the songwriting recording, it's all an evolving creative process. So we can be sitting there and he's like, 'Oh, I've got an idea.' So we just kind of stop and say 'OK, let's work on that.' We'll come back to this because it can be done. But we're kind of in the moment, figuring out what's working at that point and going with the flow on it."

Sam

"We are trying to give the students the opportunity to approach a part of the project in their own way. You know, part of what comes with creativity is that ability to have choice and to approach tasks in their own way. And since the project is about neurodiversity, that then is emphasised tenfold. So there have been a few examples of when we've suggested songs and styles of music to the students in a very open way. Over time they've been able to narrow that and really specify their approach while still staying true to the outcome that we set, which then means they've achieved that outcome because it's their own level of success. The students feel very fulfilled because if it's their approach to that task rather than us saying, 'Here's the approach, you do it, you have to do it that way.' It's allowing them to approach a task in whatever way they want."

Have you identified any needs for your own development as a tutor?

Devin

"When we did the 'Introduction to Youth Work' course with Youth Scotland – that opened my eyes to the fact that everybody works differently, but I've never experienced that until being involved in SPaRKs, not in a music situation. So learning to work with others. They won't necessarily learn how to play guitar the same way I've learned because I was self-taught. I know that I'm not playing it the right way, but other people also don't play it the right way, but it doesn't matter because it still sounds fine. I've figured out that if I'm chilled out, it'll chill everybody else out as well. I've been a bit on edge with things like, 'Oh my God, we're not getting this done. We're not moving as fast as we could have,' but it's OK. If everybody in here is happy, then everything's fine."

Sam

"I would say just remembering that the project should be flexible. It's very easy as somebody who is neurodivergent to go into my process. I think what's been positive is that I've been able to meld with other students' processes, and they're not too far different from my own. We're all different, and that means there must be a level of collaboration and patience to trust the process and let people get to the end of their sentence, as it were. And, I still have that problem. Who doesn't? One student might have an idea, you know, it might be a creative idea for a song. We try to be patient and let them get to the end of their idea to see if it works. They then can listen to our feedback and the other students' feedback and decide whether that feedback is valuable."

Developing the Programme for 2024–5

Jane was aware that it was quite a responsibility for Sam and Devin to take on their roles without any significant youth work experience, and there were occasional communication issues where Jane was asked to intervene. Sam and Devin are mature young adults and very proficient musicians, but Jane felt that it was necessary to provide a robust structure of mentoring around them, and sought help for this from Youth Borders. Towards the end of the second year, David Calver, Senior Membership Development Officer at Youth Borders, began to observe sessions and provide feedback and mentoring for Sam and Devin. This collaboration is extremely useful and provides a "critical friend."

In planning for the third year, we identified several aspects to focus on. These are also **useful questions for you** if you decide to set up experiences in your own school or educational environment:

- Is SPaRKs centred around young people enough?
- Is "performance" aimed at the quality of outcomes rather than the process?
- Could young people take more of a lead throughout?
- Are young people making authentic decisions?
- Do young people feel a sense of ownership and that SPaRKs is fully about them?

It is agreed that placing a greater emphasis on students' own decision making would lead to even greater ownership and empowerment, – potentially developing their confidence even further. This will also support a more youth-led approach, which in turn helps with youth awards and would enrich the quality of youth provision within the SPaRKs programme.

In the early stages of the project, it has been important to work closely towards a vision and a standard of excellence as a service, and so, being a performance-focused programme, there has been an element of setting a standard for the young people involved. This has supported the idea of giving students an authentic experience of the industry and what it takes to be successful and pursue a potential career. However, we recognise that there needs to be less of an emphasis on this, and the project would benefit from "letting go" a little and celebrating the imperfections, mistakes, and the journey as a whole. Teachers can strive hard for a perfect outcome from learners, and inevitably end up working harder than the learners themselves to deliver what may appear to be an excellent outcome, but this outcome is highly influenced, moulded, and orchestrated by the teacher, hence losing its authenticity. Our tutors should allow for mistakes and then facilitate a safe environment to discuss them and learn from them, which will lead to deeper, longer-term learning and confidence-building. We have discussed that sometimes less is more, and would consider measuring success as a project by the level of visibility of the team. For example, not stepping in to perform for them or model too much for them. Ask questions instead. Inculcate a culture within the programme where the young people ask questions of each other, and they learn to become "critical friends."

Over the last two years, the SPaRKs Music Project, an idea of Sam Johnston, a neurodivergent young adult musician, has flourished and developed. Success has been dependent on the vision and support of dedicated tutors, professional musicians, and school staff. It has required modest funding from the Harris Trust and appropriate spaces in schools. Students have engaged enthusiastically and have gained confidence as well as musical skills and opportunities for teamwork and peer support. Many students have achieved Dynamic Youth Awards from Youth Scotland. The project has met the aims of the Harris Trust, confirming to students that they belong, that they have a voice, and that it is valued. Areas for future development include progressing formal accreditation for students, and further youth work training for tutors.

Key Takeaways

Workshop-style learning in a flexible creative environment can be a very positive experience for neurodivergent students and can have an impact on their wider engagement with school.

Students respond well to young, skilled, neurodivergent tutors, and this should be encouraged by schools. The tutors should have access to staff who have a "light touch" neurodiversity-affirmative approach, and tutors should be encouraged to access formal youth work training.

The "behind the scenes" support for this type of musical project benefits greatly from professional musicians and industry-experienced individuals.

Reflective Activities

The following reflections are designed to help you think about what this could mean in your school or education setting when setting up workshops and creative learning experiences:

- How can we work with the people and skill sets that we already have in school to facilitate creative workshops and learning experiences?
- What can I do to make sure that we are facilitating an authentic and safe environment for learners to thrive?
- How would you integrate this into the school day or as an after-school session?

Acknowledgements

The Weir Charitable Trust for grant funding
The Macklon family for a generous donation
Billy Kennedy, Patron of the SPaRKs project
Chris Wemyss, Manager at MacArts, Galashiels

Part II Introduction: Practice and Pedagogy
Edited by Claire O'Neill

At classroom level, the quality of teaching has a profound influence on each child's learning experience. An exploration of pedagogy offers teachers insight into what practices best support learning and development. A solid understanding of pedagogy allows us as teachers not only to craft rich learning experiences, but also to connect and collaborate with our learners. An understanding of different pedagogical approaches is essential for developing an inclusive pedagogy.

The neurodiversity paradigm offers a conceptual lens for teachers wishing to interrogate the inclusivity of their pedagogical practice. Personally, learning experiences founded on the principles of the neurodiversity paradigm like the *ITAKOM* conference have been pivotal in my professional development. It is a privilege to continue to explore the neurodiversity paradigm here by bringing together a rich collection of voices to explore how to nurture and support the learning experiences of diverse body-minds at classroom and practitioner level.

Here, in this part, a cornucopia of pedagogical approaches from a diverse group of practitioners is presented. Each author has expertise which is not only truly awe-inspiring, but has also advanced my teaching practice in some way. The aim of this part is to enrich and validate good, inclusive pedagogical practice, and I am confident that it will enhance the learning experiences of all kinds of minds in our classrooms.

More specifically the learning from each contributor will support the development of neurodiversity-affirmative learning spaces. Concepts discussed in each chapter complement those explored in other chapters and parts of the book, creating a rich professional learning experience. This part will be beneficial to readers looking for a broad overview of what good neurodiversity-informed pedagogical practice looks like, affirm those already engaging in effective practices, and provide enough content for those looking for deeper dives into more specific areas of knowledge.

Vital neurodivergent-led theories like Double Empathy and monotropism are outlined in detail. Other significant educational concepts like Universal Design for Learning and Low Arousal approaches are explored through the multifaceted lens of the neurodiversity paradigm. Important considerations like learner voice and intersectionality are given attention. Finally, there is a nuanced discussion of Positive Education, which helps us challenge the rising issues of toxic positivity and neurodiversity-lite. In every case, practitioners speak directly from their own classroom knowledge as well as drawing on underlying theory and evidence.

Of course, there are umpteen topics for pedagogical consideration that could have been added here – for example, use of technology, creative methodologies and restorative practices to name a few. Rather than bemoan their absence, however, I look forward to the future conversations arising from what has and what has not been included in this part of the book.

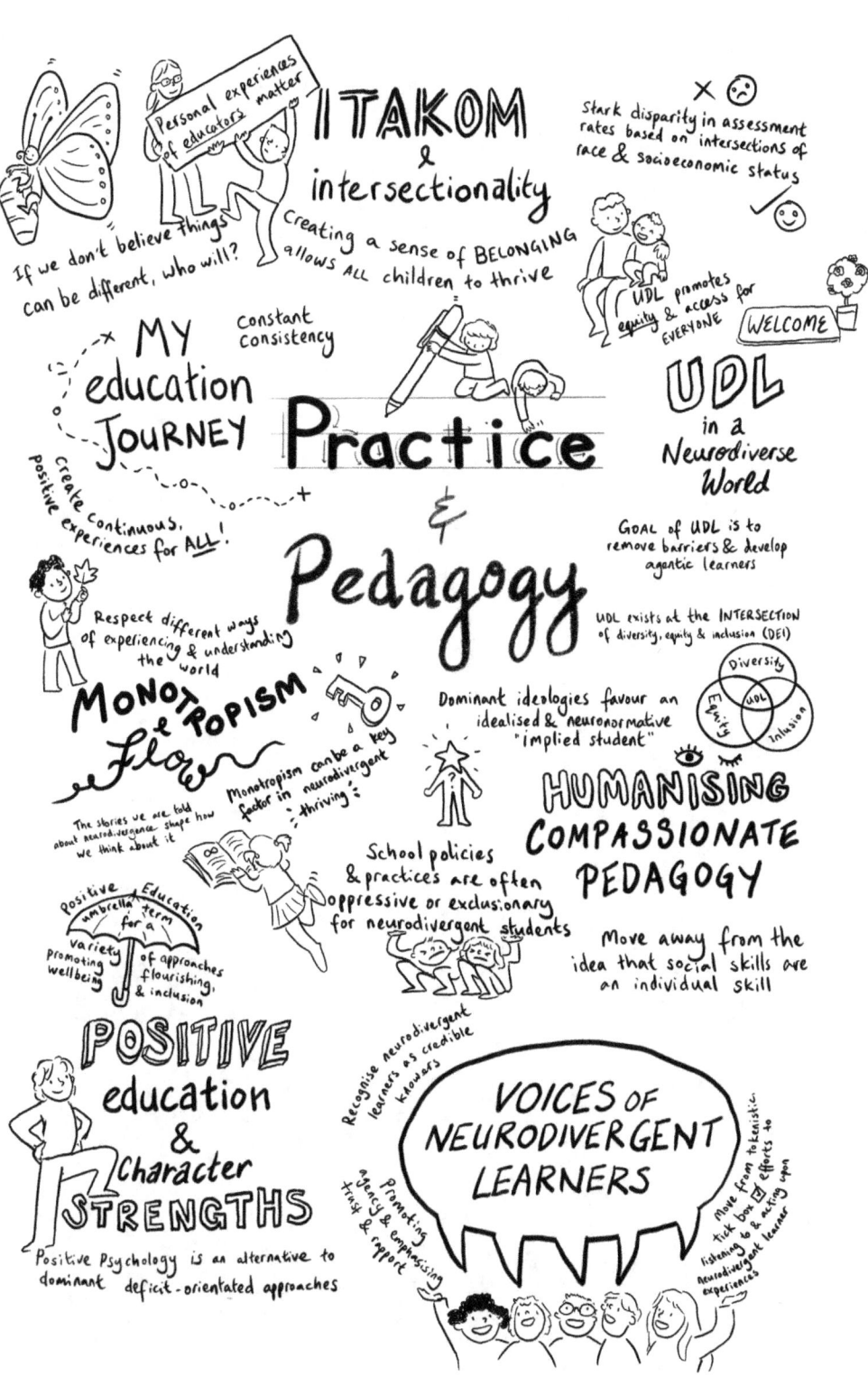

5

Creating Inclusive Learning Spaces

A Personal Journey, 30 Years in the Making

Gareth D. Morewood

Introduction

When I was asked to contribute to this exciting project, I took time to reflect and consider my personal journey and how that might be of interest to others. As with all my work, I would never claim to be an "expert" in anything, but I do have some significant personal experiences which I hope might stimulate some discussions and provide opportunities for others to reflect as well.

I often remind myself, after 30 years' working with young people, families, different professionals, and settings, that issues regularly become challenging as "we don't know what we don't know." After all, if I continued to work in ways I considered effective 25 years ago, I'd likely not be doing the best for those I am working with today – knowledge develops, understanding moves on. As outlined in the Introduction to this book, there is a paradigm shift towards understanding neurodiversity. Whilst many are very comfortable with the adoption of new terminology and thinking, others, naturally, find change difficult. I hope that my personal account of creating inclusive learning environments over the last three decades helps bring to life and make a reality some of the things with regards to inclusive pedagogy that I have experienced, the mistakes I've made, and the rich opportunities I've had working in many different contexts, countries, and circumstances. As Pooky Knightsmith writes:

> Sometimes, new knowledge can make us regretful of what we've said or done in the past. It is far better to forge ahead equipped with new knowledge than to ruminate on what we could or should have done differently, if only we'd known.
>
> **(Knightsmith, 2022)**

The Foundations

From a young age, I knew I wanted to be a teacher. I assisted in sports clubs when still at school, and did my Year 10 work experience in a local primary school and was delighted to secure a place on a three-year secondary B.Ed. (Hons) teacher training degree in the 1990s. During those three years, starting as a fresh-faced and over-excited 18-year-old, I spent at least one day per week in an educational setting. During this time, and most certainly as an enthusiastic 21-year-old newly qualified teacher in the 1990s, I made a lot of mistakes and was always trying to find ways of working that were best for the young people I was teaching, but also worked for me.

Whilst stressing the importance of not making assumptions and to avoid considering specific neuro-minorities in generic and "catch-all" strategies, I am reminded of the work of my colleague Dr Damian Milton, who succinctly surmises a core philosophy of my practice in his maxim, "personalisation, not normalisation." Milton argues that difficulties arise not from individual "deficits" in empathy and social cognition among autistic people, but from a separation in the disposition and understanding of non-autistic populations (Milton, 2012). This can be extended to the often-cited list of "impairments" associated with autism and used to prompt questions about how an autism-friendly education system might operate. How can we be more flexible in the ways in which we organise educational provision for our neurodivergent students? How can we develop new approaches and move away from historic "norms" for all neurodivergent young people?

Rather than focusing on "parking the problem within the child," we need to consider how we set up learning opportunities and be more imaginative ourselves in thinking about approaches to teaching, learning, and inclusive pedagogy. At their core, each of these questions requires us to more actively consider the perspectives of neurodivergent students.

How Can This Be Done?

For the purposes of this chapter, I have considered five core elements of my journey that have developed significantly during my 30 years (to date).

These areas are central to my global work supporting inclusive cultures and developing neurodiversity-affirmative practices, and form the basis of two structured approaches I outline later in the chapter. By exploring each of the five elements while writing this chapter, I am reminded that simple things work! In my experience, the more complex an approach, the less likely we will be able to maintain it.

Five Core Elements

1. Constant Consistency

When I first started teaching, I tried a myriad of different approaches and ways of working, ranging from many different classroom layouts to numerous ways of teaching and learning. In essence, I often made things too complex to maintain, and this variation in my approach also created confusion and uncertainty, which ultimately led to young people being unable to cope and struggling. This is one of my biggest "takeaways" from my personal journey and work with many schools both in the UK and internationally.

Creating a continuous, positive experience is the key to unlocking success for all: no one is harmed by calm, consistent, positive approaches, whereas many can experience significant distress from noisy, hectic, unpredictable, and dysregulated ones. When considering the whole day (especially transitions to and from school), it is important to proactively ensure Low Arousal approaches, described in more detail below, are consistently applied in order to prevent distress and create a calm, welcoming environment for pupils. If I am in a peaceful lesson before lunch, but I'm worried about the stampede to lunch afterwards and the noise in the canteen, I will be less well-placed to perform at my best in that lesson, even if it is a really well-established and accordant environment. Having pockets of calm and consistency (such as during certain lessons, before school, in the taxi home, etc.) gives a moment of relief from other, more chaotic times of the day, and allows young people a chance to self-regulate and better manage the demands of the rest of their day. However, this should be part of a journey to creating a "whole-day" and consistent experience, and not viewed as "success" in its own right, as pupils manage to cope better. The effort required to manage demands personally can be exhausting – for staff and young people. This might mean fewer coping mechanisms, or "spoons" (Miserandino, 2020), at my disposal later in the day, or when I arrive home. This often fuels the "they're all right in school, no idea why they're so difficult at home" narrative, and results in a fundamental failure to understand the core issues and locate concerns correctly. Failure to attempt to understand the experiences of young people can invalidate experiences, result in masking (Pearson & Rose, 2021), and lead to a sense of being forgotten.

The key to successfully improving the experiences of young people throughout their day is effective co-production, which must involve the young people and families in jointly identifying areas of challenge and finding solutions. Working collaboratively to understand a young person's physical and emotional journey through their whole day is vital. I often talk to students about their experience of their whole day – not school and home separately, or lessons and break/lunch at different times – and how they engage with it. Rather than adults or professionals assuming what individuals need, we must gather robust information together and use this to inform provision. We can then build school systems and approaches that are based on analysis and an understanding of the community rather than other assumptions and beliefs. Sometimes a small change in a school system can make a big difference to an individual and enable them to thrive. But you won't know if you don't gather information collaboratively.

An example I recall well from about 15 years ago was that of a 12-year-old pupil who, like many, found break and lunch times particularly stressful. Without really having a planned approach, we worked with the young person and their family to establish what the challenges were and jointly work on solutions. From this we identified that manga was an area of interest for this young person, and so a Manga Club was established during break and lunchtimes. By watching films, drawing, and discussing shared interests, the peer connections this shared experience allowed for gave a real sense of belonging and safety at these previously stressful times of the day, and cultivated lifelong connections. I was pleased to hear that one young man, now in his mid-20s, attended a *Comic Con* event with peers from this group recently. Rather than imposing interventions to alter and normalise neurodivergent young people, we should create safe shared spaces and allow individuals to flourish and establish real connections through a sense of belonging.

Here, a clear link between policy and practice is necessary, as disconnect creates opportunities for fragmentation regarding provision and structure. Ensuring high-quality teaching and learning for all is vital, ultimately raising the "core offer" – a concept I discuss in more detail – and ensuring young people have calm and consistent environments is important. Getting rid of noisy and chaos-inducing bells to promote and support orderly transitions, facilitating staff eating lunch with students to create that sense of belonging – all this feeds into the corporate responsibility (Morewood, 2018) model of shared expectations and consistent, inclusive ideals I wrote about a few years ago. From some recent experiences in international settings in particular, I know there are very simple things that can be changed and have significant impact; the key here is listening to the voices of young people, finding out what is challenging for them, and designing solutions together.

Additionally, it is also important to remember that every environment and community is unique. While there may be some things that have good utility, developing provision and thinking around your specific context is the key to success. Small rural primary schools, specialist settings, large comprehensive secondary schools, international schools, home-learning environments – these all have unique and different challenges, even before we consider locality and other factors. Again, personalisation is key.

2. Low Arousal

The Low Arousal approach (McDonnell, McEvoy & Dearden, 1994) emphasises a range of strategies that focus on the reduction of stress, fear, and frustration. These strategies are put in place to prevent dysregulation and avoid crisis situations. Working in this way allows us to seek understanding of the "situation" by identifying triggers and using low-intensity solutions to avoid reactive consequences for individuals, particularly those with additional needs. These approaches have been proven to enable practitioners to defuse crisis situations within a variety of settings through early identification and intervention (McDonnell, 2019). Applying these approaches to learning and educational environments seems eminently sensible to me, and it is one that I have considerable experience implementing during my career, with very positive outcomes for young people. I am often reminded of strategies and ways of working we adopted through exploration and trial and error 25 years ago; these make much more sense now as part of a framework to support putting these ways of working into action. I'd argue that a lot of this work isn't hugely surprising, yet applying these approaches consistently takes a deeper understanding that is often afforded in schools. I'd suggest that Low Arousal is essential for activated neurodivergent sensory systems.

Applying Low Arousal approaches to teaching and learning is all about the culture within the classroom being founded on a good understanding of stress and consistent proactive approaches. Maintaining a calm, consistent learning environment, and applying what the evidence would suggest is a good investment in learning, creates a purposeful environment that allows everyone the opportunity to thrive. This certainly wasn't the case when I undertook the first few years of my professional journey – this is where my experience is most certainly lived!

There is a strong emphasis on "in the moment" actions and decision making, as well as being reflective. Low Arousal is both a philosophical and practical approach to seeing the distress and the trauma, and actively taking steps to de-escalate arousal levels in the moment, and proactively create Low Arousal environments where regulation and coping are key. There's a quote I often use when talking to practitioners and families which sums things up well: "Nobody fights when they are feeling relaxed and easy-going." Physiological arousal is strongly linked to stress (McDonnell & Gayson, 2014), and both arousal and stress are important in the regulation of emotion (Reich & Zautra, 2002). In a dysregulated classroom, where stress can be significant, the arousal states of everyone (staff and young people) will be high. This does not promote positive opportunities for those involved. This doesn't need to be the case, and I have worked with many colleagues who naturally establish positive cultures for learning that are, in essence, natural Low Arousal practitioners, along with developing my own skills and strategies over the years. For those of us to whom this doesn't come naturally, I am certain that we can develop and create our own Low Arousal environments, through coaching and supervision:

> **The Low Arousal Approach is about creating a caring environment characterised by calm positive expectations aiming to decrease stress.**
>
> **(McDonnell, 2019)**

3. Stress and Coping

Stress, anxiety, and trauma are proposed as potentially significant factors regarding moments where neurodivergent young people are not able to cope (McCreadie & McDermott, 2014). While historically, I often saw the term "anxiety" used widely in schools, stress is used much less. Often, I feel the education sector was in denial that stress existed, but for me honest conversations around stress and coping allow for much more positive outcomes.

Many colleagues will have noticed that I consistently avoid the term "behaviour" when talking about creating inclusive cultures. The reason is quite simple: often, this word has developed in conversations that are negative and purely about "problematic stuff," not to mention people often framing "behaviour" against their own perceived "norms," with little understanding of neurodivergent populations. I prefer to reframe that debate around stress, regulation, and coping. My emphasis is always around minimising stress and supporting coping strategies rather than "behaviours" and trying to "correct" against a perceived "norm." Adopting this position can, almost overnight, change perceptions and open opportunities that are closed off by behaviourist beliefs.

It is our coping responses that determine how we adapt to stress. Simply reducing stressors is only part of the picture – we must also support and develop coping strategies that can, in time, become independent, self-regulatory systems.

Interventions that attempt to reduce certain types of restricted, repetitive, or stereotyped strategies because *we* perceive them as "abnormal" (e.g., stimming, doodling, movement breaks) may be taking away a person's coping mechanism without providing them with an effective alternative. We wouldn't remove a wheelchair from a student or take a pupil's hearing aid away for the day, yet we often deny young people their own coping mechanisms due to the unintended consequences of wider systems and policies. This is why policies that match our philosophy of care are integral elements of the two approaches explored later in the chapter.

Being imaginative about finding solutions to support learners with coping and arousal regulation is a must, and there are lots of resources out there with excellent suggestions for achieving and supporting self-regulation. For example, flow states, discussed in Chapter 6, are fantastic for encouraging wellbeing and managing stress.

4. An Inclusive Curriculum Offer

I believe we should think about the curriculum being offered for young people as being a curriculum for everybody, and to do that we need to ensure it is inclusive (Morewood, in Myatt & Tomsett, 2023). What we need to do is to raise the "universal offer" so it includes more young people, is appropriate, and matches the needs of a twenty-first-century neurodivergent population. This means that the limited resources we have for specific interventions can be targeted more effectively, as more is addressed through the "core offer," for all.

One example of this is using Kelly Mahler's interoception curriculum as part of the core offer for all students (Mahler, 2019), which supports children to make the connection between a physical need and an emotional need. It is important to note that you can actively teach young people to improve their interoceptive awareness, which opens doors to better self-regulation and coping with different and uncomfortable feelings.

Many sensory, fine, and gross motor skills activities can be easily woven into classroom routines with little or no equipment needed. Rather than have young people come away from class for multiple "interventions," an inclusive offer for me is one which includes that work as part of the curriculum offered to the whole class. Too often, lack of access to specialist support means young people struggle; however, there are ways we can include things previously viewed as "specialist" support or provision as part of our "universal offer." And, perhaps importantly, at very low financial cost too!

A key part of inclusive pedagogy is ensuring that minorities are represented as part of the curriculum. *Disabling Imagery* by Richard Rieser (2004) looks at different films that have disabled characters in them or portray disability. Being explicit about disability history and disablist bullying ensures that every young person in the school has access to a real opportunity to critique and to have conversations about disability and society. Similarly, with learning materials and content currently being applied, reviewing these to ensure that an inclusive society is represented is a great opportunity to ensure an inclusive and accepting school culture.

These wider elements of the curriculum can help drive an inclusive community, and I don't think that is difficult to achieve. As outlined previously, we sometimes make things too complex, whereas the simpler we can do it, the more likely we can achieve it and – perhaps most importantly – maintain it.

5. The Environment

The school environment was something I started to consider early in my career. It is important to take into careful consideration what we can do to minimise external stressors in the wider school environment – for example, temperature or lighting, the noise levels in the cafeteria – as well as the social, emotional, physical, and communication environment. Simple adjustments can make learning more accessible for neurodivergent learners and support everyone, often at little or no financial cost – it is just about how you approach things. A good example of recent work in this area is that of the Therapeutic Classroom (Knight, 2024); re-thinking simple things like furniture can change mindsets and make learning a far more enjoyable and accessible experience. These ideas are explored further int he models that follow.

Models That Use the Five Core Elements

Through a synthesis of collaborative and reflective practice and these five core elements, two overarching models have been developed. The Saturation Model (Morewood et al., 2011) and the LASER Approach (Morewood et al., 2021) provide structured approaches to supporting the journey towards creating inclusive cultures as part of systemic change in educational settings. Both of these approaches frequently contribute to my ongoing work in supporting and developing inclusive practice and pedagogy around the globe.

The Saturation Model

The Saturation Model is essentially a "model for success" developed by myself, Professor Neil Humphrey, and Dr Wendy Symes, published in 2011 as part of an Economic and Social Research Council project with the University of Manchester, UK (Morewood, Humphrey & Symes, 2011). The concept was originally devised to support autistic learners who were either being excluded from their school settings, or who were unable to attend school at a mainstream secondary school where I was the Director of Curriculum Support for 17 years.

I have used the model in many settings across the globe as a tool for school improvement and supporting systemic change. Although the model was originally conceptualised with autistic learners in mind, it is relevant to learners of other neurominorities. It has eight key elements (see Figure 5.1):

These eight elements work together to create a whole-school system of support around neurodivergent young people (and, in fact, all learners) as part of a whole-school development tool. In turn, this aims to create equal learning opportunities for all, wherever they receive education, by encouraging inclusion and belonging rather than exclusion.

1. The Agent of change
2. Developing the school environment
3. Flexible provision
4. Direct support and intervention
5. Policy development and embedding practice
6. Training and development of staff
7. Peer education and awareness
8. Creating a positive ethos

Figure 5.1 The Saturation Model (Morewood, Humphrey & Symes, 2011)

The model was so successful during its inception in my school at the time that the initial group of young people the approach was developed in partnership with all went into further education, employment, or training when they left school. Whilst the key goal is to improve outcomes for neurodivergent learners, the Saturation Model is designed to benefit everyone in the educational environment by creating a culture of calmness, consistency, and predictability. This includes a strong focus on collaborating with families to create "constant consistency" throughout the school and in the home, so that staff and family members share an approach that creates calm, predictability, and certainty for the young person, which in turn allows them to feel calmer and reduce stress (Morewood, 2020):

> Families may not have all the answers, and teachers may scratch their heads too, but your pooled experience will bring more in the way of solutions than just one person's reflections. It's essential also to listen to the voices of young people themselves, finding out what is challenging for them and designing solutions together.
> **(Elley & Morewood, 2022, p. 114)**

The Saturation Model requires that we focus on things that are "within our gift" to influence and change, rather than parking the perceived "problem" within the young person – something, upon reflection, that has been the core of my journey during the last 30 years.

The LASER Approach

The LASER Approach stands for Low Arousal Supports Educational Resilience, and is designed to be applied in a wide variety of educational settings by teachers, support workers, and families. The LASER Approach was developed by myself and Professor Andy McDonnell through my work at Studio 3 in 2019 as a new way of supporting young people to achieve their full potential as part of a whole-school (or setting) approach. This approach, again, benefits every pupil in a setting, but is particularly useful for embedding a Low Arousal ethos and practice across a whole-school setting. Low Arousal approaches include attuned, calm, and safe interactions that are less stressful for sensory systems. Low Arousal environments based on constancy, predictability, and routines help create a sense of safety and give learners more opportunities to co- and self-regulate.

The key difference between this approach and other methods is again about the fact that resilience is not "parked within the child," and applies more widely to the environment as a whole and the adults who are supporting the young person. As our colleague Elly Chapple would say, "flipping the narrative" is a key component of this approach (Chapple, 2019). This means focusing on what we can influence as parents, carers, and professionals, rather than attempting to "change" the child through a prescribed approach; as mentioned previously, it is about personalisation, not normalisation.

LASER has a strong evidence base, building on the practical experiences of educators as well as the voices and lived experience of young people and their families. Co-production and communication between the individual, their family, and the school/setting are core elements of this approach. The core elements of the LASER Approach can be adapted for a wide range of educational settings, from mainstream schools and specialist settings to young people who are educated at home. The approach provides an academic and practical understanding of key theories related to stress, dysregulation, distressed behaviour and arousal mechanisms, including:

- The Low Arousal Approach (McDonnell, 2019)
- The Saturation Model (Morewood, Humphrey & Symes, 2011)
- Co-production (Morewood, 2017a, 2019)
- Constant Consistency (Morewood, 2018)
- The PERMA Model (Seligman, 2011)
- Reflective Practice (Schon, 1987)

Whilst The LASER Approach centres around a practical focus towards eliminating the use of restrictive practices and seclusion by implementing Low Arousal Approaches within a whole school/setting framework, the pathways towards this goal should also be considered as good practice for all settings with neurodivergent and neurotypical learners. Combining this focus with positive, pro-active practice and excellence in de-escalation allows for a completely different model of working, valuing everyone's needs and goals. Working within a person-centred framework, the LASER Approach to supporting individuals in educational environments focuses on stress reduction and co-production to enable every young person within the school or setting to benefit.

Overall, there is a strong focus on the importance of stress reduction and wellbeing for all members of the school community, including staff, parents/

carers, and pupils. The individual elements of the approach can be customised based on the needs of the school or organisation. For example, a focus on restraint reduction and elimination may be a key area for one school, but less necessary for another. As such, the aims and focus of the approach can be adapted based on an analysis of the requirements of the organisation or school in question.

The LASER Approach works in conjunction with the Saturation Model to consider the whole-school environment directly as part of a systemic change model. Together, these approaches work to create a continuous positive experience throughout the school for every learner, rather than merely "pockets of calm" at certain moments in the day (Elley & Morewood, 2022). For example, what feelings might a noisy, chaotic corridor between classes evoke for a neurodivergent young person with sensory sensitivities to light, noise, and touch? Increased physiological arousal in these situations can lead to a fight or flight response and is often at the root of many instances of distress (McDonnell, 2019). Reducing the arousal levels of the school in general to create calm, controlled environments where young people are less likely to feel overwhelmed may sound out of reach for some, but it most definitely can be done.

This is entirely possible, and I have been fortunate to support settings on this journey during my 30 years in education, most recently offering advice and providing that "critical friendship" from my experiences to a variety of schools and international settings. After all, if *we* don't believe things can be different, who will?

Conclusion

Throughout this chapter I have tried to reflect upon my own personal journey and experiences and share what I find seems to work well within the opportunities I have had the privilege to experience. Within the constraints of this chapter, it is challenging to distil this concisely and with clarity; yet I hope it offers the reader an opportunity to explore things further and consider what is possible.

As a pupil once said to me, "It is great that I get to join in with things, it isn't always easy but with some changes I love being able to do the same things as my classmates." It is absolutely within our gift to make those adjustments; and in doing so provide life chances for many who would otherwise be significantly disadvantaged through no fault of their own.

Key Takeaways

- **Reflect** on past experiences and use new knowledge to adapt practices.
- Move away from "deficit" models that focus on "fixing" the child, towards a model of "**personalisation, not normalisation**."
- **Constant Consistency**: Create predictable and consistent routines and environments for all learners.
- **Low Arousal**: Minimise stress and create a calm and supportive learning environment for all.
- **Stress**: Recognise the impact of stress on learning, and support learners in developing effective **coping strategies**.
- **Inclusive Curriculum: Raise the "core offer"** of the curriculum to be more inclusive and accessible to all learners, including neurodivergent students.
- **Supportive Environment:** Create a physically and emotionally safe and supportive school environment for all students.
- **Co-production**: Work collaboratively with young people, their families, and other stakeholders to develop and implement inclusive practices.

Reflective Activities

Constant Consistency in your practice:

- Reflect on areas of your own practice where you experience high levels of consistency. Does this impact your wellbeing in any way? How?

Low Arousal in your setting:

- Identify potential stressors within your environment (noise, lighting, temperature, social interactions).
- Generate simple strategies to reduce these stressors.
- Consider how these changes might impact the wellbeing of yourself and others.

Co-production in action:

- Think of a recent situation where you involved others in decision making.
- What was the impact of this approach?

"Personalisation, not Normalisation":

- Reflect on a recent interaction with a learner or colleague.
  - Did the interaction account for individual needs and preferences?
  - Could the interaction be further personalised to make the experience more inclusive?

References

Chapple, E. (2019). *Diversity is the key to our survival: The Shoeness of a shoe.* TEDx Talk. Retrieved April 8, 2021, from https://www.ted.com/talks/elly_chapple_diversity_is_the_key_to_our_survival_the_shoeness_of_a_shoe/up-next

Elley, D., & Morewood, G. (2022). *Championing your autistic teen at secondary school: Getting the best from mainstream settings.* London: Jessica Kingsley Publishers.

Knight, S. (2024). *The therapeutic school approach. How to embed trauma-informed, attachment-aware practices to improve outcomes for all children.* London: Routledge.

Knightsmith, P. (2022). *Things i got wrong so you don't have to – 48 lessons to banish burnout and avoid anxiety for those who put others first.* London: Jessica Kingsley Publishers.

McCreadie, M., & McDermott, J. (2014). 'Tuning in': Client practitioner stress transactions in autism. In G. Jones & E. Hurley (Eds.), *GAP: Autism, happiness and wellbeing* (pp. 24–31). Plymouth: BILD Publications.

McDonnell, A. (2019). *The reflective journey: A practitioner's guide to the low arousal approach.* Peterborough: Studio III Publishing.

McDonnell, A. A., & Gayson, C. (2014). A positive approach to wellbeing: Applying the PERMA model. In G. Jones & E. Hurley, (Eds.), *GAP: Autism, happiness and wellbeing* (pp. 17–23). Kidderminster: BILD publications.

McDonnell, A. A., McEvoy, J., & Dearden, R. (1994). Coping with violent situations in the caring environment. In T. Wykes (Ed.), *Violence and healthcare professionals.* London: Chapman Hall. DOI:10.1007/978-1-4899-2863-4_11

Mahler, K. (2019). The interoception curriculum: A step-by-step framework for developing mindful self-regulation. Available from https://www.kelly-mahler.com/product/the-interoception-curriculum-a-step-bystep-guide-to-developing

-mindful-self-regulation/?gad_source=1&gclid=Cj0KCQiAgK2qBhCHARIsAGAC uzncK4Nl70kNnCCjXNrkLX9ixqZl3j54apBzgsZuDxu1KQvKWNWXGOUaApjj EALw_wcB

Milton D. (2012). On the ontological status of autism: The 'double empathy problem'. *Disability and Society, 27*(3), 883–887.

Miserandino, C. (2020). *The spoon theory* [Online]. www.butyoudontlooksick.com. Available from: https://lymphoma-action.org.uk/sites/default/files/media/documents/2020-05/Spoon%20theory%20by%20Christine%20Miserandino.pdf

Morewood, G. D. (2017a). Why is co-production so powerful? Learning from research. *Optimus Education Blog*. Retrieved April 8, 2021, from https://blog.optimus-education.com/why-co-production-so-powerful-learning-research).

Morewood, G. D. (2018). Corporate responsibility. In D. Bartram (Ed.), *Great expectations: Leading an effective SEND strategy in school* (pp. 19–21). Woodbridge: John Catt Educational Ltd.

Morewood, G. D. (2019). Working together to improve outcomes for our most vulnerable young people. *Optimus Education Blog*. Retrieved April 8, 2021, from https://blog.optimus-education.com/working-together-improve-outcomes-our-most-vulnerable-young-people).

Morewood, G. D. (2020). Why constant consistency matters: Emotional regulation as a foundation for learning. *SENCology Blog* [Online]. Available from: https://blog.optimus-education.com/why-constant-consistency-matters-emotional-regulation-foundation-learning

Morewood, G. D., Humphrey, N., & Symes, W. (2011). Mainstreaming autism: Making it work. *Good Autism Practice, 12*(2), 62–68.

Morewood, G. D., McDonnell, A. A., & McDermott, R. A. (2021). 'The LASER Approach.' In New Trends and Promising Directions in Modern Education New Perspectives 2021, Ed. By M. Aydogmus. Meram: Palet Publications.

Myatt, M., & Tomsett, J. (2023). *SEND Huh – Curriculum conversations with SEND leaders*. Woodbridge: John Catt.

Pearson, A., & Rose, K. (2021). A conceptual analysis of autistic masking: Understanding the narrative of stigma and the illusion of choice. *Autism in Adulthood, 3*(1). ISSN 2573-959X.

Reich, J. W., & Zautra, A. J. (2002). Arousal and the Relationship Between Positive and Negative Affect, Motivation and Emotion, Vol. 26, No. 3, September 2002.

Rieser, R. (2004). *Disabling imagery: A teaching guide to disability and moving image media*. London: Disability Equality in Education.

Schon, D. (1987). *Educating the reflective practitioner*. San Francisco: Josey Bass.

Seligman, M. (2011). *Flourish: A new understanding of happiness and wellbeing: The practical guide to using positive psychology to make you happier and healthier*. London: Nicholas Brealey Publishing.

6

Embracing Monotropism and Flow

Fergus Murray and Helen Edgar

What Is Monotropism?

Monotropism is a tendency to focus attention and processing resources on a relatively small number of interests at a time, leaving little for everything else. It was first described in the context of autism, but it also describes many ADHD learners, and likely others. In this chapter, we will explore how monotropism and flow provide a useful lens for understanding the barriers and strengths of many neurodivergent learners.

Monotropism was formulated as a theory of autism in the early 1990s, initially by Dr Dinah Murray (1992) with Mike Lesser, and then independently by Wenn Lawson not long afterwards. Having discovered they had hit on many of the same insights, they started working together and, in 2005, published *Attention, Monotropism, and the Diagnostic Criteria for Autism*, which showed that all of the diagnostic criteria for autism arose naturally from monotropism.

Dinah saw the mind as a system of interconnected interests: things that pull our attention in, more or less strongly. She was using "interest" in more or less its everyday sense: something a person is drawn to. At any given time, several of a person's interests are likely to be aroused, to varying degrees. A *monotropic* interest system is one where relatively few interests tend to be aroused, relatively strongly. Deep focus often follows, at the expense of easily integrating information coming in from many channels at once.

Understanding autism through the lens of monotropism means seeing it as just one way of using attention and processing information, with advantages and disadvantages. Many of the disadvantages arise from existing in a world where most people are *polytropic* processors, who have many interests aroused at any given time, and expect the same of others.

For example, polytropic communicators might expect people to simultaneously take in words, tone of voice, facial expressions, body language, and more, while bearing in mind who they are talking to. They also expect their communication partner to use all those channels simultaneously, while resolving frequent ambiguities in communication – and they infer meaning when facial expressions, intonation, or body language do not conform with their expectations.

These expectations and assumptions frequently lead to monotropic people being misunderstood: for example, being seen as rude or unempathetic due to mismatched communication styles, and for missing things because their attention was elsewhere. Many neurodivergent people learn to mask, suppressing their authentic selves in the hopes of avoiding such misunderstandings and fitting in, but this has been shown to be detrimental to mental health (Chapman et al., 2022; Pearson & Rose, 2023).

Redirecting monotropic attention once it is invested takes time, like turning a tanker. This difficulty directing and redirecting attention is key to understanding the school experiences of autistic and/or ADHD learners. For some, this is likely to manifest in "autistic inertia" – difficulty starting, stopping, or changing tracks. For others, it more often looks like the "inattention" associated with ADHD: struggling to keep attention on tasks, particularly those assigned by others. Some may develop severe demand avoidance (also referred to as pathological demand avoidance, PDA) in response to others trying to direct their attention. Difficulty splitting attention may also help explain some of the challenges faced by dyspraxic and dyslexic learners, although this has not been formally researched.

In the right environment, most monotropic learners have a powerful ability to hyper-focus on their interests, bringing joy and deep learning.

While the concept of monotropism is decades old, it is only in recent years that research has picked up steam. A group of researchers (including one of the authors) started developing the Monotropism Questionnaire in 2021, to make it possible to quantify experiences of monotropism. The initial validation study (Garau, 2023) attracted around a thousand respondents in just a week – a sign of the interest in monotropism within the autistic community. This showed clearly that most autistic people are much more monotropic than most non-autistic people, while ADHDers are significantly more monotropic than average, both with and without autism.

Significantly, most work on monotropism, including its initial formulation, has been driven by autistic people.

The Power of Framing

As Fisher (2024) suggests, "We need to think about how our education system could accommodate the whole range of developmental variation – and we need to acknowledge that this variation could be far wider than many of us appreciate."

The stories people are told about neurodivergence shape how they think about it. There is increasing evidence that developing a positive autistic identity has profound long-term effects on mental health and wellbeing. Research by Conden et al. (2021) showed that "more dissatisfaction with autistic personal identity predicted lower self-esteem, and more autism pride predicted higher self-esteem." This has also been supported by the more recent research by Heasman et al. (2024) on autistic and ADHD flow states.

Labels like autism and ADHD can help to dispel unhelpful ideas about how children who don't behave in the ways that adults want are just lazy, disobedient, slow, or disruptive. However, these differences are too often understood in purely negative terms, and such labels may simply replace one set of harmful misconceptions with another.

Monotropism not only provides deeper insight, but it avoids harmful assumptions that the learners are somehow deficient. Children seen as "lazy" might be exhausted by their environment or flummoxed by unclear instructions; children seen as "disobedient" or "unfocused" might also need clarification, or they might find it impossible to focus on tasks that seem pointless; children seen as "slow" might just need time to process, because they can't deal with so many things at once. All of these factors feed into children becoming "disruptive" when they are overwhelmed, confused, or infuriated by tasks set for them.

The theory of monotropism was initially developed before the term "neurodiversity" was coined (Botha et al., 2024). However, it was always framed around the idea that humans are naturally diverse in the ways we experience and process the world (Murray 1998, 2021): that it can be a *positive* thing that people understand and approach things so differently, even while it often contributes to misunderstandings.

The theory of monotropism can help us to move on from seeing intense interests as a "symptom": what can be seen as an obsession is often better understood as a passion. Monotropism helps us to validate learners' experiences, and identify barriers to thriving, without dismissing how disabling many environments are for monotropic people.

Can't Not Won't

Being open to the possibility that a learner *can't not won't* in a given situation is perhaps one of the most transformational acts we can undertake for neurodivergent learners. The pressure for young people to fit into normative expectations at school can cause mental health problems, attendance difficulties, and burnout. These pressures are hard for many, especially those in marginalised groups, but neurodivergent learners are often the ones most severely impacted (Nordin et al., 2023). Shepherd et al. (2024) feature descriptions of neurodivergent learners in mainstream education "feeling like they are treading water in unchartered seas," "feeling adrift," and emerging from education broken and "weathered like sea glass," highlighting the harm that can be caused due to misunderstanding and unmet needs.

A key example of *can't not won't* is school attendance. In the United Kingdom, the government exerts pressure on schools to focus on attendance metrics and applies punitive action irrespective of young people's mental and physical health. Often, it is not that children *won't* but that they *can't* attend school (Kearney et al., 2022; Fricker, 2022) due to many sensory, physical, social, communication, and cognitive differences.

In our experience as autistic teachers, a solid understanding of monotropism helps teachers shift their mindset from viewing the learner as someone who *won't* fit with normative expectations to being open to the possibility that the learner *can't* fit with expectations that are fundamentally misaligned with their way of being in the world. Too many neurodivergent children are falling through the net.

School distress is associated with poor attendance, poor academic attainment, anxiety, and extreme demand avoidance behaviour (Connolly et al., 2023). We need to consider the factors causing such distress in order to implement meaningful support rather than punitive actions. As Ross Greene (2021) states, "Children do well, when they can." We need to think about what we need to change to enable children to do well. Attendance difficulties, disengagement, and poor learning outcomes are rarely the child's fault. It is always the adults' responsibility (family and school staff) to look at the barriers a young person may be facing, and to think of ways to change teaching practice and environment. Leaning into monotropism can ignite intrinsic motivation by engaging the learner. Rather than engaging in potentially ableist practices associated with a *won't mindset*, schools need to embrace differences, a cornerstone of neurodiversity-affirmative practice. This calls for a radical conceptualisation of inclusion and involves knowledge of theories like monotropism and Double Empathy (Milton, 2012; see Chapter 7 in this book), focusing on strong relationships, adopting a pedagogy of kindness, teaching with curiosity, and creating a sense of safety for all learners. Fisher (2023) reviews why we need to change our education system, suggesting a move towards neurodiversity-affirmative and self-directed education. This sort of positive change is much needed by monotropic learners, but could benefit everyone.

Radical Inclusion

Radical inclusion goes beyond merely accepting differences and tick-box approaches to accommodations. Instead, it encourages people to work together to dismantle systemic barriers and embrace different ways of learning, allowing more equitable education in which everyone can thrive. The young people in the study by Phung et al. (2021) placed a high value on compassionate support and being able to collaborate with an adult (e.g., parent or education support) so they felt safe to be themselves and express their needs.

Monotropism can be a key factor in neurodivergent thriving. For example, monotropic people need different ways of resting and recharging to polytropic people. More flexibility and transition time may be needed around events, and more time spent with their special interests and fewer demands will all help flow and improve outcomes. Furthermore, knowledge of monotropism and flow helps educators understand relationships, both within and between neurotypes. Many monotropic people form strong relationships based on their special interests. This is often seen in schools, where young people can form intense friendships based on shared intense interests. Joining someone in their attention tunnel by engaging alongside them with a similar activity shows that you are interested and helps foster strong relationships. Parallel play (Pritchard-Rowe et al., 2024) is a powerful example of this, and working alongside someone has a similar effect – either working on the same task or "body-doubling," where two people engage in different activities at the same time. This monotropism-informed approach can be especially helpful for PDA-profile learners as there is less demand on their attention.

The needs of monotropic learners also need to be considered in the assessment process. Many benefit from quieter environments and spaces that feel safe and familiar to them, but some may work better if they can move and stim, or have access to extra sensory input. Extra time and resources may be needed for processing and creative alternative ways of engaging with assessments so that young people are not hindered by environmental factors. Being monotropic can be hard work in a world set up for polytropic people, leading to an imbalance between the "inner drive towards passions" (Rapaport et al., 2024) and the demands of everyday tasks. Interoception can also be affected, with internal signals often missed. If a person has more demands than they have capacity for, they will experience overload, leading to meltdowns/shutdowns, and may develop demand avoidance.

Without enough time to recover in ways that embrace monotropic needs, like engaging in flow with an activity of high interest, burnout and mental health difficulties can follow (Arnold et al., 2023; Raymaker et al., 2020). Friendships may be affected, and wellbeing can suffer (Fox, 2024). Burnout is a whole-mind/body experience that educators can play a huge part in preventing. We need to support young people to develop a greater understanding of their own neurodivergent identity and needs, support them to feel accepted, to make sense of their personal journey, and validate their experiences so they can feel empowered to advocate for their own needs (McGreevy et al., 2024). The ripple effects of unaddressed needs can spiral into disengagement with school, non-attendance, a drop in grades, and problems at home.

Supporting Radical Inclusion

- Ensure flexibility with seating and spaces (e.g., sitting and standing options).
- Provide access to alternative and augmentative communication.
- Provide universal access to a wide range of sensory tools.
- Adopt a flexible timetable with scope for child-led sensory/movement breaks.
- Cushioning around transition times allows monotropic people to adjust and regulate.
- Adaptable uniform policy – uncomfortable clothing makes people focus on discomfort rather than learning.
- Breaktimes must give space for recovery, regulation, and leisure so that learners and staff return to class regulated and ready to learn.
- Eating difficulties are very common among neurodivergent people. Provide options for quiet spaces with few demands, especially when eating. Young people need to feel safe to eat the foods they can in comfort.
- Incorporate special interests in curriculum planning, but never weaponise them. Using interests as part of a reward system can reduce intrinsic motivation and cause alienation.
- Foster intrinsic motivation through autonomy and relevant learning.
- Collaborate with learners and staff to ensure continuity, and celebrate what works.

Meeting Needs through Flow

The concept of flow is central to an understanding of monotropism, and harnessing the power of flow with neurodivergent learners is a strengths-based approach in action.

Flow states are arguably essential for human wellbeing in general. Csikszentmihalyi (1992), a pioneer of flow research, describes *flow* as when an individual is performing at their peak: losing themselves in a meaningful activity that is just challenging enough. For monotropic people, flow is even more vital (Heasman et al., 2024).

As autistic scholar Damian Milton (2017) first observed, Csikszentmihalyi's descriptions of flow states bear a striking resemblance to descriptions of monotropism: total absorption, to the exclusion of outside stimuli; time losing its meaning; a highly rewarding sense of being in control. If someone has experienced the sense of being in flow, "in the zone," they may be able to make more sense of the experience of monotropic learners. In particular, if they have ever been jerked out of something they were totally absorbed in, that might help them understand the distress of neurodivergent children who are forcefully pulled out of their attention tunnels multiple times every day. A timetable that is rigidly divided into many separate periods, each one subdivided into segments, means regular interruptions to potential flow; adding scheduled sensory breaks can potentially make the situation even worse.

Despite educationists like Montessori, Froebel, and Piaget developing approaches that are conducive to flow, most schools are not set up to facilitate this way of learning, or to respect it when it happens. Barriers to flow in typical schools include scarce opportunities for self-direction; distracting physical environments; task overload; and rigid time periods. Thankfully, there is a huge amount of overlap between the things that facilitate flow and the things that can make an educational experience accessible for many neurodivergent learners.

Curriculas that ignite intrinsic motivation and flow enable monotropic learners to deep-dive into their interests and expand their learning rhizomatically. Many monotropic students thrive in settings where they can embrace self-directed learning, as autonomy is usually required for flow states. When monotropic learners can latch onto a topic, they may find ways into a subject that would otherwise be difficult to maintain focus on (Wood, 2019). However, teachers have sometimes caused real harm by trying to use learners' passions as ways to reward compliance, through a behaviourist approach. There is mounting evidence that behaviourist approaches can be detrimental to a person's wellbeing, and over time such practice can add to mental health difficulties (Kohn, 2018; Boren, 2024).

Neurodivergent school staff – not just teachers, but support assistants and others – are more likely to have insight into the role of intense interests and flow states, and the dangers of blocking them or trying to use them to control behaviour. When these adults are being open about their own differences, it can also help to create a sense of belonging and feeling "seen" for neurodivergent young people (Wood, 2023; O'Neill & Kenny, 2023).

Trust and Belonging

Monotropic learners work best when they feel empowered to embrace their natural flow and learning style. Autonomy to move, communicate, and learn in ways that work for them can all help maintain flow and support energy management. To feel empowered, you need people around you who can validate your experiences, respect your boundaries, and give you the opportunity to advocate for your needs. If a child or a parent/carer says it is too bright, too noisy, or too uncomfortable to work, staff should believe them – not invalidate their needs by telling them to "get on with it" or "stop making a fuss." Similarly, the use of transitional and comfort items may be a source of great safety, and shouldn't be taken away until the child is ready (Norman, 2024).

Educators "must genuinely value everyone's presence. There must be an ongoing recognition that everyone influences the classroom dynamic, that everyone contributes" (bell hooks, 1994). This means a whole-school approach, with young people's voices at the centre, and parent/carer concerns and ideas also taken seriously. In order to work collaboratively, students, staff, and parents/carers all need to respect different ways of experiencing and understanding the world.

Neurodivergent students will often have at least one neurodivergent parent (Sandin, 2017), so schools need to offer a variety of spaces and methods of communication. Emails and text are no less valid than in-person meetings, and often more accessible for monotropic people, among others.

Recommendations for the Classroom

Multiple Channels

Anticipate that monotropic learners may miss information others take for granted. Words, gestures, tone, and subtext might be missed; be explicit, and do not rely on any one channel. Working independently, one-to-one, or in small groups with familiar people may be easier than larger groups.

Filtering

Distractions and multiple streams of input make concentrating harder and contribute to the risk of overwhelm, meltdowns, and shutdowns. Common distractions in school environments include noises, visual clutter, lights, smells, and uncomfortable clothes.

Sensory tools and stimming can help learners to focus, flow, and regulate, providing extra input when needed and helping with filtering. Some focus better when listening to music; others may need ear defenders to block out sound.

Changing Tracks

Sudden changes can cause feelings of instability and inertia, so give notice of upcoming changes and time for transitions. Having to juggle information from multiple subjects, delivered by multiple people, makes it hard to maintain flow. Routines can provide predictability and reassurance, but rigid timetables can cause anxiety.

Intense Experiences

These can be positive or negative. Learners are likely to get deeply absorbed in tasks that motivate them, and intensely distressed by things that frustrate and overwhelm them. Never shame somebody for responding more strongly to something than you would.

Looping Back

Many thought loops are harmless, but some can cause anxiety. Unresolved questions are a major source of rumination for monotropic learners, and they may not be able to let something go if they can't make sense of it. Rumination can create cycles of anxiety: "loops of concern" (Hallett, 2021). Reliable adults can help neurodivergent learners feel safe to talk things through and get to the root of why they are stuck.

Things Drop Out

Monotropic people may seem forgetful or disorganised, since executive functioning often depends on holding on to multiple pieces of information. Reminders, timers, and visual aids can all be helpful, especially if people have agency and autonomy in their use. Flexible routines and written instructions mean less to remember.

Conclusion

Since the Monotropism Questionnaire (Garau, 2023) was published, there has been a wonderful surge of interest in monotropism. However, currently, research is predominantly focused on adults' experience of being monotropic, and research that captures the child's experience is much needed. Moreover, there is a need for more of an understanding of monotropism as it relates to neurodivergent presentations other than autism and ADHD.

Monotropic learners need schools to validate and value their ways of being, and understand their passionate interests as a gateway into expansive learning opportunities. Recognising the relationship between monotropism, sensory systems, social interaction, communication, and wellbeing is also important. Validating the experience of young people and their families by listening and collaborating together can make a world of difference to a young person's experience at school. It is the difference between merely surviving and being able to thrive. A regulated monotropic mind will help support and balance the sensory system, leading to joyful flow states, intrinsic motivation, and improved learning outcomes.

Adopting a radically inclusive approach to monotropism and flow in the school environment benefits everyone. Schools cannot be neurodiversity-affirmative unless they are meeting the needs of all, and that means understanding the needs of monotropic learners.

Key Takeaways

Key differences between monotropic and polytropic learners and strategies for working with the former are summarised in the following table and its bullet points, based on Murray's six starting points for understanding monotropism (Murray, 2019a; Murray, 2019b).

	Monotropic Learners	Polytropic Learners
1.	Coping with multiple channels is hard – this can be sensory channels or other information streams.	Having multiple attention channels makes integrating information easier.
2.	Filtering is tricky and error-prone – it can be difficult to tune things out, other times people may filter them out completely.	Filtering takes less energy. Distractions are less of a problem, while important interruptions are less likely to be missed.
3.	Changing tracks is destabilising – task-switching is hard, and new plans take work.	Changing tracks is more manageable, requiring less investment of attention – often faster and less jarring.
4.	People often experience things intensely – especially things that relate to interests and concerns.	With more diffuse attention, experiences are less often so intense and absorbing. Energy levels are easier to manage.
5.	Monotropic people often loop back to interests and concerns – it's hard to let things drop.	Attention is easier to redirect, so even when people are anxious there is more capacity to move on.
6.	Things that drop out of awareness tend to stay dropped – reminders may be needed.	Having wider and multiple channels to organise thoughts and actions means there is greater scope for memory recall from multiple entry points.

Reflective Activities

Personal Reflection

- Reflect on your own attentional style: Use the table highlighting the key differences between monotropic and polytropic learners to reflect on your own attentional style.
- Consider how your attention is reflected in daily life: how does it show up in your work and your leisure activities?
- Identify your own "flow" states: when do you feel most engaged and absorbed in an activity? What characteristics do these activities share?

Analysing Classroom Practices

- Observe a classroom setting:
- How is attention managed in this classroom?
- Are there opportunities for students to engage in deep focus and explore their interests?
- Are there opportunities for student choice and autonomy?
- Consider how the classroom environment might be adapted to better support monotropic learners: What changes could be made to the physical environment, the curriculum, or teaching methods to reduce distractions and promote flow?

Exploring "Can't Not Won't"

- Think about a situation a learner found challenging in some way.
- How did you respond?
- Does the reframing of "can't not won't" apply to the situation?
- What alternative approaches could you have taken?

Fostering Flow

- Generate ways to incorporate flow states into your own practice.
- How can you create opportunities for students to engage in deep, meaningful work that aligns with their interests?
- How can you minimise distractions and create a supportive environment for focused learning?

References

Arnold, S. R., Higgins, J. M., Weise, J., Desai, A., Pellicano, E., & Trollor, J. N. (2023). Towards the measurement of autistic burnout. *Autism, 27*(7), 1933–1948. https://doi.org/10.1177/13623613221147401

Boren, R. (2024, July 7). *Behaviorism - Stimpunks Foundation*. Stimpunks Foundation. https://stimpunks.org/glossary/behaviorism/

Botha, M., Chapman, R., Onaiwu, M. G., Kapp, S. K., Ashley, A. S., & Walker, N. (2024). The neurodiversity concept was developed collectively: An overdue correction on the origins of neurodiversity theory. *Autism, 28*(6), 1591–1594. https://doi.org/10.1177/13623613241237871

Conden, K., Brewer. R., & Cage, E. (2021). Personal identity after an autism diagnosis: Relationships with self-esteem, mental wellbeing, and diagnostic timing. *Frontiers in Psychology, 12*(699335). https://doi.org/10.3389/fpsyg-2021

Chapman, L., Rose, K., Hull, L., & Mandy, W. (2022). 'I want to fit in. . . but I don't want to change myself fundamentally': A qualitative exploration of the relationship between masking and mental health for autistic teenagers. *Research in Autism Spectrum Disorders, 99*, 102069. https://doi.org/10.1016/j.rasd.2022.102069

Connolly, S. E., Constable, H. L., & Mullally, S. L. (2023). School distress and the school attendance crisis: A story dominated by neurodivergence and unmet need. *Frontiers in Psychiatry, 14*. https://doi.org/10.3389/fpsyt.2023.1237052

Csikszentmihalyi, M., & Csikszentmihalyi, I. S. (1992). *Optimal experience: Psychological studies of flow in consciousness*. Cambridge: Cambridge University Press.

Fisher, N. (2023). *A different way to learn: Neurodiversity and self-directed education*. London: Jessica Kingsley Publishers.

Fisher, N. (2024). What does neurodiversity really imply for education? *BPS*. https://www.bps.org.uk/psychologist/what-does-neurodiversity-really-imply-education

Fox, L., Williams, R. B., & Asbury, K. (2024, January 9). *Experiences of friendships among autistic children in UK schools: A qualitative meta-synthesis*. https://doi.org/10.31234/osf.io/zm76n

Fricker, E. (2022). *Can't not won't: A story about a child who couldn't go to school*. London: Jessica Kingsley Publishers.

Garau, V., Murray, A., Woods, R., Chown, N., Hallett, S., Murray, F., Wood, R., & Fletcher-Watson, S. (2023). Development and validation of a novel self-report measure of monotropism in autistic and non-autistic people: The Monotropism Questionnaire. OSF Preprints. https://doi.org/10.31219/osf.io/ft73y

Greene, R. W. (2021). *The explosive child updated and revised edition: A new approach for understanding and parenting easily frustrated, chronically inflexible children*. New York: Harper Paperbacks.

Hallett, S. (2021). *Loops of concern*. Available at: https://medium.com/@sonnyhallett/loops-of-concern-ff792eebad03

Hallett, S. (2022, January 5). *Loops of concern - Sonny Hallett - medium*. Medium. https://medium.com/@sonnyhallett/loops-of-concern-ff792eebad03

Heasman, B., Williams, G., Charura, D., Hamilton, L. G., Milton, D., & Murray, F. (2024). Towards autistic flow theory: A non-pathologising conceptual approach. *Journal for the Theory of Social Behaviour*. https://doi.org/10.1111/jtsb.12427

hooks, bell. (1994). *Teaching to transgress: Education as the practice of freedom*. Routledge. https://doi.org/10.4324/9780203700280

Kearney, C. A., Benoit, L., Gonzálvez, C., & Keppens, G. (2022). School attendance and school absenteeism: A primer for the past, present, and theory of change for the future. *Frontiers in Education, 7*. https://doi.org/10.3389/feduc.2022.1044608

Kohn, A. (2018). *Punished by rewards: The trouble with gold stars, incentive plans, A's, praise, and other bribes*. New York: HarperOne.

McDonnell, A., & Milton, D. (2014). Going with the flow: Reconsidering 'repetitive behaviour' through the concept of 'flow states'. In Glenys Jones & Elizabeth Hurley (Eds.), *Good* autism practice*: Autism, happiness and wellbeing* (pp. 38–47). Birmingham: BILD. ISBN 978-1-905218-35-6

McGreevy, E., Quinn, A., Law, R., Botha, M., Evans, M., Rose, K., Moyse, R., Boyens, T., Matejko, M., & Pavlopoulou, G. (2024). An experience sensitive approach to care with and for autistic children and young people in clinical services. *Journal of Humanistic Psychology*. https://doi.org/10.1177/00221678241232442

Milton, D. E. (2012). On the ontological status of autism: The 'double empathy problem.' *Disability & Society, 27*(6), 883–887. https://doi.org/10.1080/09687599.2012.710008

Milton, D. E. (2017). *Going with the flow: Autism and 'flow states'* - Kent Academic Repository (n.d.). https://kar.kent.ac.uk/63699/

Murray, D., Dr. (1992). Attention tunnelling and autism. In Living with autism: The individual, the family, and the professional (Durham Conference). https://monotropism.org/dinah/attention-tunnelling-and-autism/

Murray, D., Dr. (1998). Mind as a dynamical system: Implications for autism. In Psychobiology of autism: Current research & practice (Durham Conference). https://monotropism.org/dinah/mind-as-a-dynamical-system/

Murray, D. (2021). Dimensions of difference. In *Routledge eBooks* (pp. 34–41). https://doi.org/10.4324/9781003056577-5

Murray, D., Lesser, M., & Lawson, W. (2005). Attention, monotropism and the diagnostic criteria for autism. *Autism, 9*(2), 139–156. https://doi.org/10.1177/1362361305051398

Murray, F. (2019a). Starting points for understanding autism. *Medium*. https://oolong.medium.com/starting-points-for-understanding-autism-3573817402f2

Murray, F. (2019b). Autism tips for teachers - by an autistic teacher. *Tes Magazine*. https://www.tes.com/magazine/archive/autism-tips-teachers-autistic-teacher

Nordin, V., Palmgren, M., Lindbladh, A., Bölte, S., & Jonsson, U. (2023). School absenteeism in autistic children and adolescents: A scoping review. *Autism, 28*(7), 1622–1637. https://doi.org/10.1177/13623613231217409

Norman, A. (2024). *Transitional objects in early childhood: The value of transitional objects in the early years*. London: Routledge.

O'Neill, C., & Kenny, N. (2023). 'I saw things through a different lens. . .': An interpretative phenomenological study of the experiences of autistic teachers in the Irish education system. *Education Sciences, 13*(7), 670. https://doi.org/10.3390/educsci13070670

Pearson, A., & Rose, K. (2023). *Autistic masking: Understanding identity management and the role of stigma.* London: Pavilion.

Phung, J., Penner, M., Pirlot, C., & Welch, C. (2021). What i wish you knew: Insights on burnout, inertia, meltdown, and shutdown from autistic youth. *Frontiers in Psychology, 12.* https://doi.org/10.3389/fpsyg.2021.741421

Pritchard-Rowe, E., De Lemos, C., Howard, K., & Gibson, J. (2024). Diversity in autistic play: Autistic adults' experiences. *Autism in Adulthood, 6*(2), 218–228. https://doi.org/10.1089/aut.2023.0008

Rapaport, H., Clapham, H., Adams, J., Lawson, W., Porayska-Pomsta, K., & Pellicano, E. (2024). "In a state of flow": a qualitative examination of autistic adults' phenomenological experiences of task immersion. *Autism in Adulthood, 6(3),* 362–373. https://doi.org/10.1089/aut.2023.0032

Raymaker, D. M., Teo, A. R., Steckler, N. A., Lentz, B., Scharer, M., Santos, A. D., Kapp, S. K., Hunter, M., Joyce, A., & Nicolaidis, C. (2020). 'Having all of your internal resources exhausted beyond measure and being left with no clean-up crew': Defining autistic burnout. *Autism in Adulthood, 2*(2), 132–143. https://doi.org/10.1089/aut.2019.0079

Sandin, S., Lichtenstein, P., Kuja-Halkola, R., Hultman, C., Larsson, H., & Reichenberg, A. (2017). The heritability of autism spectrum disorder. *JAMA, 318*(12), 1182. https://doi.org/10.1001/jama.2017.12141

Shepherd, J., Sutton, B., Smith, S., & Szlenkier, M. (2024). 'Sea-glass survivors': Autistic testimonies about education experiences. *British Journal of Special Education.* https://doi.org/10.1111/1467-8578.12506

Wood, R. (2019). *Inclusive education for autistic children: Helping children and young people to learn and flourish in the classroom.* London: Routledge

7

Embedding a Humanising, Compassionate Pedagogy for Collaborative Learning in the Neurodiverse Classroom

Elaine McGreevy

Introduction

In every classroom, students differ in their neurocognitive functioning, linguistic and communication skills, and cultural and other social identities. Currently, the dominant ideologies in education favour an idealised "implied student" (Ulriksen, 2009) influenced by neuronormativity and other forms of supremacy. School policies and practices are often oppressive or exclusionary for neurodivergent students, making the conditions for their participation much more difficult. Group working is one of the most challenging learning contexts for neurodivergent students. This chapter will explore how to create a culture of compassion and inclusivity in the classroom.

A Strained, Inequitable Education System

Teachers have the greatest potential to influence a student's flourishing in education. Globally, teachers experience work-related stress, burnout, anxiety, and depression (Agyapong et al., 2022). They are significantly overburdened, and subjected to conflicting pressures from governmental and local policies and regulatory frameworks, staff shortages, teacher attrition, increasing class sizes, limited resources, and financial pressures, to mention just a few (Citaristi, 2022). New teachers may not access sufficient induction support to successfully include children with diverse needs, and may experience a "reality shock" as they try to embed inclusive pedagogy in these complex systems (Mintz et al., 2020). Neurodivergent staff face additional pressures. Autistic staff in the UK face barriers and discrimination arising from a lack of understanding, sensory impacts, mental health issues, and impact of the disclosure of an autistic identity (Wood & Happé, 2021).

Neurodivergent students face serious barriers in accessing education. Recent statistics on school exclusions in England (Department for Education, 2024) have found disproportionate exclusion rates for students with special educational needs and disabilities compared to non-disabled students. It is not surprising then that many autistic pupils do not realise their academic potential (Serratore et al., 2025) and have "poor" post-secondary outcomes too (Fleury et al., 2014). ADHD students, including those who are sub-threshold, have similarly poor educational outcomes (Zendarski et al., 2020). Moreover, the All-Party Parliamentary Group on Autism (2017) found that 50 per cent of autistic children were unhappy at school and felt that their needs were not being met. In a UK study, 92.1 per cent of the 1,096 children experiencing school distress and attendance difficulties were neurodivergent, and 83.4 per cent of this cohort were autistic (Connolly et al., 2023). Fielding at al. (2024) reported themes of inaccessible and distressing school environments. Neurodivergent students described harrowing experiences of school, reporting that difficulties with peer relations, bullying, difficulties communicating with and being understood by teachers, inconsistent provision of supports, sensory overwhelming spaces, and a lack of predictability made school intolerable and psychologically harmful for a majority. Auditory differences and noise impact learning most often (Jones et al., 2020; Wood, 2018).

School spaces, policies, and practices tend to be designed for the "implied" student (Uliksen, 2009). This ideal type of learner is based on a white, non-disabled, and non-marginalised student. These implicit biases arise from a neurotypical hegemony (Radulski, 2024), and often unexamined racism and ableism which uphold the idea of normalcy (DeMatthews, Serafini & Watson, 2021). Consequently, the neurodivergent student encounters an exclusionary and unrelenting socially, emotionally, culturally, and/or sensorily assaulting experience. Such oppressive systems cannot support neurodivergent flourishing – it is a matter of surviving, and not thriving (Shepherd et al. 2024). The neurodivergent student's right to attend mainstream education is more vulnerable and dependent on their ability to meet the ableist and subjective notions of demonstrating acceptable behaviour that does not disrupt the education of others (Lalvani & Osieja, 2024, Ferguson, 2021). The lack of acknowledgement of how these same environments disrupt the education of the neurodivergent student perpetuates the assumption that they are always at fault and the only one who needs to change or improve. This fixed mindset can lead educators to use a medical model "intervention" approach and place more controls and sanctions on the neurodivergent student rather than looking to address barriers in the environment.

A "Them and Us" Context Thwarts Acceptance and Belonging for Marginalised Classmates

Current educational practices often reinforce ableist and capitalist ideals about ability, excellence, productivity, desirability, and conformity. This contributes to stigma and a devaluing of neurodivergent and disabled ways of being which is ultimately absorbed by all students. Negative bias, based on initial "thin slice judgements," affects the willingness of social partners to interact with autistic adults and young people (Sasson et al., 2017). These biases influence how educators perceive and treat autistic and other neurodivergent students in the classroom, which may in turn influence how their peers view them – for example, the ADHD child who receives the most frequent corrections from the teacher may be perceived by the other students as naughty or not likable, and someone they don't want to work with. Children identified as having special educational needs and disabilities may be separated out and may receive ableist interventions such as social skills- and attention-building groups, emphasising their perceived "brokenness" in the eyes of their peers, and they may come to believe this too. A "them and us" division influences the self-perception of students and negatively impacts others' perceptions of those who are othered. Commonplace motivational strategies such as time pressures, rewards and sanctions, testing, and competition increase stress for students, but worryingly, increase self-centredness and reduce sense of justice, moderation, and kindness (Pyyry & Sirviö, 2024). A "sink or swim" or "dog eat dog" mentality can develop under such conditions. These conditions foster exclusionary attitudes about those who are seen as other, deficient, or undesirable.

Wellbeing and intrinsic motivation are essential factors in fostering thriving for all students, and education staff too. We all do well when we feel psychologically safe and when we have the support and resources to do what is meaningful and what motivates us. Social Determination Theory (SDT) (Ryan

& Deci, 2000) outlines the importance of three fundamental psychological requirements of relatedness, competence, and autonomy. People have a need to be accepted by others and to have a sense of personal relatedness – students should feel socially connected in their classrooms. Everyone should be able to achieve their goals and control their outcomes through a sense of personal competence. Everyone should be free to have personal autonomy and act in ways that express their "true" self. Small changes and bigger changes through school policy which enable the fulfilment of these requirements will improve conditions for all.

The Double Empathy Problem in the Classroom

Neurotypical privilege (Walker, 2021) describes the unearned privilege that neurotypical people possess by virtue of being the majority. Those who are in positions of power will never have to address or acknowledge their own empathy deficits or poor communication skills when interacting with neurodivergent people – all failures of empathy, understanding, and communication are attributed to the so-called "deficits" of the other. The attitudes and beliefs held by educators may lead them to dismiss the perspectives of the neurodivergent student and/or their neurodivergent parent/carer. They may view the neurodivergent student or their parent as wrong, deficient, needy, over-anxious, undeserving of support, or unnecessarily consuming too much of the finite resource. This increases the barriers many parents face in advocating for their disabled children, with parental blame a continuing narrative (Clements & Aiello, 2021). The cost of these relentless battles is high, with a recent study identifying an increased suicide risk for parent/carers (O'Dwyer et al., 2024).

Given the potential harms of neurotypical privilege, it is imperative that educators look at ways of minimising these risks. The Double Empathy Problem (DEP) (Milton, 2012), describes the shared misunderstanding and communication difficulties between autistic and non-autistic people due to a mismatch in each one's social expectations and lived experience, which also leads to an imbalance of power and responsibility. Neurotypical privilege is at play in the DEP, with communication problems mis-located in the autistic person – the non-autistic person fails to consider their role in the communication breakdown. The DEP can be extended beyond autistic and non-autistic dyads – for example, Sisskin, (2021) explored the DEP in the context of stammering. Some examples of the DEP in the classroom are:

- The teacher dismisses the student's request to repeat or request for help based on the assumption that if the student had listened, they would already know what to do.
- The neuromajority student assumes the child with speech, language, and communication differences has nothing to contribute or doesn't want to contribute an idea in a group task because they cannot speak clearly or do not speak.
- The well-meaning support adult advises the stammering child to slow down instead of addressing their own listening and communication partner skills.
- The neuromajority students ignore the neurodivergent student in the group.
- The autistic student has trouble getting their point acknowledged in the small group activity and feels their peers are not listening.
- The ADHD student is corrected by the teacher for speaking first before putting their hand up.
- The autistic student interprets a peer's friendly joke as teasing.
- The teacher expects that all students pay attention best by having quiet bodies and while looking at the teacher's face.
- The teacher interprets the student's behaviour and inability to meet the adult and academic expectations as a choice.
- A student is labelled as "lazy," "stubborn," "aggressive," or "unable to share and take turns" without consideration of the barriers to participation and the role of others in the shaping of these narratives.
- The child with auditory hyperacusis interprets the teacher's raised voice as shouting.
- Adults misunderstand or fail to recognise the impact of the physical and sensory environment on the participation or physical and emotional well-being of the student with sensory differences or physical disability.
- The range of linguistic, cultural, and neurodivergent identities within the school are not represented.

Addressing the DEP in the classroom requires attention to enable fairer conditions for everyone's participation, and this should form part of ongoing educator reflective practice sessions.

Towards a Socially Just, Neuro-Inclusive, Compassionate Pedagogy

Florian and Camedda (2019) describe Scotland's Inclusive Practice Project (Rouse & Florian, 2021), which considers facilitating learning as apprenticeships of the head (theoretical knowledge), the hand (technical and practical skills), and the heart (attitudes and beliefs). Emphasizing the heart in the work of education generates empathy and compassion. A rights-based education (UNICEF) ensures respect, dignity, and equity of opportunity for all, affirming each student's worth and the value of all identities. Ortega (2024) describes the relationship between critical education and humanising pedagogy, which is based on four key ideas:

1. Holding shared values of inclusion and valuing student agency, empowerment, and the development of critical consciousness.
2. A holistic approach which prioritises student wellbeing and socio-emotional learning.
3. Recognition of intersectionality of identities and culturally responsive classrooms.
4. The importance of action and praxis, encouraging students to apply learning to real-world contexts.

Embedding these values and ideas is putting the "head, hand, and heart" into creating inclusive school communities. There are some resources available to schools which can support this work. The Learning About Neurodiversity at School (LEANS) programme teaches children (aged 8–12 years) about neurodiversity, including ideas about equity, which increases positive attitudes and intended actions (Alcorn et al., 2023 – see Chapter 12). *Belonging in School* is a school-level resource to develop inclusive policy which emphasises a focus on the pupils' sense of belonging and their subjective sense of whether they feel part of their school community and feel safe and valued (Alcorn, Zdorovtsova & Astle, 2023).

A compassionate and neurodiversity-inclusive pedagogy produces conditions for students to feel safe, calm, and secure so that they can engage with learning in a way that recognises their strengths, supports their needs, and allows for sensory regulation, as and when they need it. Students learn to appreciate their similarities and differences when accessibility is built in through UDL (see Chapter 11). This creates a hopeful, positive, and compassionate classroom culture – a place where all students can belong, flourish, play, and work together in a culture of togetherness.

Bridging the Double Empathy Gap

Building in policies and practices and through modelling, educators can bridge communication gaps to promote better understanding, empathy, connection, and an accessible environment. The following points can guide educators in addressing the Double Empathy gap:

1. Listen well. Many adults overestimate how good they are at listening. Listening is an art crafted over time, and is an essential feature in creating a culture of care and working well together. Shannon and Hackett (2024) explore that how and what children communicate about varies according to the place where they're situated. They make suggestions for expansive listening – listening to hear and understand rather than to meet the narrow agenda and convenience of the system and the adult. Listening requires space and time, and especially multi-modal communication for students who cannot rely on speech alone to be heard and understood (e.g., visual, tactile, vocal, verbal, and non-verbal means of communication). The adult is actively involved in bridging any communication misunderstandings and is open to facilitating and listening to all the ways the student communicates, and then checks back for understanding.
2. Build positive relationships based on emotional safety so that the students can express their perspectives and needs without fear of judgement or dismissal. One of the most useful things education staff can do is to not make assumptions about a student's perspectives and needs. Get to know the student well, and include parents/carers.
3. Consider the environment. The classroom belongs to all its members, therefore the students should have a say on the conditions they need to feel comfortable, able to learn, and work together. Working collaboratively with the students over shared space reduces the power differential in the hierarchical teacher–student relationship. The teacher could conduct a classroom sensory audit with the students and give opportunities for them to describe their preferences and needs. This is a great way for

students to develop empathy and understanding of each other's preferences and problem-solve how to address competing needs.
4. Consider instructional inadequacy (Donnellan, 1984). Effective teachers are those who can teach all students. If a student does not do well, the quality of the instruction should be questioned rather than assuming the student is wrong or non-compliant. Improve access through UDL. Build in more flexibility regarding the length of time students can have to complete tasks.
5. Proactively check for understanding instead of placing the burden on the neurodivergent child to ask for help. Neurodivergent children learn over time to stop asking for help due to previous experiences of help being denied when they asked for it or when help was given in a way that made things worse for the student. Build emotional safety by welcoming a student's self-advocacy in a non-judgemental manner.
6. Promote social equality and a flexible "can do" approach. Support the individual student's needs and make adjustments that are accessible to all, rather than relying on clinical diagnostic pathways or working through legislative time frames which unfairly limit access to support. Leadership should support teachers' autonomy to discover their own best ways of doing things in relation to the diversity represented in the classroom (Cook, 2024).
7. Prioritise continuing professional development and reflective practice as a cornerstone of pedagogy to unsettle fixed mindsets, biases, and rigid rules and allow for more personalised and responsive teaching (Cook, 2024).
8. Consider the impact of emotions on relationships and motivations. Emotions are transactional and may be caught – emotional contagion impacts the regulation and participation of students and contributes to staff feelings of satisfaction or stress. The excited educator may dysregulate some students. The exhausted, angry, or anxious teacher may negatively impact the development of positive relationships with students (Frenzel, Daniels & Burić, 2021). A wellbeing approach and an environment that brings out the best in all will foster quality relationships and emotional regulation that sets everyone up to be their best self.
9. A compassion-informed approach requires adults to be attentive to signs of distress. Educators should consider the cognitive, emotional, and physical impact of masking, which develops in childhood and is not limited to autistic people (Miller, Rees & Pearson, 2021). Educators should rely on

reports of distress from parents/carers to help them attune to the "quiet" student who may need more support but does not feel safe to express their needs or concerns.

Creating the Conditions for Positive Peer Relations and Neurodiversity-Inclusive Collaborative Learning

Group working or collaborative learning is a common approach in education at all stages. The Education Endowment Foundation (July, 2021) states that collaborative learning is a low-cost approach that can have a positive impact on attainment; however, overall, there is low-quality evidence for the effectiveness of collaborative learning. Collaborative learning may take different forms, and choosing the format that best suits the learners in a class is essential.

Key points to consider in setting up neuro-inclusive groups in the classroom:

- Structure and predictability – provide clear, explicit and non-ambiguous instructions in different modes (e.g., a model, text, pictures, or video). There should be clarity in roles and expectations.
- Group tasks should be meaningful and motivating.
- Adult support should be provided to the group, rather than singling out the neurodivergent child unnecessarily.
- Match the individual to the optimum group size for them. Some students may feel safer in a large group. Others may feel more regulated and able to process and participate in a small group. Some students may work best in a paired group, with a preferred partner.
- Skilled adult monitoring of the group at work will ensure the neurominority student feels safe, supported, and not abandoned. Should adult support be required, this should be directed to all group members, taking account of the Double Empathy Problem.

Applying Self-Determination Theory to Collaborative Learning

The psychological needs of personal relatedness, competence, and autonomy are important to consider when trying to create a group that works well together. The members of the group should feel a sense of personal relatedness. Friendships facilitate peer interactions, whereas negative peer interactions create barriers to participation. All students benefit emotionally and socially from having a friend who understands them, and this safe partner can be a conduit to developing interactions with other peers. Neurodivergent children tend to gravitate naturally towards each other. Shared interests and experiences increase communication effectiveness, connection, and rapport. Research has shown this to be true for autistic people in same-neurotype interactions (Chen et al., 2021, Crompton et al., 2020). In mixed groups of autistic and non-autistic members, autistic people expressed reduced rapport when in the minority, which was not experienced by the non-autistic members (Foster et al., 2024). Considering matching peers based on how well they get along, shared interests, and the same neurotype may be positive factors in a successful and harmonious group.

Where the content and task design provide a just-right level of challenge, group members are likely to feel more engaged, confident, and competent. A strengths-based and multi-sensory approach enables neurodivergent learners to access different modes of expression and avail of a range of choices for participation. The flexibility in task design underpinned by UDL principles creates more motivating and less frustrating conditions, which will likely reduce frustrations. Some students might choose to work on their own for part of the group task so they can get into their monotropic flow state, in deep concentration or total absorption (Heasman et al., 2024). Having the opportunity to move away to complete an element of the group task on their own might be an effective way to support the individual's need to work without interruption and might aid self-regulation. When the group has autonomy in making decisions on how to complete the task, this enables ownership of the task, and increases predictability for students, giving them more control over their context.

Some group tasks (and learners) will require clearly defined roles. The teacher should aim to match the student to the role, focusing on their strengths

Expanding Ideas about Group Playing and Working

Neurodivergent intersubjectivity has been studied between autistic people (Heasman & Gillespie, 2018) and in autistic and non-autistic conversation partners (Williams, Wharton & Jagoe, 2021). Intersubjectivity involves the interactive co-construction of meaning and social relating, moving away from the idea that social skills are an individual skill. Social skills are the coming together and attuning to each other through language, body language, and actions, in a shared context and across different timescales. In autistic pairs, shared interests and experiences lead to greater flow and synchronicity and in autistic–non-autistic pairs, even though the interaction flow may be lower and have less symmetry in turns, connection is enabled through warm curiosity and common ground (Williams et al., 2021). A neuro-inclusive classroom values and creates space for diverse interactions. Common ground and positive regard significantly help peers to build connection. Group activities where there is a fixed outcome or objective to be achieved within a short time frame can limit opportunities for authentic relationship-building and connection. Parallel play or parallel group working should be seen as valuable as interactive group work for building connection and establishing relationships.

Educators can also draw on insights from neurodivergent students' social preferences and incorporate them into the classroom. Gaming is a popular social and play activity for many children and young people. Autistic youth have described how gaming enables autonomy, provides a place to make friendships, and doesn't require speaking to participate (Pavlopoulou, Usher & Pearson, 2022). The asynchronous and parallel features of communication and interaction in gaming support engagement for those who need more processing time or physical space or who struggle with the intensity of face-to-face interactions. Leaning into a neurodivergent strength and interest in media and technology is a way to increase social opportunities and collaborative, non-competitive working that is enjoyable for all students.

Key Takeaways

- Teachers have the greatest potential to influence a student's flourishing in education, and are often working in stressed and overburdened systems.
- Teachers need to be able to exercise agency in their classrooms to provide a humanising, compassionate, and flexible pedagogy

that benefits all. To do this, they need time, space, and support for reflective practice.
- Reflecting on how the Double Empathy Problem manifests in the classroom with students from diverse backgrounds and intersectional identities should be a regular focus for educators.
- Embedding values and ideas of inclusive and socially just pedagogy through policy and practice has the potential to make classrooms feel safer and accessible for all students.
- The outworkings of inclusive pedagogy should lead to positive relationships and feelings of connectedness in a place where all students feel they belong and can benefit from equality of opportunity to engage in different ways of learning alongside and with each other.

Reflective Activities

Think about a student in your class or whom you've previously taught who was/is least able to meet the academic challenges, social or communication demands, or behavioural expectations of your classroom.

1. Identify examples of the Double Empathy Problem in interactions:
    - between adults and this student
    - between this student and other students

What was the impact of the Double Empathy Problem on this student? On you?

What steps can you take to bridge the gap in understanding, empathising, and communicating with this student?

2. Evaluate a recent group activity. Reflect on the accessibility factors that enabled participation for the neurodivergent students.

Consider the impact of the following aspects. Identify challenges or barriers that you observed and that the students reported:

- The sensory environment before and during the task (e.g., consider auditory, lighting, room temperature, movement, physical space)
- Resources (e.g., consider preparedness, sufficient resources, relevant to the task, easy to use, organised and accessible)
- Instructional context (e.g., multiple modes of instruction used, supports to access instructions throughout, specificity of instructions, and clarity of task, including clearly defined roles)
- Relationships (e.g., familiarity and comfort between peers in the same group, impact of staff/student relationship on seeking or giving support)
- Motivation (e.g., ability to feel competent with the task, intrinsic motivation, and relevance and meaningfulness of the task)

Consider if the learning objectives were appropriate to be achieved through group learning. What can you do to improve the experience for the students the next time?

References

Alcorn, A. M., Zdorovtsova, N., & Astle, D. E. (2023). *Belonging in school part 1: An introduction to school-level approaches for developing inclusive policy*. Medical Research Council Cognition and Brain Sciences Unit, University of Cambridge.

Alcorn, A. M., McGeown, S. P., Mandy, W., Aitken, D., & Fletcher-Watson, S. (2023, September 1). Learning About Neurodiversity at School (LEANS): Evaluation of the LEANS resource pack in mainstream primary schools. https://doi.org/10.31219/osf.io/fhc2k

All Party Parliamentary Group on Autism. (2017). *APPGA report: Autism and education in England*. All Party Parliamentary Group on Autism, London.

Agyapong, B., Obuobi-Donkor, G., Burback, L., & Wei, Y. (2022). Stress, burnout, anxiety and depression among teachers: A scoping review. International Journal of Environmental Research and Public Health, 19(17), 10706. https://doi.org/10.3390/ijerph191710706

Chen, Y.-L., Senande, L. L., Thorsen, M., & Patten, K. (2021). Peer preferences and characteristics of same-group and cross-group social interactions among autistic and non-autistic adolescents. *Autism, 25*(7), 1885–1900. https://doi.org/10.1177/13623613211005918

Citaristi, I. (2022). United Nations Educational, Scientific and Cultural Organization—UNESCO. In *The Europa Directory of International Organizations 2022* (pp. 369–375). Routledge.

Clements, L., & Aiello, A. L. (2021). Institutionalising parent carer blame. *Cerebra*

Connolly, S. E., Constable, H. L., & Mullally, S. L. (2023). School distress and the school attendance crisis: A story dominated by neurodivergence and unmet need. Frontiers in Psychiatry, 14, Article 1237052. https://doi.org/10.3389/fpsyt.2023.1237052

Cook, A. (2024). Conceptualisations of neurodiversity and barriers to inclusive pedagogy in schools: A perspective article. *Journal of Research in Special Educational Needs, 24*(3), 627–636. https://doi.org/10.1111/1471-3802.12656

Crompton, C. J., Hallett, S., Ropar, D., Flynn, E., & Fletcher-Watson, S. (2020a). 'I never realised everybody felt as happy as I do when I am around autistic people': A thematic analysis of autistic adults' relationships with autistic and neurotypical friends and family. *Autism, 24*, 1438–1448. https://doi.org/10.1177/1362361320908976

Deci E. L., & Ryan, R. M. (2000). The 'what' and 'why' of goal pursuits: Human needs and the self-determination of behavior. Psychological Inquiry, 11(4), 227–268. https://doi.org/10.1207/S15327965PLI1104_01

DeMatthews, D. E., Serafini, A., & Watson, T. N. (2021). Leading inclusive schools: Principal perceptions, practices, and challenges to meaningful change. *Educational Administration Quarterly, 57*(1), 3–48. https://doi.org/10.1177/0013161X20913897

Department for Education. (2024). *Suspensions and permanent exclusions in England: 2022 to 2023*. Department for Education, London, England. GOV.UK (www.gov.uk)

Donnellan, A. (1984). The criterion of the least dangerous assumption. *Behavioral Disorders, 9*, 141–150

Education Endowment Foundation. (2021, July). *Collaborative learning approaches*. EEF. educationendowmentfoundation.org.uk

Ferguson, L. (2021). Vulnerable children's right to education, school exclusion, and pandemic law-making. *Emotional and Behavioural Difficulties, 26*(1), 101–115. https://doi.org/10.1080/13632752.2021.1913351

Fielding, C., Streeter, A., Riby, D. M., & Hanley, M. (2024, May 3). Neurodivergent pupils' experiences of school distress and attendance difficulties. https://doi.org/10.31219/osf.io/425sq

Fleury, V. P., Hedges, S., Hume, K., Browder, D. M., Thompson, J. L., Fallin, K., El Zein, F., Reutebuch, C. K., & Vaughn, S. (2014). Addressing the academic needs of adolescents with autism spectrum disorder in secondary education. *Remedial and Special Education, 35*(2), 68–79. https://doi.org/10.1177/0741932513518823

Florian, L., & Camedda, D. (2019). Enhancing teacher education for inclusion. *European Journal of Teacher Education, 43*(1), 4–8. https://doi.org/10.1080/02619768.2020.1707579

Foster, S., Ackerman, R. A., Wilks, C., Dodd, M., Calderon, R. M., Ropar, D., ... Sasson, N. (2024, July 9). Rapport in same and mixed neurotype groups of autistic and non-autistic adults. https://doi.org/10.31219/osf.io/efvbc

Frenzel, A. C., Daniels, L., & Burić, I. (2021). Teacher emotions in the classroom and their implications for students. *Educational Psychologist, 56*(4), 250–264. https://doi.org/10.1080/00461520.2021.1985501

Heasman, B., & Gillespie, A. (2018). Perspective-taking is two-sided: Misunderstandings between people with Asperger's syndrome and their family members. *Autism, 22*(6), 740–750. https://doi.org/10.1177/1362361317708287

Heasman, B., & Gillespie, A. (2019). Neurodivergent intersubjectivity: Distinctive features of how autistic people create shared understanding. *Autism, 23*(4), 910–921. https://doi.org/10.1177/1362361318785172

Heasman, B., Williams, G., Charura, D., Hamilton, L. G., Milton, D., & Murray, F. (2024, June 3). Towards autistic flow theory: A non-pathologising conceptual approach. *Journal for the Theory of Social Behaviour.* https://doi.org/10.1111/jtsb.12427

Jones, E.K., Hanley, M., & Riby, D. M. (2020). Distraction, distress and diversity: Exploring the impact of sensory processing differences on learning and school life for pupils with autism spectrum disorders. *Research in Autism Spectrum Disorders, 72*, 101515. ISSN 1750-9467, https://doi.org/10.1016/j.rasd.2020.101515

Lalvani, P., & Osieja, E. (2024). Battle fatigue: Parents, institutionalized ableism, and the 'fight' for inclusive education. *Research and Practice for Persons with Severe Disabilities, 0*(0). https://doi.org/10.1177/15407969241259365

Miller, D., Rees, J., & Pearson, A. (2021, December 1). 'Masking is life': Experiences of masking in autistic and nonautistic adults. *Autism Adulthood, 3*(4), 330–338. https://doi.org/10.1089/aut.2020.0083. Epub 2021 Dec 7. PMID: 36601640; PMCID: PMC8992921.

Milton, D. E. M. (2012). On the ontological status of autism: the 'double empathy problem.' *Disability & Society, 27*(6), 883–887. https://doi.org/10.1080/09687599.2012.710008

Mintz, J., Hick, P., Solomon, Y., Matziari, A., Ó'Murchú, F., Hall, K., Cahill, K., Curtin, C., Anders, J., & Margariti, D. (2020). The reality of reality shock for inclusion: How does teacher attitude, perceived knowledge and self-efficacy in relation to effective inclusion in the classroom change from the pre-service to novice teacher year? *Teaching and Teacher Education, 91*,103042. ISSN 0742-051X, https://doi.org/10.1016/j.tate.2020.103042

O'Dwyer, S. T., Sansom, A., Mars, B., Reakes, L., Andrewartha, C., Melluish, J., & Janssens, A. (2024). Suicidal thoughts and behaviors in parents caring for children with disabilities and long-term illnesses. *Archives of Suicide Research*, 1–18. https://doi.org/10.1080/13811118.2024.2363230

Ortega, Y. (2024). 'Un futuro mejor para todos': Towards a critical humanizing English language teaching. *Language Teaching Research, 0*(0). https://doi.org/10.1177/13621688241262618

Pavlopoulou, G., Usher, C., & Pearson, A. (2022, May 28). 'I can actually do it without any help or someone watching over me all the time and giving me constant instruction': Autistic adolescent boys' perspectives on engagement in online video gaming. *British Journal of Developmental Psychology, 40*(4), 557–571. https://doi.org/10.1111/bjdp.12424

Pyyry, N., & Sirviö, H. (2024). Landscape of competition: Education, economisation and young people's wellbeing. *Environment and Planning A: Economy and Space, 56*(2), 491–507. https://doi.org/10.1177/0308518X231197303

Radulski, E. (2024). *A Sociology of Autistic Masking and Camouflaging: The Intersectionality of Neurotypical Privilege and the Neuroarchy.* Thesis. University of Melbourne. Available at: https://orcid.org/0000-0002-6301-1319

Rouse, M. & Florian L. (2021). Inclusive Practice Project: Key Lessons for Schools. UNiversity of Aberdeen. Available at: https://www.autismtoolbox.co.uk/wp-content/uploads/2022/09/Inclusive-Practice-Programme-key-Lessons-for-schools-Aberdeen-University.pdf

Sasson, N., Faso, D., Nugent, J., Lovell, S., Kennedy, D. P., & Grossman, R. B. (2017). Neurotypical peers are less willing to interact with those with autism based on thin slice judgments. *Scientific Reports, 7,* 40700. https://doi.org/10.1038/srep40700

Serratore, T., Berdelmann, K., & Schmiedek, F. (2025). Which barriers do autistic and non-autistic children experience in inclusive classrooms? An experience sampling approach. *European Journal of Special Needs Education,* 1–16. https://doi.org/10.1080/08856257.2025.2474842

Shannon, D. B., & Hackett, A. (2024). The entanglement of language and place in early childhood: A review of the literature. *Critical Inquiry in Language Studies,* 1–24. https://doi.org/10.1080/15427587.2024.2312142

Shepherd, J., Sutton, B., Smith, S., & Szlenkier, M. (2024, June). 'Sea-glass survivors': Autistic testimonies about education experiences. *British Journal of Special Education, 51*(2), 142–155. https://doi.org/10.1111/1467-8578.12506

Sisskin, V. (2021, March 31). Power imbalances and stuttering: The double empathy problem [Blog post]. Retrieved from https://www.redefiningstammering.co.uk/power-imbalances-and-stuttering-the-double-empathy-problem/

Ulriksen, L. (2009). The implied student. *Studies in Higher Education, 34*(5), 517–532. https://doi.org/10.1080/03075070802597135

UNICEF. (n.d.). Your guide to a rights respecting classroom. Rights Respecting Schools Award. Retrieved July 19, 2024, from unicef.org.uk

Walker, N. (2021). *Neuroqueer Heresies: Notes on the Neurodiversity Paradigm, Autistic Empowerment, and Postnormal Possibilities.* Autonomous Press. ISBN-10:1945955260

Williams, G. L., Wharton, T., & Jagoe, C. (2021, April 29). Mutual (mis)understanding: Reframing autistic pragmatic 'impairments' using relevance theory. Frontiers in Psychology, 12, 616664. https://doi.org/10.3389/fpsyg.2021.616664. PMID: 33995177; PMCID: PMC8117104.

Wood, R. (2018). The wrong kind of noise: Understanding and valuing the communication of autistic children in schools. *Educational Review, 72*(1), 111–130. https://doi.org/10.1080/00131911.2018.1483895

Wood, R., & Happé, F. (2021). What are the views and experiences of autistic teachers? Findings from an online survey in the UK. *Disability & Society, 38*(1), 47–72. https://doi.org/10.1080/09687599.2021.1916888

Zendarski, N., Sciberras, E., Mensah, F., & Hiscock, H. (2020). Factors associated with educational support in young adolescents with ADHD. *Journal of Attention Disorders, 24*(5), 750–757. https://doi.org/10.1177/10870547188043

Zendarski, N., Guo, S., Sciberras, E., Efron, D., Quach, J., Winter, L., Bisset, M., Middeldorp, C. M., & Coghill, D. (2022). Examining the educational gap for children with ADHD and subthreshold ADHD. *Journal of Attention Disorders, 26*(2), 282–295. https://doi.org/10.1177/1087054720972790

8

Informing Educational Practice by Supporting, Listening to, and Acting upon the Voices of Neurodivergent Learners

Craig Goodall

Introduction

In referring to research and practice, this chapter discusses why it is crucial to support, listen to, and act upon the voices of neurodivergent learners. As educators, we can recognise their autonomy and agency, but we can also champion learners to be central actors in developing our understanding of their educational experiences. Without seriously engaging these perspectives and everyday experiences, we will struggle to develop classroom practice and pedagogy which ensures these learners thrive in a system that educates *with* them, not only *to* them. Examples of supporting, listening to, and acting upon the voices of neurodivergent learners focuses on the processes used to garner voices of primary-age autistic learners within the autism support service where the author is an advisory teacher.

Why Is It Important to Elicit the Voices of Neurodivergent Learners?

The power of eliciting the voices of neurodivergent learners is exemplified within a growing body of research, particularly drawing on examples with autistic children and young people (see Goodall, 2020; Horgan et al., 2023). The importance of being listened to and feeling respected is reflected by learners within several studies (see Gray et al., 2023; Goodall, 2018; Hummerstone & Parsons, 2021). However, Lewis, Hamilton, and Vincent

(2023, p.2) suggest that "first-person perspectives of neurodivergent children and young people are still largely absent from the literature."

One study by Howe et al. (2023) explores the perspectives of eight 10–14-year-olds and how they experience camouflaging (an aspect of masking), with findings highlighting that "autistic children and adolescents … engage in camouflaging behaviour which can be pervasive and automatic, and that this can be a stressful, confusing, and energetically draining experience" (p.1). This demonstrates why we need to hear the perspectives of neurodivergent learners, as without their insight we will always be "second-guessing": there may be a mismatch between what we see and what is experienced by the learner.

Mutual understanding between teachers and learners is emphasised in research by Gray et al. (2023), who report that "fundamentally empathetic interactions appeared to have positive implications on autistic pupils' mental health and well-being and their academic progress" (p.12). These interactions strive to overcome what Milton (2012) calls the Double Empathy Problem: the idea that there is a misalignment between the minds of autistic and non-autistic people (perhaps the non-autistic teacher and autistic learner). Gray et al. (2023) conclude that schools and local authority professionals should seek to work in partnership with autistic pupils to secure the necessary support for their inclusion in mainstream education.

Mirroring this call to action, a systematic review of educational experiences of autistic learners conducted by Horgan et al. (2023, p. 526) suggests that "further research that prioritises the voices and perspectives of this cohort is essential as inclusive policy and practice continues to develop." Rights-informed research by Goodall (2020) demonstrates that when we move beyond tokenistic endeavours to ensuring learners have multiple means to share their voice, then new perspectives can be developed (as will be revisited later). Voice is a matter of practice and of rights.

Lundy and Kilpatrick (2006) highlight that the rights of children with special needs (under Article 12 of the United Nations Convention on the Rights of the Child) have been ignored or underplayed due to a reported lack of resources and capacity within schools to provide adequate provision, including limited opportunities for children to express themselves through non-verbal modes of communication (Robinson et al., 2020). Irrespective of their perceived competence, children of all ages have useful insights on matters that are important to them, such as their education. This is not only a matter of supporting their rights, but seeking the voices of neurodivergent learners about their education to ensure that "decision makers" are guided by the experts – the young people – and not by ideological crusades. Before considering how we can authentically support neurodivergent learner voices, we will consider some barriers and some pitfalls to avoid.

Pitfalls to Avoid

1. Using perceived capacity as a denial of voice:

There is a danger in neurodivergent learners being "multiply marginalised" (Parsons et al., 2021, p. 163) and denied participation in decision making due to a "double denial" of their voice (Lundy, 2007, p. 935) – that is, doubts about their competence to form and express a view because of being a child, and a disabled child. Neurodivergent learners communicate in a range of different ways, so creating opportunities for facilitating their voices must consider multi-modal expression. Consequently, efforts need to be made to value all forms of expression so that barriers to voices being represented and facilitated can be removed. This, in part, begins with considering the learner's communicative preference (as emphasised in point 3), and not limiting our understanding of voice as only meaning speech.

2. Limiting our understanding of voice to the spoken word:

Although recent research estimates that 25–30 per cent of autistic individuals are non-speaking or have limited speech (Brignell et al., 2018), we must not limit their "voice" by conflating an absence of verbal speech with an absence of communication. Hence, as suggested, non-speaking autistic children may require support to help them communicate effectively via other means. Voice must be conceptualised beyond spoken or verbal expression; all forms of communication are valid forms of communication.

3. Not prioritising relationships, but expecting voice:

We cannot expect learners to feel comfortable, confident, and safe to share their perspectives before connections are established and trust and rapport are developed. Whether in research or within the classroom, time spent building rapport, developing relationships, showing empathy, and, as highlighted in point 2, acknowledging that the neurodivergent learner may prefer to share their voice through different ways will help us avoid this pitfall. Listen and learn through co-constructing knowledge with neurodivergent learners; address potential power imbalance or apprehensiveness by connecting early and showing that you are a person with whom it is worth sharing voice with (see Lundy's model described below). And, as emphasized in point 1, avoid assumptions about the learners' capabilities by positively recognising them as experts in their lives, as credible knowers.

4. Misinterpreting hesitation or silence:

In a fast-paced school environment, hesitation to share thoughts can easily be overlooked – or misconceived – as a lack of capacity, a lack of want, or as their having nothing to say. Silence or lack of engagement can easily be equated with the learner being content with decisions being made.

Also be mindful of how and when we ask for the learner's opinion. For example, will a neurodivergent learner who may already be operating at a high level of anxiety feel comfortable to raise their hand to show they require help, or give their opinion verbally in front of peers; most likely not.

5. Prioritising our communication style:

Time constraints and classroom pressures can often mean that we prioritise verbal conversation as it is quick, spontaneous, and convenient for us, but for the child we need to adapt our approach to maximise their opportunity to demonstrate their agency (much like the Double Empathy Problem). Neurodivergent differences are not inherently pathological, but can be disabling in interactions with approaches that are not optimal for neurodivergent ways of being (see Heasman et al., 2024). Understand current communication preferences and adapt communication to meet the child where they are at, not how we want them to engage based on convenience for us.

For example, verbally discussing a scenario may be better approached through a comic strip visual approach. In the author's own research (see Goodall, 2020), a participatory approach which was cognisant of participant communication was adopted, using flexible methods and approaches which provided multiple means of representation to support the autistic children and young people to informed views. Likewise, as outlined later, in our classrooms we can adapt approaches for supporting voice and hopefully changing for the better attitudes, understanding, policy, and practice. Being mindful of Lundy's participation model, discussed below, will help us authentically garner the voices of neurodivergent learners. As argued by Lundy (2007, p. 927), and touched upon already, "voice [by itself] is not enough."

Authentically Garnering the Voices of Neurodivergent Learners

If we consider the rights argument alone, the impact of Article 12 of the UNCRC is potentially diminished by being represented by simplistic phrases such as "the voice of the child" and "the right to participate" (Lundy, 2007) – we must move beyond tokenistic, tick-box efforts for supporting, listening to, and acting upon the voices of neurodivergent learners. A progressive and ubiquitous participation model proposed by Lundy (2007) magnifies understanding beyond these phrases and demonstrates the complexity that the above phrases do not convey. Lundy's model considers four interconnected factors: voice, space, audience, and influence. For meaningful and effective participation, attention must be applied to all four aspects of this model, which in part provides us with a framework to build upon:

- Learners should be provided with appropriate information, guidance and means to express their views, (voice).
- Learners should be provided with a safe and inclusive space to express their views (space).
- These views should be communicated to someone with the responsibility to listen (audience).
- The views should be taken seriously and acted upon when appropriate (influence).

Voice, Space, Audience, and Influence in Practice

The author is an advisory teacher within the Autism Advisory and Intervention Service (AAIS), one of several pupil support services currently within the Education Authority Northern Ireland. Recently, greater importance has been afforded to hearing the educational experiences of children and young people referred to AAIS. When heard, these perspectives then inform the advice and recommendations provided to school staff. How does Lundy's model apply?

Voice (Facilitating the Learner's View)

Through a structured conversation approach, using two resources (pupil conversation and wellbeing resource), autistic learners are supported to form their views. The pupil conversation initially focuses on interests and things they are good at ("I am good at ..."), before focusing specifically on school experiences (best and worst things about school, who helps them at school, friendships, areas they might want further help with, what they would change about school, and future aspirations and dreams). Early within the conversation learners are asked to choose from five emojis (angry, sad, worried, OK, happy). This structured choice provides a point from which further conversation can be developed – for example, asking "What would help you feel happy/when have you felt happy in school?" if the learner chooses 'OK.' It also provides an early opportunity to reinforce that the five emojis presented are some of the feelings we all experience, and none of these are wrong to feel. This helps establish deeper awareness of the learner, such as their understanding of emotions.

The wellbeing resource seeks feelings on various aspects of the school day, including how they feel before school, on arrival at school, in class, about schoolwork, at break and lunch, at home time, and about homework. They choose an emoji for each, and within each further discussion can be developed.

Some reveal that a certain day is more challenging due to a change in teaching personnel, overwhelming events (assembly), or it being Monday and the shift from home routine to a school routine. Pupils might outline that they are apprehensive when arriving at school as the entrance area is an overwhelming sensory and social environment, and some have described how they can find breaktime challenging as they feel awkward and do not know what to do within this unstructured social period (this worry for some begins in advance of breaktime). Learners also outline self-developed strategies for coping, such as doodling or fidgeting to aid concentration, or seeking movement by finding an excuse to escape the classroom (e.g., visiting the toilet) to help them engage again.

Importantly, this resource provides a springboard from which the learner can be supported to provide further insights and serves as a third-party focal point, reducing the potential pressure of a one-to-one discussion. Often, class teachers and special educational needs co-ordinators are positively surprised at the (untapped) insight these learners have, and at times the strategies they bring to the discussion for improving their educational experience.

Exploring the wellbeing resource can bring realisation for the learner, who initially portrays their school experience as totally negative, that there are many positive aspects to their school day – for example, when exploring school work they may initially choose the "awful" emoji, but on discussion realise, on balance, that only literacy is challenging, numeracy is "OK," and several aspects of their curriculum (school work) are "good" or "great." This resource asks about their feelings at home time. "Great" is often chosen, but for some they find the end of the school day rushed and unsettling, which is then reflected in negative focus regarding school when they reach their caregiver (which in turn can paint the picture that the school day has been negative throughout), leading to discussion around possible supports (such as a school to home transition buffer – e.g., time within a Low Arousal area).

In short, the wellbeing resource has proved effective in exploring pupil experiences across the journey of the school day in a structured way. Schools can then revisit the wellbeing resource to get another snapshot of how the learner is experiencing school. Furthermore, these resources not only provide structure to support conversation, they also give insight into the learner's communication differences and how these may apply within the classroom environment – for instance, how meaningful and accessible open response questions are, or if the learner is currently better supported with limited choices.

The wellbeing resource, as well as a third resource (a pupil evaluation), is used pre- and post-direct support to gauge the learner's opinion on the programme of support (such as developing emotional understanding, brick-based group work, or supporting emotional-based school non-attendance). Although not perfect, potential barriers of having to write are removed, and within the pupil evaluation they are encouraged to write, draw, or discuss verbally their experiences regarding what they learnt from support sessions, and how the support could be improved – their communication preference is respected.

These resources are not rigid, and can be adapted to support the communication of the child. For example, the child can complete the wellbeing aspect using an interactive presentation on a laptop or tablet device, reducing the communicative risk a learner who experiences (situational) mutism might experience (choosing from limited choices is lower-risk than open conversation). This has also been adapted further to be a matching/choosing game, thus breaking the task into chunks (one aspect at a time), which can be a preference of neurodivergent learners who may find too much information overstimulating or too much to process.

This mirrors Lewis, Hamilton and Vincent (2023, p. 2), who state that "engaging children in practical tasks of their choosing empowers them to voice their experiences in ways which are meaningful to them and not reliant on verbal competencies." Further, to help redress potential power imbalances within the pupil conversation, as highlighted earlier, rapport building is considered. Prior to the session, the author forwards a social narrative about himself to help prepare the learner. The author encourages his being addressed on first name terms, and also models example responses to help build confidence. The space for completing this conversation is considered.

Space

Spaces embody certain norms, rules, and expectations (Goodall, 2020). There needs to be a valued space within which the learner can feel comfortable to be supported in providing their voice. For practical and geographical reasons, this is perhaps the most challenging aspect of Lundy's model to satisfy within busy school environments. Some schools visited by the author have adequate facilities to provide a quiet, comfortable space, others are limited in the space they can offer – and "making do" is the best that can be hoped for.

Based on information given prior to the school visit, the author incorporates an element of structured choice for the learner, with cognisance of sensory differences and sensitivities – do they need a space with minimal external stimuli which might impact on information processing, do they need a visual support such as comic strip cartoons to help structure conversation and provide a concrete reference point (and a less formal, perhaps less intense situation to face-to-face discussion), and would they benefit from the session being chunked further or interspersed with movement opportunities to support focus and concentration? Which space is optimal? For instance, if the child enjoys using the sensory space that is suggested which can allow for further observation of how they interact within this space, alternative aspects of voice and experience can be considered. These considerations promote agency, emphasise trust and rapport, and provide the foundations for authentically garnering the voice of neurodivergent learners.

Audience

The sessions are conducted one-to-one. In the author's experience, rarely will learners request that the additional adult support they have (classroom assistant) or a trusted peer accompany them within the session, but this would be accommodated. As the professionals tasked with providing guidance to schools to better support the learner, their views are communicated to someone with the responsibility to listen, in keeping with Lundy's model, and these views are then used to (hopefully) influence practice.

Influence

Aspects of what the learner has said are incorporated, often verbatim, within written recommendations for the school staff to consider in developing the understanding they have of – and support they might develop for – the individual learner. This often helps reshape attitudes and understanding. For example, one learner was described as being disruptive and not being able to sit appropriately during carpet time, yet the learner advised that they found it difficult when sat between too many people (tactile sensitivities) and would prefer sitting slightly off to the edge of a row (the child offered the strategy and brought accuracy to what was being observed by those "outsiders looking in"). Further, for the same child, it was advised that many strategies had been employed with minimal positive impact. However, when exploring just one of these with them, the use of a visual "first and then" on their desk was not understood by the child – their voice had not been sought or heard regarding their understanding of and impact of the strategy.

Similarly, another child advised that their approach within numeracy lessons was to calculate internally before presenting this on paper. They spoke of being regularly interrupted by staff who equated – without seeking the child's voice – a lack of writing with being "off task." The learner expressed that this resulted in frustration – the reason why the school had sought advice. The learner advised that they would benefit from completing their independent numeracy work in a quieter space just outside the classroom. Taking time within the busy day to ask "How do you feel, what is making you frustrated?" would have hopefully revealed this learner's experience. Similarly, another learner advised that they dreaded daily mindfulness sessions and that these were proving counterproductive, yet despite having additional adult support, was not permitted to use this time to "regulate" in a manner which best suited them (he would have preferred a walk with his classroom assistant) – his non-engagement was characterised as defiance. Several learners have detailed to the author that they can worry about not knowing what is coming up in the school day, adding to general feelings of overwhelm when arriving at school (and throughout the day). They spoke of how having a whole-class visual timetable would help provide predictability, and allow them to focus on upcoming subjects of interest and be able to better appraise how long was left. The importance of this simple whole-class approach was further underscored when some learners also advised that using the analogue classroom clock was difficult so they could not accurately gauge when key points of the day were (e.g., breaktime and lunchtime).

Often, particularly for learners who may be experiencing anxiety-based school non-attendance, the author emphasises the power of supporting the learner in exploring why they are finding school attendance difficult. Many resources exist which can be used to map the school and uncover potential anxiety triggers, from which strategies and adjustments can be developed (with the learner, at each stage) to hopefully re-engage them with education in school.

Supporting and championing these autistic voices, which are often not included readily enough in discussion regarding autism-competent educational approaches, have been instrumental in underpinning advice for school staff. Understanding how each pupil experiences being autistic within the classroom and wider school environment (and across the school day) can help underpin the supportive strategies schools can employ to ensure each child can thrive. Many pupils offered ideas and strategies on how to better support them in school, demonstrating that, when asked, children themselves may have the solution.

What is clear is that each autistic child, albeit sharing a diagnostic label, is (autistically) unique and experiences school in an individual way (and this experience can change across the day, week, month, and year, depending on the demands placed upon them and the supports they can draw on). And as the autistic young people in the study by Goodall (2020, p. 114) present, "they want to be respected and valued as an individual person and not viewed as part of a homogeneous group because of a shared diagnostic label" – as with classroom strategies, a "one size fits all" approach to support and listen to the voices of neurodivergent learners is unlikely to work.

Further, these sessions demonstrate to classroom teachers and other adults supporting autistic learners that they have insight into their educational experiences, and have thoughts regarding strategies or support measures which can help them within the classroom environment. Often when discussing and championing their responses, the author receives comments from teachers that they were not aware of that, or that they did not think the pupils were so aware of themselves (the pitfall of assuming too little, as noted earlier). Listening to the voices of these neurodivergent learners is central to broadening our knowledge, and doing so can challenge ingrained and often damaging assumptions.

Other Practical Approaches

A framework has been detailed for authentically supporting, listening to, and acting upon the voices of neurodivergent learners through the process of using autistic educational experience to inform advice and guidance within a pupil support service. We now turn to everyday approaches within the classroom which could be adapted for use with neurodivergent learners, and are also cognisant of and respect different communicative preferences.

- A *walk and talk* approach can allow the learner to move from the busy classroom environment to a preferred area, such as the school garden, to then explore within a space and with an undistracted audience. This can also facilitate us in utilising learner interests as a "way in." As Wood (2019, p. 152) writes:

    enabling autistic children to focus on areas that interest them could have a significant, positive influence on how they express themselves, also resulting in an important shift in the power dynamic, with the child taking a more confident and assertive role in communication exchanges.

- *Draw (or create) and talk* – simply engaging in doodling alongside the learner may help reduce the communicative pressures that can be associated with one-to-one, face-to-face discussion, thus helping them to realise their voice (the focus is on the paper and the doodles both are drawing). This may lead to the adult drawing stick figures to represent the learner to gently approach a recent situation, then they can add speech and thought bubbles together to find solutions to possible problems. Humour can be brought in, and this approach can support a neurodivergent learner for whom speech is not their preferred communication style. Mini-figures or plasticine could be used to re-create situations to support learners in exploring their perspectives and exploring solutions together (co-production). The balance of power can shift by placing the learner in the position of expert, and this moves us away from communicating *to* to communicating *with*.

- *Participatory activities* that are not reliant on speech alone could be embedded to support learner voice. Two examples are "beans and pots" and diamond ranking.
  - The "beans and pots" approach can help capture learner opinions in an active manner by placing a bean or ball in a pot. For instance, in research by Goodall (2020), this approach was used to garner the opinions of autistic young people on a set of prepared statements (e.g, "I feel happy being at school"). Another simple use of this approach might be to seek learner perspectives on a recently embedded class initiative, voting on a class treat, the impact of sensory supports (such as a range of fidget items), or in involving learners in deciding on equipment being requisitioned for a new sensory space.
  - Similarly, diamond ranking can provide another approach for learners to rank statements or ideas into levels of preference. This again could be used to help co-construct a neurodivergent learner's experience of using a range of sensory exercises or items on sensory breaks to develop a learner informed inventory.
- Use *structured choice* rather than open-ended questions such as "are you OK/how do you feel about this/what do you want to do?" One lovely example is supporting a child's voice when they transition from one primary class to the next by providing time for them to explore their new classroom and have a say in where they will sit – respecting their wishes and needs, and also taking a further step to build a relationship and trust which will hopefully further support them in feeling able to have their voice heard.
- *Embed non-verbal opportunities or responses* during teaching. For example, a "fist to five" approach can be effective for learners who do not wish to be spotlighted for requiring help. Learners place their heads down, raise one hand, and indicate their level of understanding of a topic (a closed fist indicating that they do not understand it at all, and five open digits indicating confidence). Similarly, other strategies could include the learner

using a specific pencil topper or placing a specific pen on work to indicate subtly that they might need help (or a brain break). The author is noticing, anecdotally, that less invasive, subtler approaches are being sought by autistic learners who are apprehensive about appearing different to peers.

Key Takeaways

- **Centre the Learner's Voice:** Prioritise and value the perspectives of neurodivergent learners in all aspects of education.
- **Authenticity is Key:** Move beyond tokenistic efforts, and ensure genuine participation and meaningful influence.
- **Lundy's Model:** Utilise Lundy's participation model as a framework for effective practice.
- **Diverse Communication:** Acknowledge and respect diverse communication styles and provide multiple means for learners to express themselves.
- **Build Trust and Rapport:** Foster strong relationships and create a safe and inclusive environment for learners to share their experiences.
- **Act on Learner Feedback:** Use learner input to inform and improve educational practices, policies, and interventions.

Reflective Activities

Considering the neurodivergent learners within your classroom:

- How do you currently enable them to share their voices? List these, and consider if your practice is aligning to Lundy's model (voice, space, audience, and influence).
- Consider how you might gain further understanding of their school experience – how can you adapt your communication approach? Can time be scheduled into the school week to engage with these learners?
- Consider one aspect of the curriculum within which you could embed further opportunity to learn from them.

Practical Resources

- *Autism NI School Anxiety Triggers* – to explore in a structured manner aspects of the school day which may cause anxiety: https://autismni.org/assets/resources/education-resources/school-anxiety-triggers-PDF.pdf
- You can map the landscape of your school using Lancashire County Council's *Emotionally Based School Avoidance Guidance* to support a learner in exploring aspects of their school to understand their experience of emotionally based school avoidance: https://www.lancashire.gov.uk/media/930428/lancashire-ebsa-guidance-strategy-toolkit-2023-update.pdf
- For various strategies that can be adapted for research into classroom practice, see Goodall (2020).

References

Brignell, A., Chenausky, K. V., Song, H., Zhu, J., Suo, C., & Morgan, A. T. (2018, November 5). Communication interventions for autism spectrum disorder in minimally verbal children. Cochrane Database of Systematic Reviews, 11(11), Article CD012324. https://doi.org/10.1002/14651858.CD012324.pub2. PMID: 30395694; PMCID: PMC6516977.

Goodall, C. (2018). 'I felt closed in and like I couldn't breathe': A qualitative study exploring the mainstream educational experiences of autistic young people. *Autism & Developmental Language Impairments*, 3. https://doi.org/10.1177/2396941518804407

Goodall, C. (2020). *Understanding the voices and educational experiences of autistic young people: From research to practice*. Oxon: Routledge.

Gray, L., Hill, V., & Pellicano, E. (2023). 'He's shouting so loud but nobody's hearing him': A multi-informant study of autistic pupils' experiences of school non-attendance and exclusion. *Autism and Developmental Language Impairments, 8*, 1–17. https://doi.org/10.1177/23969415231207816

Heasman, B., Williams, G., Charura, D., Hamilton, L. G., Milton, D., & Murray, F. (2024). Towards autistic flow theory: A non-pathologising conceptual approach. *Journal for the Theory of Social Behaviour, 54*(4), 469–497. https://doi.org/10.1111/jtsb.12427

Horgan, F., Kenny, N., & Flynn, P. (2023). A systematic review of the experiences of autistic young people enrolled in mainstream second-level (post-primary) schools. *Autism, 27*(2), 526–538. https://doi.org/10.1177/13623613221105089

Howe, S. J., Hull, L., Sedgewick, F., Hannon, B., & McMorris, C. A. (2023). Understanding camouflaging and identity in autistic children and adolescents using photo-elicitation. *Research in Autism Spectrum Disorders, 108*. https://doi.org/10.1016/j.rasd.2023.102232

Hummerstone, H., & Parsons, S. (2021). What makes a good teacher? Comparing the perspectives of students on the autism spectrum and staff. *European Journal of Special Needs Education, 36*(4), 610–624. https://doi.org/10.1080/08856257.2020.1783800

Lewis, K., Hamilton, L. G., & Vincent, J. (2023). Exploring the experiences of autistic pupils through creative research methods: Reflections on a participatory approach. *Infant and Child Development*. https://doi.org/10.1002/icd.2467

Lundy, L. (2007). 'Voice' is not enough: Conceptualising article 12 of the United Nations convention on the rights of the child. *British Educational Research Journal, 33*(6), 927–942. https://doi.org/10.1080/01411920701657033

Lundy, L., & Kilpatrick, R. (2006). Children's rights and special educational needs: Findings from research conducted for the Northern Ireland commissioner for children and young people. *Support for Learning, 21*(2), 57–63. https://doi.org/10.1111/j.1467-9604.2006.00405.x

Milton, D. E. M. (2012). On the ontological status of autism: the 'double empathy problem'. *Disability and Society, 27*(6), 883–887.

Parsons, S., Ivil, K., Kovshoff, H., & Karakosta, E. (2021). 'Seeing is believing': Exploring the perspectives of young autistic children through Digital Stories. *Journal of early childhood research, 19*(2), 161–178. 2https://doi.org/10.1177/1476718X20951235

Parsons, S., Kovshoff, H., & Ivil, K. (2022). Digital stories for transition: Co-constructing an evidence base in the early years with autistic children, families and practitioners. *Educational Review, 74*(6), 1063–1081. https://doi.org/10.1080/00131911.2020.1816909

Robinson, C., Quennerstedt, A., & I'Anson, J. (2020). The translation of articles from the United Nations convention on the rights of the child into education legislation: The narrowing of article 12 as a consequence of translation. *Curriculum Journal, 31*(3), 517–538. https://doi.org/10.1002/curj.6

Wood, R. (2019). Autism, intense interests and support in school: From wasted efforts to shared understandings. *Educational Review*. https://doi.org/10.1080/00131911.2019.1566213

9

ITAKOM and Intersectionality

Frances Akinde

Background and Positionality

This chapter on neurodivergence and intersectionality starts with a detailed background where I share my context and positionality with the reader. Both my personal and professional perspectives inform how I visualise a neurodiversity-inclusive, ITAKOM classroom. My professional experience is rich and varied, and is relevant to the topic of neurodiversity and intersectionality. I am writing from the geographical context of the United Kingdom, but I believe my experiences apply to jurisdictions beyond the UK. Some of the terminology I use in the chapter is the official terminology of England's Department of Education and might not always align with the language of the neurodiversity paradigm which underpins this handbook.

For example, my official title is Inspector and Advisor for Special Educational Needs and Disabilities (SEND). I work in a large local authority in England. Most of our schools (457 out of 530) are still maintained by local authorities. In this role, I provide guidance and support to schools to ensure they meet the needs of students with SEND. My role involves working across primary, secondary, specialist, and secure provision centres in my local authority area. This work is varied and gives me rich opportunities to share good practices across my local authority and beyond. Previously to this role, I was a headteacher of a special school in Kent, a county in South East England.

I have worked in education for over 20 years, 15 of those in inclusive education. Over the years I have worked in mainstream secondary, primary, and alternative provision, and have been a specialist advisory teacher for speech, language, and communication needs, an inclusion lead, and assessment centre lead. My subject specialism is in Art and Design.

ITAKOM and Intersectionality

My favourite aspect of my role is supporting students who are struggling in some way in their educational setting. These challenges in my context are commonly referred to as social, emotional, and mental health (SEMH). Throughout my career I have continued to be motivated to use my intersectionality to help discover, understand, and support the underlying causes of distress and difficulties learners experience in school and other educational settings.

In this chapter, I will draw from my own personal lived experience of intersectionality, as well as professional expertise (particularly advisory work), to highlight some common challenges experienced by marginalised neurodivergent learners in schools. I will follow these insights by sharing successful and actionable strategies to support the inclusion of all kinds of minds to ensure that everyone within the school environment truly feels that they belong, matter, and are understood. The discussion includes ways to support speech and language differences, working memory difficulties, the role of technology, the importance of play, and the need for supportive learning environments.

Introduction: The Personal Experiences of Educators Matter

The opening paragraphs of this chapter describe a successful and experienced educational professional. However, this opening section only paints a partial picture of the expertise I bring to the topic of neurodivergence and intersectionality.

When I was around 3 years old, I contracted meningitis. This is an infection and inflammation of the protective membranes around the brain. My mum knew that I was ill because I had lost my appetite; I have always been a good eater. I was fortunate that it was caught early, and I seemed to recover well. My mum said that after they had operated on me and cleared the infection, I seemed to make a full recovery. I had one follow-up appointment, and that was it. Although meningitis can lead to hearing loss, memory problems, challenges with cognitive development, and seizures, I received no monitoring or special treatment, I just got on with it.

At the time, I didn't appear to have any lasting difficulties. I simply managed through school. However, with the benefit of hindsight, the signs of a neurodivergent body-mind were clear. I was seen as bright (but lazy), and left with a good range of GCSEs. I chose teaching art as my career because I was creative and I could get lost in drawing for hours.

I enjoyed teaching, and worked my way up to headship. It wasn't until I was in my mid-40s, after 20 years in leadership positions, after a build-up of stress after a devastating sequence of events, that I began to experience what I now know to be the early signs of a neurodivergent burnout.

I had spent my whole career in high-pressure educational roles, concentrating on supporting other people's children as well as my own children's needs.

They say that your body keeps a score – mine was certainly trying to tell me something, but I never had the time to look inwardly to find out what was happening within me. There were signs that something was not quite right, as is common after a period of acute stress, but I ignored it and carried on the best I could regardless of my own health. Moreover, my school community had just experienced a number of devastating events. As the school leader, I had to show that I was strong for my staff and for my pupils, so I carried on going to work, day after day, showing up for them.

I felt like I had to carry on for my pupils and staff, but then I began to have vertigo, dizzy spells, and fatigue. It wasn't until May 2022, when I began to experience more and more dizziness and fatigue, that I had to admit something was seriously wrong. I ended up, for the first time in years, being off work ill. I was subsequently told that I had all the symptoms of Ménière's disease, a vestibular condition. I didn't know that there was a link between Ménière's disease and having meningitis 40 years earlier. A growing awareness of the intersectionality of chronic disease, high stress, and neurodivergence was slowly emerging.

Previously, people had made jokes about me showing traits of ADHD. My executive functioning differences were so apparent that I chose working memory as the subject for my masters dissertation. Through my research I discovered the links between working memory difficulties and ADHD. Up to this point I had not made the connection between this and my own challenges with learning and concentration. I decided to try and figure out so many other things about myself as a learner and neurodivergent individual. The same questions always seemed to be in the back of my mind:

1. Why did I find it so hard to concentrate, unless it was something I was really interested in?

2. Why was I always getting myself into trouble as a child, and still as an adult?
3. Why did I always get bored so easily and have so many things on the go at any one time?
4. Why did I find it so hard to maintain friendships?
5. Why did I struggle to maintain what is considered "typical" eye contact? Was it just due to cultural differences (another intersectionality that I will come to soon)?

I know more now that some of these traits or differences I had noted in myself are common neurodivergent traits, and some are considered traits of neurotypes like ADHD, autism, and dyslexia. I received a confirmation of ADHD in the summer period of 2022; my assessor said to me that she suspected that I was dyslexic as well. So, in the space of six months, I went from having a concept of self based on having no formally assessed neurodivergence to being multiply neurodivergent. I knew autism would be next on the list, but I wasn't in the right headspace to investigate anymore. Instead, I started a process of looking at myself introspectively, my whole world felt as if it had been turned upside down. I started to use the lens of assessed neurodivergence to reflect on all the difficulties I had encountered navigating my way through life. I commenced therapy and began building the second version of myself with a better understanding of who I was and how I showed up fully in this world – a world that I previously felt like I didn't belong in. So many things started to make sense to me.

I paid to be assessed privately, and I acknowledge that I had the financial privilege to be able to pursue a private assessment. I had felt the urgency to be assessed to stop myself from spiralling into depression, However, when I then went to my doctor for support, I was told that my private diagnosis would not be accepted by the National Health Service (NHS).

I then began the arduous process of being reassessed to have my neurodivergence recognised by the NHS. I was fortunate that the waiting time was only seven months (at the time of writing, this has increased to two years). So, within seven months, I was assessed as being an ADHDer twice!

My journey to diagnosis is not unusual, and I know that my experience is far from unique. I speak to many parents, carers, and newly assessed adults who share similar experiences. In terms of intersectionality, I found that my ethnic minority background (I am Black, British African) added an additional barrier when it comes to searching for support, and an extra layer of struggle to my quest for understanding and information.

Intersectionality

My intersectionality of being female, Black, multiply neurodivergent, and experiences of chronic illness are part of who I am. Attending the 2022 *It Takes All Kinds of Minds* conference was the learning experience I needed to synthesise all this knowledge I had about my way of being in the world. Here, I delved deep into the challenges and stereotypes surrounding neurotypes like ADHD, autism, dyslexia, and dyspraxia. A pressing issue that resonated with me was the stark disparity in assessment rates based on intersections of race and socioeconomic status.

In any discussion of intersectionality as a phenomenon, it is essential to revisit the origin of intersectionality as a concept. Kimberlé Crenshaw, an American feminist scholar, introduced the term in the late 1980s to address the unique challenges faced by Black women (Crenshaw, 1991). Since then, the concept has evolved to refer to the overlapping identities and experiences that intersect to shape an individual's life.

My research has led me to some unsettling discoveries about intersectionality and how a knowledge of intersectionality can help us understand the troubled history of systemic discrimination. My growing awareness allowed me to critically reflect on discrimination, stigma, and biases I had experienced on a personal and professional level. It also helped me recognise the significance of intersectionality from racial, gender, cultural, health, and neurodiversity perspectives. My critical reflections include these questions:

1. Why are Black, Caribbean, and Gypsy Roma Traveller children in the demographics most frequently excluded from school in the UK?
2. Why do children from minority ethnic groups constitute 34 per cent of the school population (and rising), and yet, Black school leaders and teachers are significantly under-represented?
3. What does it mean in our ITAKOM classrooms that most teachers and even fewer school leaders do not look like me?
4. What role does intersectionality play with other systemic issues within our education system to prevent marginalised children from aspiring to educational careers?

Moreover, research indicates that White, middle-class children are the most likely to receive accurate assessments confirming neurotypes like autism and ADHD. Conversely, Black children are more often misdiagnosed with SEMH conditions.

Knowing this and applying this to my professional and lived experiences has been a significant focus of my work more recently. This includes ongoing advocacy to highlight the shortcomings in the behavioural approaches often used as a first port of call in understanding, assessing and "supporting" children's/young people's needs, leading to not only a fundamental misunderstanding, but also an over-diagnosing of SEMH needs and conditions in Afro-Caribbean communities in the UK.

Intersectionality is a pertinent concept when critically reflecting on the institutional racism pervasive in UK schools. The recent case of Child Q illustrates this troubling reality (Gamble & McCallum, 2022). When considering intersectionality and institutional racism, it helps to form some critically reflective questions. For example, why does it seem as though some educators do not see *all* children as their own? Reflective questions like this are deeply personal to me, especially when viewed through an intersectional lens. I am a Black, multiply neurodivergent mother of five Black boys. Moreover, a key feature of my role as a local authority inspector and advisor is to support specialist settings in ensuring the best education for *every child* in their care.

Key readings like Barton and Packer (2024), raised further critical questions that inform my reflective practice. These include:

1. What does the makeup of ethnic groups in specialised education look like?
2. Why are boys more frequently assessed as neurodivergent while neurodivergence in girls from marginalised groups remains under-identified?

These intersectionality-related disparities demand our attention and action.

Supporting the Intersectional Learner

Having shared my background and my lived experience of intersectionality, the chapter now turns in another direction. Continuing with intersectionality as the focus, here I share from my experiences of what works when supporting learners with intersecting identities. To write theichapter for this book, there were lots of questions in my mind.

I knew I wanted to focus on intersectionality (neurodivergence, ethnicity, and other educational challenges), but I also knew that there were a lot of things I could share from my experiences over 20 years of education. As an educator, I have a keen interest in communication differences and how they are often misunderstood as behavioural difficulties. Moreover, I am passionate about the potential of assistive technology and artificial intelligence and how to use technology equitably to support all our students to succeed. Additionally, I am also interested in creativity and the role it plays in relieving anxiety, supporting mental health difficulties, and finally ways of improving working memory function, particularly visual memory.

Intersectionality and Communication Differences

Studies based in England show that in primary schools, difficulties related to speech and language development require the greatest level of support. (Department for Education, England, 2024). In my previous advisory role as a specialist speech and language advisory teacher, I would regularly meet children in both primary and secondary schools presenting primarily with behaviour difficulties. Time and time again, behavioural difficulties would be highlighted to me as their most pronounced area of need. On closer observation, the underlying and often unmet need was some difference in language and communication.

Typically, I would see a child or young person struggling with expressive language, such as spoken word (in particular, word-finding, vocabulary, and word confusion). When this difficulty intersects with other demands like increased need for attention, these challenges start to affect working memory and auditory processing. In my experience, as these children grow older, their needs are often misinterpreted as SEMH issues. The external presentation looks like anger, frustration, withdrawal, ignoring, or not following instructions, all of which can be mistakenly attributed to behaviour rather than speech and language differences often intersecting with neurodivergence. Misinterpretation of a child's needs can lead to inappropriate interventions that do not address the root cause of the child's difficulties. This is a classic example of learners who *cannot* conform in a certain way of being in school, rather than children who *will not* comply with classroom expectations. This can present in a classroom as a child not following instructions or seemingly ignoring them altogether. These signs of underlying differences in social communication and attention skills are too commonly misinterpreted as behavioural difficulties.

In my experience, the best approach in the first instance is to support these learners through creativity and play. Through play, teachers can monitor attention skills and receptive and expressive language skills in a way that does not cause additional anxiety. After the early years, the demands on working memory and auditory processing increase. This is where neurodivergent children struggle to acquire new information. If a child has difficulties with phonics and does not pass the phonics screening check test first time, there is merit in looking for further dyslexic traits by using screeners and including gathering family history. As a child moves up into Years 1 and 2, we may see increasingly more difficulties around attention and listening, particularly around following instructions. Indeed, the typical age for identifying many differences, including neurodivergence, is around age 7. Once again, this is where certain intersectionality can influence the identification and support of needs. For example, White boys are more likely to have their needs accurately assessed early on (Strand, 2019). This is much later for girls and children from minority ethnic backgrounds, especially if they also use English as an additional language (Varsik & Gorochovskij, 2023). Early and accurate identification of needs is crucial to supporting all learners. If a child's needs are not correctly assessed in primary school, they will transition to secondary school without their underlying needs being recognised. It is much harder to get an assessment of needs at secondary school age unless a child presents with noticeable challenges.

Supporting the speech and language differences of neurodivergent learners requires an individualised approach. However, the reality in many systems is that there is a shortage of speech and language therapists to support these needs. We know that this is a significant issue driven by several factors. Moreover, in my experience, teachers can do a lot to provide individualised support, but again, resourcing and staffing are common school-level barriers to providing this support. An individualised approach must begin with thorough assessments to understand each child's specific needs, allowing for the creation of personalised learning plans that outline tailored goals and strategies. Best practice advocates for collaborative approaches, including one-on-one support from speech and language therapists, engaging parents and carers in the process, skilled use of technology, regular monitoring and feedback, and a supportive environment across different settings. By focusing on these individualised strategies, a more effective support system for children with speech and language differences in primary schools can be established. Unfortunately, the reality is that many schools face challenges such as limited resources, insufficient training for staff, and large class sizes, which hinder the implementation of these tailored approaches.

Technology

Technology plays a significant role in providing personalised support and enhancing accessibility in education. It equips educators with tools and resources to cater to the diverse needs of neurodivergent students, empowering them to create inclusive learning environments. As an assistive technology trainer, I show students how to use technology to support their relearning. I have seen first-hand the difference it can make and the knock-on effect of not having the right technology has on a student's wellbeing and self-esteem. IBM put it best in 1991 when they said: "The power of technology lies in its ability to transform lives and create opportunities for all" (Bryant & Seok, 2017).

The use of assistive technology in education should not be limited to those who know about it and/or can afford to use it. We must make assistive technology accessible to all. Tools like speech-to-text software, interactive learning apps, and adaptive learning platforms powered by artificial intelligence allow educators to be more supportive and adapt easily to an individual learner. This goes beyond differentiation and add-on approaches, and moves towards what we all should be striving for: equity, more in keeping with approaches like Universal Design for Learning.

IBM's training manual from 1991 states: "For people without disabilities, technology makes things easier; for people with disabilities, technology makes things possible" (Bryant & Seok, 2017). This simple statement really highlights the truly transformative power of technology in the lives of people with disabilities. Assistive technology enables disabled people to perform tasks that might otherwise be impossible.

Working Memory and Neurodivergence

Working memory is a key research interest of mine, and my research shows that supporting working memory difficulties in the classroom by reducing cognitive load is one of the most effective methods of support and can be done effectively within the classroom. However, the evidence gathered from classroom observation demonstrates that working memory difficulties are generally not fully supported in the classroom, therefore classroom practice needs to change, or at least needs to improve.

A truly neurodiversity-inclusive learning environment supports working memory. "Working memory" refers to how we hold on to and work with information stored in short-term memory. It concerns the manipulation of information that short-term memory stores. (In the past, the term "working memory" was incorrectly used interchangeably with the term "short-term memory.") It is a skill students use to learn, and is needed for tasks like following multi-step directions or solving a maths problem in your head. Working memory and processing difficulties are common for many people who are neurodivergent (McLeod, 2023).

Often overshadowed by more observable traits and behaviours in the classroom, working memory is a critical yet misunderstood challenge for many neurodivergent learners. This cognitive function, responsible for holding and manipulating information over short periods, plays a pivotal role in tasks such as following instructions, problem-solving, and planning. Differences in working memory can look like difficulties in maintaining focus, organising thoughts, and processing information efficiently. These challenges can significantly impact academic performance, social interactions, and daily functioning. Despite its importance, working memory is frequently overlooked in favour of more apparent behavioural symptoms, leading to a gap in effective support strategies. Although there is little evidence to support that working memory can be improved, scaffolding strategies can be beneficial to learners. Techniques such as chunking, visuals, keywords, and breaks can help neurodivergent students manage their cognitive load and improve their learning experiences (Rhodes, 2019). Similarly, teachers engaged with my study reported that using visual cues and keywords and limiting teacher talk were the most beneficial support strategies. Furthermore, learners with working memory difficulties and anxiety saw an improvement in their anxiety when their working memory difficulties were effectively supported. That supporting working memory helps reduce anxiety is a key finding in the wider literature (Kalanthroff et al., 2016).

Intersectionality, Neurodivergent Staff, and Inclusive Schools

Inclusion as it relates to neurodiversity involves creating a learning environment that welcomes and supports all learners and their intersectionalities, especially emphasising the strengths of those with neurological differences. This is not just a goal, but a responsibility we all share as stakeholders in the field of education. It allows us to build a more diverse and inclusive society, one where everyone can contribute their unique talents and perspectives. However, for schools to be truly inclusive for their students, it must also be for their staff. Given that it is estimated that approximately 20 per cent of the population is neurodivergent, it is likely that at least 20 per cent of school staff are too (Doyle, 2020). Attention to inclusive school culture, however, does not just refer to neuro-inclusion. An understanding of intersectionality contributes further to inclusive school culture. Establishing an authentically inclusive school environment for staff is paramount to creating an inclusive educational setting for students. The claim of a neurodiversity-inclusive school must encompass all members of the school community, including the wellbeing and support of staff.

Conclusion

My experience across many domains of the education system have certainly given me ideas of how to better support the diversity of learners in the classroom. It is undoubtedly my lived experience of the intersectionality of being a multiply neurodivergent, Black learner and educator that utterly convinces me that supporting educators in becoming more inclusive and neurodiversity- and intersectionality-informed is an essential aim of this chapter.

Creating a sense of belonging allows *all* children to thrive and feel valued, understood, and supported in their learning journey. This leads to increased engagement and participation in classroom activities, improved academic performance, and enhanced social and emotional wellbeing. Neuro-inclusive schools that celebrate diversity help all individuals within them to thrive both academically and socially. It creates a supportive and safe learning environment where learners and staff feel empowered and prepared for successful futures. I was that student; I am that adult. I know the power of inclusion and getting the right support. My extensive experience as an inspector advisor for SEND and my background as a headteacher and various roles in special education have given me a deep understanding of the challenges and effective strategies for supporting marginalised students.

By understanding the strengths and difficulties of neurodivergent children, educators can create more inclusive and supportive learning environments, ensuring that all students are afforded the opportunity to thrive and reach their potential.

In conclusion, creating an inclusive learning environment for *all* students involves a combination of individual support and whole-school strategies. By focusing on early identification of areas requiring support, and concrete learning opportunities coupled with cultural sensitivity, schools can significantly enhance the learning experience for *all* and ultimately create a true sense of belonging for all our learners.

Key Takeaways

Here are some practical suggestions that I hope will help the reader support all learners, including those learners with marginalised intersectionality:

1. Be curious about the intersectionalities that inform learners' experiences and identity.
2. Centre learning experiences around creativity, play, and joy.
3. Embrace technology.
4. Engage in approaches that foster a sense of **belonging** for every member of the school community. These include restorative practices, mentoring, and explicit support for self- and co-regulation.
5. Provide opportunities for **concrete learning** opportunities
6. Be aware of **key policy and legislation**. In the Englishcontext, this includes:

- **SEND Code of Practice 6:14**, which outlines the need for clear approaches to identifying and responding to learners requiring educational support.
- **The Equality Act 2010**, which aims to protect learners and school staff, and outlines an anticipatory duty to provide equitable opportunities and support.

Reflective Activities

Personal Reflection

Reflect on how your personal background shapes your practice and pedagogy.

What disadvantages have you experienced in your life, perhaps due to your gender, sexuality, neurotype, ethnicity, nationality, or physical body. How can you use that lived experience of disadvantage – perhaps discrimination, perhaps feeling you don't belong – to develop empathy and solidarity with pupils, parents, or colleagues who don't share your specific background?

What advantages have you had, again relating to your identity, background and upbringing? How can you recognise your privilege? What can you do to make any positive experiences from which you have benefited more universal, for both your pupils and your colleagues?

Classroom Application

Analyse a lesson plan or classroom activity through the lens of accessibility and intersectionality. Consider how the activity might be adapted to meet the needs and backgrounds of neurodivergent learners, not only with diverse sensory needs, communication styles, and learning preferences, but also from a range of cultural backgrounds and with a range of identities.

References

Barton, D., & Packer, N. (2024). *Beyond boundaries: Leading great SEND provision across a trust*. United Kingdom: Hodder Education.

Bryant, R., & Seok, S. (2017). Introduction to the special series: Technology and disabilities in education. *Assistive Technology, 29*(3), 121–122. https://doi.org/10.1080/10400435.2016.1230154

Crenshaw, K. (1991). Mapping the margins: Intersectionality, identity politics, and violence against women of color. *Stanford Law Review, 43*(6), 1241–1299. https://doi.org/10.2307/1229039

Doyle N. (2020). Neurodiversity at work: A biopsychosocial model and the impact on working adults. *British Medical Bulletin, 135*(1), 108–125. https://doi.org/10.1093/bmb/ldaa021

Gamble, J., & McCallum, R. (2022). *Local child safeguarding practice review child Q*. Available at: www.chscp.org.uk. Accessed 28th November 2024.

Government, United Kingdom. (2024). *Statistics on pupils with SEN, including information on educational attainment, destinations, absence, exclusions, and characteristics*. Available at: Statistics: special educational needs (SEN) - GOV.UK. Last Accessed 28th November 2024.

Kalanthroff, E., Henik, A., Derakshan, N., & Usher, M. (2016). Anxiety, emotional distraction, and attentional control in the Stroop task. *Emotion* (Washington, D.C.), *16*(3), 293–300. https://doi.org/10.1037/emo0000129

McLeod, S. (2023). Working memory model (Baddeley and Hitch). *Simply Psychology*. Available at: www.simplypsychology.org. Last Accessed 28th November 2024.

Rhodes, S. (2019) *The EPIC Strategy Booklet: A Guide for Teachers*. University of Edinburgh. Available at: https://edwebcontent.ed.ac.uk/sites/default/files/atoms/files/epic_strategy_teachers.pdf

Strand, S. (2019). Ethnicity and the identification of SEN. National Association for Special Educational Needs (NASEN), *Connect*, (17), 24–25.

Varsik, S., & Gorochovskij, J. (2023). Intersectionality in education: Rationale and practices to address the needs of students' intersecting identities. *OECD Education Working Papers*. https://doi.org/10.1787/19939019

10

Character Strengths

Changing the Language to Change Expectations

Clara O'Byrne

Introduction

This chapter focuses on an exploration of how strength-based Positive Education approaches can be aligned with neurodiversity-informed pedagogy, exploring the language of Positive Education as a tool to support inclusive culture in schools. A distinction is made between a neurodiversity-lite approach to strengths which can veer into toxic positivity, and a Character Strengths approach which is supported by evidence from the field of Positive Psychology. A particular focus is on the use of the language of Character Strengths as a tool to embed inclusive practices, support cross-neurotype communication, and highlight the common experience of shared humanity regardless of neurotype. The chapter concludes with practical suggestions for teachers wishing to start capitalising on Character Strengths in their classroom.

Positive Psychology and Positive Education

Background

Positive Psychology was conceptualised as an alternative to the dominant medicalised and deficit-oriented approach common in psychology (Seligman & Csikszentmihalyi, 2000). This shift prompted research that explored the factors that contribute to a thriving and flourishing life, and this research has influenced education. Positive Education seeks to develop and embed the core principles of wellbeing and flourishing in school systems (Boniwell & Tunariu, 2019). Seligman and colleagues (2009) refer to Positive Education as a reconsideration of the purposes of education. The initial applications of Positive Education centred around wellbeing programmes and classes, but this focus solely on students was seen as ineffective without including the teachers in the wellbeing initiatives (Kern & Wheymer, 2021). The second wave of Positive Education prioritised the importance of a nurturing learning environment. This aligns with Armstrong's (2010) conceptualisation of neurodiversity-affirmative approaches which he called "niche construction." Niche construction is concerned with modifying the environment to enhance opportunities for success and highlights the importance of strength-based learning strategies. Current third wave approaches in Positive Education centre both content and pedagogy, and view Positive Education as an umbrella term encompassing a variety of approaches to promote flourishing, wellbeing, and inclusion.

A criticism of Positive Psychology approaches in education has been the focus on individualised intervention rather than systemic change (Becker & Marecek, 2008). The primary focus of most interventions is on students, and these have often been singular interventions, usually categorised under the umbrella of pastoral care (Waters, 2011). This results in inclusion strategies being othered and seen as an "add-on." Waters and colleagues (Brunzell et al., 2016) instead trained teachers in trauma-informed principles to promote the strength of self-regulation, which showed positive results. When the focus on wellbeing moves beyond worksheets and into teacher training, it legitimises wellbeing interventions and invites teachers to be more flexible about constituting teaching content.

Positive Education and the Neurodiversity Paradigm

Positive Education approaches can take a neurodiversity-affirmative lens when embedded alongside neurodiversity paradigm concepts across the curricula and within the school structure. It is essential that school staff develop a cultural competency about neurodivergent culture and thus have the knowledge and skills to challenge "diversity-lite" approaches, where neurodiversity terminology may be deployed, but fundamental understanding and change is not implemented (Thomas, 2024). The acceptance of neurodiversity as a core concept underpinning inclusive practice can act as a protective factor against the oppression of normative standards in schools. There is a well-evidenced connection between wellbeing and social connectedness (O'Connell et al., 2016), and positive social relationships are a central component of Seligman's (2018) PERMA (Positive Emotions, Engagement, Relationships, Meaning, and Accomplishment) model. Schools are ideally placed to implement Positive Psychology approaches within a social context, whilst respecting the level of social connection that varying neurotypes may seek.

Like the neurodiversity movement, Positive Education offers an alternative to medical model-based approaches. Critics of the medical model comment that this approach does not consider the social and cultural factors that disable and disempower individuals (Campbell & Oliver, 2013; Lalvani, 2015). Traditionally, special education provision has reinforced this model because of its tendency to focus on deficits within the child rather than on deficits at structural or systemic level (Lalvani, 2015). A common thread running through more recent conceptualisations of disability is a focus on the social construction of disability and imbalances of power and agency (Gallagher et al., 2014). Within the neurodiversity paradigm, neurodiversity-affirmative practices include those that respect, validate, and support the myriads of ways in which people process information, communicate, and experience their environment.

The evolution of thinking about disability towards more socially contextualised and competency-based models coincides with the evolution of the field of Positive Psychology and its focus on human virtue and flourishing. The emphasis on "what is strong" rather than just on "what is wrong" (Mayerson, 2015) is central to Positive Psychology interventions such as Character Strength training. Niemiec and colleagues (2017) identified that there are opportunities to embed Character Strengths approaches into existing practices – for example, inclusive education practices. Interestingly, they argue that a Character Strength approach at the level of those working with disabled people provides an opportunity to reframe staff thinking to be more strength-based (Niemiec et al., 2017). Character Strength approaches promote qualities that are beyond skills and capacities, and value characteristics that are integral to human identity. Twenty-four Character Strengths have been identified in Positive Psychology, and are outlined in Figure 10.1.

24 CHARACTER STRENGTHS	
1. CREATIVITY	13. TEAMWORK
2. CURIOSITY	14. FAIRNESS
3. JUDGMENT	15. LEADERSHIP
4. LOVE OF LEARNING	16. FORGIVENESS
5. PERSPECTIVE	17. HUMILITY
6. BRAVERY	18. PRUDENCE
7. PERSEVERANCE	19. SELF-REGULATION
8. HONESTY	20. APPRECIATION OF BEAUTY & EXCELLENCE
9. ZEST	21. GRATITUDE
10. LOVE	22. HOPE
11. KINDNESS	23. HUMOUR
12. SOCIAL INTELLIGENCE	24. SPIRITUALITY

Figure 10.1 24 Character Strengths (Peterson and Seligman, 2004)

Character Strengths

It is important for any teacher wishing to work with Character Strengths to have a nuanced understanding of Character Strengths and how they differ from similar concepts. The phrase "play to your strengths is perhaps common to readers, but what *are* strengths? Strengths can be talents, skills, and positive character traits. Talents and skills such as excelling at football, music or art are tangible and visible, and rewarded as such. While celebrating achievements is a lovely thing to do, exclusive focus on these kinds of strengths risks emphasis on normative definitions of success, straying into neurodiversity-lite.

In contrast, Character Strengths are integral to the individual and impact how you think, feel, and behave (Peterson & Seligman, 2004). Although integral to who we are, they are not always easy to identify. Seligman and Peterson have painstakingly identified and formally classified 24 positive human traits that everyone possesses. These traits, seen as values in action (VIA) became to be known as VIA Character Strengths (Figure 10.1). Each person's Character Strength profile is different; some people have a strength profile that leans towards creativity and curiosity, others to leadership, others to humour and zest for life. When a person does something well, with energy and with frequency, there is a good chance that this is evidence of a Character Strength. A strength is more nuanced than being good at something. For example, many children can develop a good level of competency at playing a musical instrument, but it does not excite them, and they do not become immersed in the activity. This phenomenon of becoming fully immersed in an activity or task is called flow (Csikszentmihalyi, 2014) and is a good indicator that a strength is in use. This sense of being immersed in an activity that is meaningful, and satisfying is protective of emotional wellbeing. Flow states are linked to a concept known as monotropism, and this is explored further in Chapter 6.

Evidence Base for the Efficacy of Character Strengths Approaches in Schools

VIA Character Strengths have been widely used in education settings (Waters, 2011; Mendes de Oliveira et al., 2022). Training teachers in Character Strength approaches provides an effective roadmap to inclusion and more sustainable and positive changes. Furthermore, research shows that the efficacy of strength interventions is improved when delivered by teachers (Bressoud et al., 2018). Bressoud's team examined how Character Strength activities could promote wellbeing for all students in an inclusive setting which included autistic students. They found that teacher belief in the efficacy of an approach is a key variable to its implementation. Similarly,

Quinlan and colleagues (2019) examined whether student outcomes were mediated by teacher strength spotting. This study revealed that the efficacy of strength spotting activities was influenced by teachers. These studies support the need to develop an integrative framework to ensure multilevel Character Strengths approaches in schools (Lavy, 2020).

Character Strength approaches can contribute to the collective wellbeing in schools by enhancing shared social connections and providing a common language. The importance of social connections and the shared social identity of cohesive group membership is critical in the promotion of wellbeing (Boniwell & Tunariu, 2019; Lomas, 2015). A whole-school Character Strengths approach casts the teacher as an agent of change in the classroom rather than a person who must implement a stand-alone intervention. Allison and colleagues (2021) argue that a flourishing classroom could involve group-level Character Strength activities such as strength spotting and strength awareness, integrated into the classroom culture by the teacher and wider school community.

Language, Character Strengths, and the Neurodiversity Paradigm

The language used by teachers in relation to inclusive practices reflects the dominant discourse of school culture, as the ways in which we talk and think reflect our cultural context (Rodden et al., 2019; Rapley, 2004). Language influences power imbalances, inequity can be naturalised in everyday discourse, and ability or disability can be perceived through talk (Lester et al., 2024; Williams, 2011). Disabled people are largely described in terms of their disability as their defining attribute (Clark & Marsh, 2002).

Everyday language forms and sustains the status quo in schools, and deficit-based and ableist language is not only unhelpful to, but at odds with, inclusive practices. Universally used language in school communities that promotes an inclusive and neurodiversity-affirmative mindset is a challenge to this status quo. Certainly, using the lexicon associated with the neurodiversity paradigm challenges pathologising and deficit-based biases (Cleary et al., 2024). Similarly, research indicates that using the language associated with strength-based approaches challenges deficit thinking. Research on barriers to improved health outcomes for indigenous populations in Australia found that strength-based approaches provided a solution-orientated and positive language narrative which contrasted with traditional deficit discourse that was commonly used (Fogarty et al., 2018).

The efficacy of Positive Education approaches like Character Strengths greatly improves when delivered by teachers who are on site and develop relationships with students (Mendes de Oliveria et al., 2022). This relational piece is a vital element in promoting the use of Character Strengths terminology as a common language across the school community. Recent research on the success of integrating strength-based approaches into school practice has found that success was more likely when teachers were trained in these approaches (Quinlan et al., 2019).

However, providing information to teachers about language is not sufficient, and embedding new language and practices in the school culture can be challenging. Woodcock and Nicoll (2022) found that teachers who held personal beliefs in favour of inclusive education were more encouraging in their student feedback. This study measured teachers' attribution responses, and found that embedding inclusive practices in schools is insufficient; teachers must also believe in inclusive practices to make them sustainable and impactful. This highlights the challenge that would arise in schools for those who might be tempted to "do" wellbeing in a one-off seminar about Character Strengths, as the research illustrates that more sustained support is required. Wellbeing interventions that target the staff in a school community as well as the students are far more likely to be effective than focusing solely on students (Wells et al., 2003). In practical terms, this suggests that Character Strengths interventions should begin with staff and extend to include the whole school community over time, increasing the efficacy of the interventions through staff modelling.

The use of strengths-based language can change an individual's perspective on disability. Carter, Carlton, and Travers (2020) utilised a Character Strength intervention with the siblings of intellectually disabled young people. They found that when given the opportunity and the language, siblings did not use deficit language, but rather engaged readily in strength spotting and positive descriptors of their siblings. These findings align with the author's experiences of supporting teachers in using Character Strengths language in classrooms, thereby providing teachers with a lexical toolkit that challenges deficit thinking while providing them with a means of advocating for their students. Neurodiversity-affirmative and strengths-based language helps to develop a culture of inclusivity and acceptance of diversity. Crucially, the integration of strength-focused language into school culture sends the message that being different is OK and it is not necessary to aspire to be neurotypical.

Character Strengths approaches can help disrupt teachers labelling and inadvertently othering learners, by using a different lens (Kang, 2009). Efforts to construct strength-based language as a positively oriented common language for use in school is consistent with the position taken by Niemiec and colleagues (2017), who proposed using the common language of Character Strengths as relevant for all whether disabled or not. By using a common language, Character Strengths can be understood across multiple levels – for example, learners, parents, teachers, leaders, and outside professionals. The use of a common language of strengths could be particularly helpful for students who are traditionally "othered" and viewed through a deficit lens (Lalvani, 2015). Shared language can also perform as a means of communication across neurotypes, thus supporting communication difficulties associated with the Double Empathy Problem (Milton, 2012).

The Struggle to Implement Changes

Moreover, teachers' beliefs and attitudes towards the needs and challenges of learners are often found to be consistent with a medical model approach to disability (Lalvani, 2012; O'Byrne & Muldoon, 2018). Lalvani (2013) found that teacher discourse about inclusion is influenced by the dominant discourse present at a societal level about disability and marginalised learners, and this discourse is characterised by "otherness" and deficit. Aas (2019) explored teacher talk during support planning meetings for students. This study found that teachers generally had a positive attitude towards inclusion. However, when examined more closely, adaptations for diversity were not welcomed, and the focus was on academic learning rather than the development of students' pro-social skills. Similarly, Rodden and colleagues (2019), examined teacher discourse about the inclusive practices for autistic students. They found that teachers expressed a willingness to develop their knowledge about inclusive practices, but they reported low self-efficacy in relation to the implementation of inclusive practices in their schools. Teacher discourse was also found to reflect the dominant discourse in their school communities, where inclusive education issues were perceived as separate to their responsibilities as class teachers. This othering of "special education" as not mainstream is a barrier to inclusive practices. The neurodiversity paradigm challenges the older and problematic categories of disability approach that were prevalent in school until recent times, (pre-2017 in Ireland). In the past, access to a support teacher was diagnosis-led, and consequently those privileged with the task of "labelling" were in effect gatekeepers to resources. The reality is that learners and their needs are complex and diverse, and often overlap and change in intensity over time.

This ambivalence towards inclusive practices and learning needs is commonly found in research into teacher attitudes towards inclusive practices (Lalvani, 2012; Rodden et al., 2019; Browning, 2018). Shankland and Rosset (2017) acknowledge teacher hesitation when implementing Positive Psychology approaches in their classrooms. Their review of brief interventions included Character Strengths. They suggested that this approach was perceived by teachers to meet the criteria of being easily integrated, requiring no special equipment, and adaptable to school contexts.

Taking a Balanced View: The Overuse and Underuse of Strengths

Character Strengths are not clearly delineated skills, but rather are expressed in degrees. Character Strengths can be expressed in different ways, and can also be overused or underused by individuals. Teaching students that a balanced approach is ideal is also a great way to develop self-awareness and reflective capacity. Discussion around the overuse and underuse of strengths can prevent an inadvertent toxic positivity (Bhattacharyya, Bhattacharyya & Sharaff, 2021), where a determination to present as cheerful, strong, and positive is rewarded and prioritised, making it difficult for learners to share their challenges or uncomfortable feelings. Within this framing, problems are stepping stones towards developing or discovering a Character Strength. There is a danger that only those strengths that are seen to have academic utility – for example, self-regulation or determination – are promoted, rather than "soft" strengths (Waters, 2021). The school environment and culture are essential to the successful implementation of neurodiversity-affirmative pedagogies, as Positive Education approaches are of little use in a toxic environment.

Character Strengths and Inclusive Education

The literature relating to using Character Strength approaches as a type of inclusive practice in schools is limited (Shogren, 2013). Some studies (Samson & Antonelli, 2013) explored the strengths profile of autistic adults and found that they are largely intellectually driven and are consistent with autistic and neurodivergent traits such as special interests and attention to detail. It is likely that the use of Character Strength approaches with neurominority groups will lead to distinct neurodivergent strengths profiles being highlighted. Character Strength approaches acknowledge and account for both the overuse and underuse of signature strengths. In this way, a traditionally described trait like fixated interests could be reframed as Love of Learning. This type of reframing offers a more flexible conceptualisation of a common and often-pathologised trait associated with neurodivergent learners.

Reframing Traits Using Character Strengths Language	
Bossy, own agenda	Leadership
Blunt, tactless	Honest
Rule-bound	Fairness
Know-it-all	Love of Learning

Character Strengths are a resource to enable positive reframing of deficits in school settings. By shifting the focus to Character Strengths, there is an opportunity for staff to model a positive reappraisal of behaviours and actions. Character Strengths language fosters an inclusive mindset which focuses on strengths and ability rather than deficit and disability. Whilst children are necessarily in the process of Becoming, school staff can also benefit from intentionally beginning a journey to becoming a more authentic version of themselves. A Character Strengths approach is neurodiversity-affirmative in that it gives staff a language that is not grounded in deficit and a vocabulary that enables them to welcome, celebrate, and support all neurotypes. In an environment where the language of strengths is centred, adaptations and accommodations are de-stigmatised because difference is accepted.

Key Takeaways

- Strengths are about both being and doing. They are positive traits that can be developed and improved. They can be overused or underused, and their use is dynamic and context-dependent.
- Strengths approaches in schools give teachers a language toolkit to challenge deficit-oriented thinking.

- Strength interventions support the development of positive identity, are protective of emotional wellbeing, and deepen social connection.
- *Character strengths are positive personality traits that reflect our basic identity, produce positive outcomes for ourselves and others, and contribute to the collective good (Niemiec, 2018).*

    The intentional use of a Character Strengths approach in schools is about being aware of the language of strengths, strength spotting across the school community, and intentional use of named strengths. This supports wellbeing at an individual level and builds and deepens relationships at a school level. Character strengths are things we do well, often, and with energy.

- Fundamentally, a Character Strengths approach is about working on what is working well. What does that feel like?

Reflective Activities

Try this reflective activity. Write your name on a piece of paper. Now write your name with your non-dominant hand. Which was easier? Which was frustrating and slow?

Learning and living using strengths is like using your dominant hand – it is just easier. Focusing only on weakness or need is like always writing with a non-dominant hand, it is tiring. In a neurotypical world or metaphorically right-handed world, many neurodivergent children are metaphorically left-handed, and this is tiring. A Character Strengths approach gives teachers the tools to reframe situations.

Instead of thinking what needs to be fixed, think of what strengths are needed to handle this situation. When staff put on strengths "goggles," they can see that children do well if they can. For example, if a child is resisting putting away a project/toy, looking at this situation through a strengths lens would mean recognizing that the child is deploying their strength of Perseverance. For many neurodivergent children, transitioning between tasks is hard. They can be fully immersed in an activity, demonstrating their Love of Learning, Perseverance, Enthusiasm, etc. Instead of pointing out the negative (e.g., the child is being disobedient), a strengths lens reminds us to take the conscious effort to put on our strengths glasses and look for the good (Niemiec, 2018). For example, instead of saying to the child something like "I've told you, it's time to clean up. This is your last warning," one could say "Let's finish this up so that I can see your energy on the playground."

The language of Character Strengths gives teachers tools to amplify small successes and link them to the use of strengths – "Well done finishing your homework, that showed great determination." Teachers can use their knowledge of an individual's unique strengths profile to cultivate connection and promote engagement.

The concept of strengths can be difficult to grasp for some young people, particularly those with limited vocabulary or limited understanding of concepts such as perseverance. It may be helpful to start with the visible or tangible and focus on the body, such as "I can stand on one leg, touch my nose" etc., then identifiable skills such as "I can write," "I can type," and gradually move that into strengths such as creativity, determination, Love of Learning, etc. The VIA Character Strength Questionnaire and its adaptations are useful first steps tools for diverse student groups.

Classroom Applications

Here are some activities that not only explore Character Strengths, but also strengthen social connections. Social connectedness is a central pillar of Seligman's PERMA model (Seligman, 2018), and also the Social Wellbeing Model (Keyes, 1998). We know that group-based activities are a source of social support and protective of wellbeing (O'Shea & Gallagher, 2014).

- Strength of the week – take a strength spotting approach to a named strength each week.
- Regular gratitude activity – have staff and students name or draw three things they are grateful for.
- Nominate a student or staff member who embodies a certain strength.

- Support students to recognise their contributions to a team, such as their family, class, sports team, etc.
- Who sees you? How would someone in your life describe you? What strengths would they say you have?
- Make a list of "little" Character Strength uses. Sometimes strength use is present in small doses in daily life. Can students/staff spot examples of everyday strengths used – for example, remembering to brush teeth (self-regulation), holding a door (kindness).

Recommended Reading

i. Niemiec R. (2017) *Character Strengths Interventions: A Field Guide for Practitioners*. Hogrefe Publishing.
ii. O'Neill C. (2022) *The Strength-based Guide to Supporting Autistic Children*. Jessica Kingsley Publishing.
iii. Proctor C. & Eades J. (2019) *The Strength Gym*. Positive Psychology Research Centre.

References

Aas, H. K. (2019). Teachers talk on student needs: exploring how teacher beliefs challenge inclusive education in a Norwegian context. *International Journal of Inclusive Education, 26*(5), 495–509. https://doi.org/10.1080/13603116.2019.1698065

Allison, L., Waters, L., & Kern, M. L. (2021). Flourishing classrooms: Applying a systems-informed approach to positive education. *Contemporary School Psychology, 25*(4), 395–405. https://doi.org/10.1007/s40688-019-00267-8

Armstrong, T. (2010). *Neurodiversity: Discovering the extraordinary gifts of autism, ADHD, dyslexia, and other brain differences*. Toronto: ReadHowYouWant.com

Becker, D., & Marecek, J. (2008). Positive Psychology: History in the Remaking? *Theory & Psychology, 18*(5), 591–604. https://doi.org/10.1177/0959354308093397 (Original work published 2008)

Bhattacharyya, R., Bhattacharyya, M. N., & Sharaff, M. S. (2021). Toxic positivity and mental health–It is ok to not be ok. *Design Engineering*, 8, 5109–5127.

Boniwell, I., & Tunariu, A. D. (2019). *Positive psychology: Theory, research and applications*. Maidenhead: McGraw-Hill Education (UK).

Bressoud, N., Shankland, R., Ruch, W., & Gay, P. (2018). Character strengths and children with special needs: A way to promote well-being all together. Well-being in education systems, Well-being in Education Systems Conference Abstract Book.

Locarno. Available at: https://www.researchgate.net/profile/Jenny-Marcionetti/publication/334697135_Well-being_in_education_systems_Conference_abstract_book_Locarno_2017/links/5d5cde1892851c37636e6407/Well-being-in-education-systems-Conference-abstract-book-Locarno-2017.pdf#page=267

Browning, T. D. (2018). Countering deficit discourse: Preservice teacher experiences of core reflection, *Teaching and Teacher Education, 72*, 2018, 87–97. https://doi.org/10.1016/j.tate.2018.01.009.

Brunzell, T., Stokes, H., & Waters, L. (2016). Trauma-informed positive education: Using positive psychology to strengthen vulnerable students. *Contemporary School Psychology, 20*(1), 63–83. https://doi.org/10.1007/s40688-015-0070-x

Campbell, J., & Oliver, M. (2013). *Disability politics: Understanding our Past, Changing our Future.* Routledge. https://doi.org/10.4324/9780203410639

Carter E.W., Carlton M.E. & Travers H.E. (2020). Seeing strengths: Young adults and their siblings with autism or intellectual disability. *Journal of Applied Research in Intellectual Disabilities, 33*(3): 574–583. doi: 10.1111/jar.12701. Epub 2020 Jan 9. PMID: 31919930; PMCID: PMC7160005.

Clark, L., & Marsh, S. (2002). Patriarchy in the UK: The language of disability. The Disability Archive UK.

Cleary, M., West, S., McLean, L., Johnston-Devin, C., Kornhaber, R., & Hungerford, C. (2024). When the Education System and Autism Collide: An Australian Qualitative Study Exploring School Exclusion and the Impact on Parent Mental Health. *Issues in Mental Health Nursing, 45*(5), 468–476. https://doi.org/10.1080/01612840.2024.2328251

Csikszentmihalyi, M., Csikszentmihalyi, M., Abuhamdeh, S., & Nakamura, J. (2014). Flow. In M. Csikszentmihalyi (Ed.), Flow and the foundations of positive psychology: The collected works of Mihaly Csikszentmihalyi (pp. 227–238). New York: Springer.

Fogarty, W., Lovell, M., Langenberg, J., & Heron, M.-J. (2018). Deficit Discourse and Strengths-based Approaches: Changing the Narrative of Aboriginal and Torres Strait Islander Health and Wellbeing.

Gallagher, D., Connor, D. & Ferri, B. (2014). Beyond the far too incessant schism: Special education and the social model of disability. *International Journal of Inclusive Education, 18*. 10.1080/13603116.2013.875599.

Kang, J. G. (2009). A teacher's deconstruction of disability: A discourse analysis. Disability Studies Quarterly, 29(1). doi: https://doi.org/10.18061/dsq.v29i1.173

Kern, M. L., & Wehmeyer, M. L. (2021). *The Palgrave Handbook of Positive Education* (p. 777). Cham: Springer Nature.

Keyes, C. L. M. (1998). Social well-being. *Social Psychology Quarterly, 61*(2), 121–140. https://doi.org/10.2307/2787065

Lalvani, P. (2012). Privilege, compromise, or social justice: teachers' conceptualizations of inclusive education. *Disability & Society, 28*(1), 14–27. https://doi.org/10.1080/09687599.2012.692028

Lalvani, P. (2015). Disability, Stigma and Otherness: Perspectives of Parents and Teachers. *International Journal of Disability, Development and Education, 62*(4), 379–393. https://doi.org/10.1080/1034912x.2015.1029877

Lalvani, P. (2015). "We are not aliens": Exploring the Meaning of Disability and the Nature of Belongingness in a Fourth Grade Classroom. *Disability Studies Quarterly, 35*(4) doi: 10.18061/dsq.v35i4.4963

Lavy, S. (2020). Perspectives: The Dance of Love and Fear in the Middle East: An Invitation for Change?. Middle East *Journal of Positive Psychology, 6,* 36–40. Available at: https://www.middleeastjournalofpositivepsychology.org/index.php/mejpp/article/view/115

Lester, J., O'Reilly, M. & Furlong, D. (2024). Analyzing constructions of disability in everyday talk: Methodological applications of discursive psychology. *Qualitative Research in Psychology* VL - 21 DOI - 10.1080/14780887.2024.2367589

Lomas, T. (2015). Positive social psychology: a multilevel inquiry into sociocultural well-being initiatives. *Psychology, Public Policy, and Law, 21*(3), 338. Available at: https://psycnet.apa.org/buy/2015-24690-001

Mayerson, N. (2015). "Characterizing" the Workplace: Using Character Strengths to Create Sustained Success. VIA Institute on Character. Available at: https://www.viacharacter.org/pdf/CHARACTERIZING%20THE%20WORKPLACE-USING%20STRENGTHS%20TO%20CREATE%20SUSTAINED%20SUCCESS.PDF

Mendes de Oliveira, C., Santos Almeida, C. R., & Hofheinz Giacomoni, C. (2022). School-based positive psychology interventions that promote well-being in children: A systematic review. *Child Indicators Research, 15*(5), 1583–1600. https://doi.org/10.1007/s12187-022-09935-3

Milton, D. E. M. (2012). On the ontological status of autism: the 'double empathy problem.' *Disability & Society, 27*(6), 883–887. https://doi.org/10.1080/09687599.2012.710008

Niemiec, R. M., Shogren, K. A., & Wehmeyer, M. L. (2017). Character strengths and intellectual and developmental disability: A strengths-based approach from positive psychology. *Education and Training in Autism and Developmental Disabilities, 52*(1), 13–25. Available at: https://www.jstor.org/stable/26420372

Niemiec, R. M. (2018). *Character Strengths Interventions: A Field Guide for Practitioners.* Hogrefe. ISBN 9781616764920

O'Byrne, C., & Muldoon, O. T. (2018). The construction of intellectual disability by parents and teachers. *Disability & Society, 34*(1), 46–67. https://doi.org/10.1080/09687599.2018.1509769

O'Connell, B. H., O'Shea, D., & Gallagher, S. (2016). Mediating effects of loneliness on the gratitude-health link. *Personality and Individual Differences, 98,* 179–183. https://doi.org/10.1016/j.paid.2016.04.042

O'Shea, D., & Gallagher, S. (2014). The role of positive social interactions in improving wellbeing: A randomised controlled pilot trial. *European Health Psychologist, 16.*

Peterson, C., & Seligman, M. E. (2004). *Character Strengths and Virtues: A Handbook and Classification.* Washington: American Psychological Association.

Quinlan, D., Vella-Brodrick, D. A., Gray, A., & Swain, N. (2019). Teachers matter: Student outcomes following a strengths intervention are mediated by teacher strengths spotting. *Journal of Happiness Studies, 20*(8), 2507–2523. https://doi.org/10.1007/s10902-018-0051-7

Rapley, M. (2004). *The Social Construction of Intellectual Disability*. Cambridge University Press. https://doi.org/10.1017/CBO9780511489884

Rodden, B., Prendeville, P., Burke, S, and Kinsella, W. (2019) Framing secondary teachers' perspectives on the inclusion of students with autism spectrum disorder using critical discourse analysis. *Cambridge Journal of Education, 49*(2), 235–253. DOI: 10.1080/0305764X.2018.1506018

Samson, A. C., & Antonelli, Y. (2013). Humor as character strength and its relation to life satisfaction and happiness in Autism Spectrum Disorders. *Humor, 26*(3), 477–491. https://doi.org/10.1515/humor-2013-0031

Seligman, M. E., & Csikszentmihalyi, M. (2000). *Positive psychology: An introduction* (Vol. 55, No. 1, p. 5). Washington: American Psychological Association.

Seligman, M. E., Ernst, R. M., Gillham, J., Reivich, K., & Linkins, M. (2009). Positive education: Positive psychology and classroom interventions. *Oxford Review of Education, 35*(3), 293–311.

Seligman, M. (2018). PERMA and the building blocks of well-being. *The Journal of Positive Psychology, 13*(4), 333–335. https://doi.org/10.1080/17439760.2018.1437466

Shankland, R. & Rosset, E. (2017). Review of Brief School-Based Positive Psychological Interventions: a Taster for Teachers and Educators. *Educational Psychology Review, 29*. 10.1007/s10648-016-9357-3.

Shogren, K.A. (2013). Positive Psychology and Disability: A Historical Analysis', in Michael L. Wehmeyer (ed.), *The Oxford Handbook of Positive Psychology and Disability*. Oxford Academic. https://doi.org/10.1093/oxfordhb/9780195398786.013.013.0003, accessed 21 Aug. 2025.

Thomas, E. (2024). Why critical psychology and the neurodiversity movement need each other. *Frontiers in Psychology, 15*, 1149743.

Waters, L. (2011). A review of school-based positive psychology interventions. *The Australian Educational and Developmental Psychologogy, 28*(2), 75-90. https://doi.org/10.1375/aedp.28.2.75

Waters, L. (2021). Positive education pedagogy: Shifting teacher mindsets, practice, and language to make wellbeing visible in classrooms. In M. L. Kern & M. L. Wehmeyer (Eds.), *The Palgrave handbook of positive education* (pp. 137–164). Cham: Springer International Publishing.

Wells, J., Barlow, J., & Stewart-Brown, S. (2003). A systematic review of universal approaches to mental health promotion in schools. *Health Education, 103*(4), 197–220. https://doi.org/10.1108/09654280310485546

Williams, V. (2011). *Disability and discourse: Analysing inclusive conversation with people with intellectual disabilities*. Wiley Blackwell. https://doi.org/10.1002/9780470977934

Woodcock, S. & Nicoll, S. (2022). "It isn't you": Teachers' beliefs about inclusive education and their responses toward specific learning disabilities. *Psychology in the Schools, 59*, 765–783. https://doi.org/10.1002/pits.22643

11

Universal Design for Learning in a Neurodiverse World

Margaret Flood

Thinking about Neurodiversity and Variability in Education

From the outset, it is important to note that we all contribute to neurodiversity. The concept of neurodiversity applies to every student, because no two students in our classrooms, indeed on the planet, are the same or learn in the exact same way. Each student has different skills, interests, perspectives, abilities, and areas where they need support (Myer, Rose & Gordon, 2014). In advocating for variability in learning, teaching, and assessment, we acknowledge the importance of recognising a broad understanding of neurodiversity and the unique variations within each individual's neurological makeup to embrace a more inclusive understanding of human diversity.

Variability and Universal Design for Learning

Universal Design for Learning (UDL) exists at the intersection of diversity, equity, and inclusion (DEI), social justice, and accessibility. In a world where potential is often left unrealised due to barriers imposed by systems – including our curriculum and how we teach it, and society – we must scrutinise our teaching methods, tools, and materials to ensure they minimise bias based on identity, race, culture, language, gender, disability, or class. Such biases inevitably limit access, participation, engagement, and success. UDL is an approach specifically designed to address and reduce these inequities by removing barriers for all students (Chardin & Novak, 2020). This ensures that every student has genuine and engaging opportunities to learn and succeed. Importantly, variability in education encompasses both the diversity of students we design for as a group, regardless of pre-assigned labels, and the diversity within each student. This means that we no longer teach to the "average" student. Rather, we design with intentional options included that enhance the educational experiences of every student.

As teachers, we must move away from narrowly categorising students (e.g., bright, average) and assigning support or challenges based on these categories. Instead, we should focus on variability. Variability is a fundamental aspect of UDL because it mirrors the inherent diversity of the human nervous system (Meyer, Rose & Gordon, 2014; CAST, 2018). There is no single way that a brain will respond to the learning environment. Since there is no "average" or typical brain and thus no "average" or typical student, it is imperative to abandon planning, teaching, and assessment methods based on the concept of an average student.

UDL and variability consider the "jagged profile" (Rose, 2017) as a more comprehensive means of understanding each student's strengths and areas for support. This approach to variability considers the context and environment, facilitating intentional design to remove barriers to learning. By recognising the jagged profile of each individual, we can start designing for the person rather than the subject or topic. This does not mean more work. In fact, once we adopt this new way of thinking, we realise that variability is predictable. With intentional design, we can anticipate which options, supports, and challenges to incorporate into specific learning experiences. Thus, as educators, we can create a toolbox of strategies from which we can apply the ones that will work best in the context of a particular learning experience.

Teachers might feel daunted by the prospect of designing for the variability of a class of up to 30 students. However, the UDL Guidelines, which align with the concept of identity in addition to the organisation of the brain, support teachers in addressing the predictable variability in learning that will be present in any environment (Meyer et al., 2014; CAST, 2018; CAST, 2024). UDL encourages teachers to shift their focus from thinking in terms of ability and disability to thinking in terms of variability. Through this UDL mindset, students are not defined by their disability, social background, gender, race, or any other category. UDL is not solely for students with higher support needs or neurodivergent students; it is for every student.

What Is UDL?

UDL offers three principles for designing for learning, teaching, and assessment that provide a map for teachers as we strive to create meaningful and purposeful learning experiences for every student: Engagement, Representation, and Action and Expression, the goal being to develop agentic students. At its core, UDL emphasises the importance of designing multiple pathways (choice and flexibility) so that every student can engage with and understand the content of the lesson or topic.

Thus, UDL starts with a shift in mindset. It serves as an approach for fostering inclusion, and the UDL Guidelines function as a valuable tool to facilitate inclusive practices. It shifts the focus away from viewing students as the source of learning barriers. Instead, barriers are recognised as environmental, curricular, or contextual factors that can be intentionally addressed. UDL takes a proactive approach to designing learning experiences, teaching methods, and assessments that cater to the diverse identities, competencies, learning strengths, and needs of every student within our classrooms and school community. Variability becomes a key consideration in instructional design. Thinking in terms of variability encourages us to go beyond conventional boundaries and look past the student alone. By acknowledging that barriers to learning exist within the environment, curriculum design, and even among teachers, we gain insight into the multifaceted challenges faced by students. This awareness allows us to apply the UDL Guidelines strategically, aiming to eliminate these barriers and create more inclusive educational experiences.

But What Does This Mean in Practice for Teachers?

Often, when teachers think about neurodiversity, they are thinking about their neurominority students. However, we now know that neurodiversity means *all* our students. Here we are going to explore the goal of each of the UDL principles, looking at some examples of strategies that we might use for neurominority students but are in fact beneficial for each of our students. In doing so, it is hoped that we will recognise that we are already applying aspects of UDL to our learning, teaching, and assessment practice. In some instances, this may be an accommodation aimed at just one cohort of students, but if offered as a choice for every student, it becomes UDL. In other instances, it is something we do without thinking that means we are supporting every student. Taking a UDL approach, we can design our lessons to ensure that all aspects of the lesson are accessible to the range of neurovariability in our classrooms, so that every student can participate, engage, and achieve in a meaningful and authentic way.

Multiple Means of Engagement

Multiple means of engagement refers to designing options for welcoming interests and identities, sustaining effort and persistence, and emotional growth. We recognise that our students have diverse identities, interests, and perspectives in addition to engagement and motivation patterns, and that these patterns are impacted by external influences. To promote student engagement, we should account for these various influences that impact how students participate, including neurology, culture, personal relevance, subjectivity, and background knowledge. It is essential to recognise that there is not a one-size-fits-all approach to engagement; different students respond differently. Some may immediately disengage from a task or topic, while others eagerly participate. Some may tire quickly due to cognitive effort, while others thrive on practical elements. By intentionally offering multiple engagement options, we can cater to each student's unique needs. Below are some examples of multiple means of engagement in practice. It is important to note that while all three principles are interwoven, engagement threads through all aspects of UDL, as engaging students in their learning is at the core of what we do as teachers.

Foster Belonging and Community

For learning to occur, relationship-building and a sense of belonging and community are essential. This starts with us. Teachers need to be approachable and available to their students. This means knowing and using student's names, welcoming questions and alternative perspectives, and responding compassionately. Fostering belonging and community also requires opportunities for collaborative learning and social interactions, and developing students' awareness of themselves and others. For some students this may require pre-teaching certain skills or having visual cues and reminders before and during activities and interactions. For example, autistic students might have communication or processing differences and might benefit from using straightforward language, explaining new terms or phrases in the context they are used, and giving practical examples. These changes are also of benefit to students who are learning and interacting in a language that is not their home language and students with different cultural backgrounds. Building community through ensuring understanding and engagement for every student also builds compassion and awareness within every student in the classroom or community.

Optimise Choice and Autonomy

Providing choice and autonomy for students increases motivation and a sense of control and ownership for our students. Offer a menu of project options related to the topic or goal. For example, students might choose between creating a video, writing an essay, or making a poster to learn about a significant character in a period of time in History. For older students, there should be greater autonomy. For example, the topic is still a specific era in history, but rather than assign the choices, we can engage students in design. This can be as straightforward as:

> Next, we are learning about ancient civilisations. These are the civilisations we can choose from. What ones are you interested in? I am thinking about including choices such as creating a video, making a poster, or writing an essay. Would you like those choices, or do you have any other ideas we can consider.

Of course, as teachers, we are limited timewise, so give what time you can when you can, and it is OK if sometimes you cannot offer students this choice.

Optimise Relevance and Value

Ensuring the choices we design are relevant and hold value for students will provide opportunities to engage different interests and perspectives. This can be achieved through offering choice and autonomy, as discussed earlier. It can also be offered through inviting discussion. For example, when learning about different currencies in maths, invite students to talk about the countries they would like to visit that do not use the euro. How will they manage their money? Or when introducing climate change in geography, asking students their thoughts on sustainability, what they have learned in other subjects or at home about the topic, or by having a walking debate, or who they think is responsible are invitational ways to invite students' perspectives (without their being wrong), bringing the topic into their lived and learned experiences.

Embed Predictable Routines and Clear Expectations

Having predictable routines and expectations within your classroom can reduce anxiety, support students' organisation, and increase focus.

Having a routine or structure to your lesson provides students with a road map to help them engage. Start your class with a clear agenda, the focus of learning or learning intentions for the lesson, and consistently structure the class time. For example, class might begin with a warm-up or relaxation exercise, followed by the learning intentions or goals with a connection to prior knowledge, new content, an activity, a check-in of understanding and achievements, and ending with a summary of key points.

Supporting students' sensory requirements is a prerequisite to engagement. For some students, this may be having time in a quiet area, wearing headphones during a noisy activity, using a fidget, or stretching. While these strategies are most commonly associated with students with autism and ADHD, providing these strategies to every student will benefit students who are anxious, have a headache, like to move, or just need space that day. Some of these, like the headphones and fidgets, can be options individual students take as they feel they need them. Others, such as calming and quiet exercises or movement breaks, can be embedded into your lesson routine. For example, the ADHD student may need time to settle after lunch break, while the autistic student may be sensory-overloaded and need time to re-regulate. A quiet breathing exercise with the lights off in the classroom will help both students and benefit the rest of the class in preparing for their next lesson. Another example is the student who has a token or signal for their need to take a movement break, often outside the classroom. Not only is this othering the student, but it also means the student is missing learning. In an environment where our students spend most of their day sitting, embedding movement breaks in our lessons benefits everyone. One way of embedding movement breaks is through learning activities such as station work, walking debates, floor work, and physical engagement with the content. For example, for measurement in maths, we can use the furniture, building, and outdoor space to measure – something we already do if teaching this topic. Another way to embed movement breaks is to use them to signal transitions within the lesson through simple one-minute activities as students move through the lesson. An example that I got from a student teacher is to offer variety in these and make them fun for the students. As that student teacher said, they mix it up. One transition might be to stand up and bow to the person beside you, another might be chair press-ups, and one might be students' choice.

Multiple Means of Representation

Multiple means of representation refers to designing options for perception, language, and symbols, and building knowledge. It is how information is presented and made accessible and meaningful for students. We recognise that our students perceive and comprehend information differently, and that we must consider how they engage with the content we present. Our goal is to ensure that all students have access to learning. Just as there is no one-size-fits-all approach to engagement, there are multiple ways to represent content. Some students may struggle with text-based information and benefit from visual or auditory modes. Others thrive when independently exploring content, while some prefer accessing instructions step-by-step as they work through tasks. Taking a UDL approach, we can design our lessons to ensure that all aspects of the lesson are accessible and comprehensible to the range of variability in our classrooms. Below are some examples of multiple means of representation in practice. It is important to note that it is good practice to provide students with the option of materials in both physical and digital formats, but not all schools will have the resources to provide this. It is also important to note that the examples given are not an alternative to traditional modes of presenting content. Rather, they should be offered as options in addition to these traditional modes, and as teachers we will know what options are suitable within a lesson for students to engage and achieve their goals.

Using Multiple Media and Formats

Presenting information using text, images, audio recordings, and hands-on materials supports students to access the content, but also to enhance their focus.

Using subtitles in our presentations can provide access and focus to a student who has difficulty hearing or remove a barrier where the acoustics in the room are a distraction. It also can remove language barriers for students who are learning through a language that is not their home language. If students who are new to the language can access the content through their own home language while listening through their new language, students can not only access and comprehend the lesson better, but they can also build proficiency in their new language.

Designing media and format options for how students will engage with the lesson content ensures that every student has a medium in which they can access and therefore achieve the goal. It is important to note that this is not about differentiation or dumbing down the lesson content for some. For example, let us say the goal of a series of literature lessons is to read texts for understanding and appreciation. If we only provide a written text, we are excluding many of our students. For example, if a dyslexic student cannot access the text at the rate or level of their peers, it often results in them appearing to not understand. If within these literature lessons we offer the choice of the traditional text, an audio version, visual storyboards, or where available an acted-out version or tactile scenes from the text, the dyslexic student can choose which format suits them best, as can every other student in the classroom. By designing these options from the outset, we are ensuring access to the learning strategy that best suits the student in the context of this lesson.

Using Visual Cues and Systems

Using visual systems and cues aids learning for many students within our neurodiverse classrooms. At an access level, it provides clear signposting and structure – for example, our timetables or schedules. In school, our timetables offer a degree of predictability and routine for our students. However, the formats in which timetables are presented to students, particularly in post-primary, are often inaccessible in terms of information overload, font size, and the space in which information is presented. For some students the timetable is unreadable, for others it is a cause of anxiety, while for others it adds an unnecessary barrier to their organisational capacity. Now, what if students had a range of timetable formats to choose from?

- A colour-coded timetable with each subject having its own colour
- A daily timetable as an option, instead of a weekly one
- A "now/next" timetable
- A timetable with a visual representation of the subject or teacher
- A digital timetable with text-to-speech or screen reader capability
- A sensory schedule – this type of schedule is predominantly used in special schools and classes for our students with the most complex needs

Each of these timetables could be designed in consideration of a particular cohort of students, but if offered as a choice to every student, each student can navigate the school structure in a way that suits their organisational capacity best.

At a knowledge and comprehension level, visual strategies can be used to highlight critical features. This helps students focus on key information, improving their understanding. Use colour-coding, underlining, and bullet points to emphasise new or key words, information, and concepts. Use visual cues for new words and phrases and to support decoding of these words. For example, in a history lesson on World War Two, students could highlight the important countries on the map and provide a summary/key points sheet. Levels of challenge can be embedded in this. They might involve dividing the map into allied forces and Nazi/fascist forces, or colour-coding in accordance with timelines of occupation and liberation. Students could also create a visual timeline of the war's events, or a statistical mind map or poster of key information.

In some subjects, such as maths, visual codes may start with the visual symbol rather than the word. For example, when teaching subtraction, students start with numbers and symbols (9 – 2), but we need to ensure that they understand the purpose and meaning of "–" and all the terms used to explain it. This could involve a maths word wall, where the minus sign would be in the centre with key terms such as "minus," "take away," "subtract," "decrease," and "less than." As students move from numerical maths problems to language-based problems, they will know the symbol that coincides with the language, facilitating them to solve the problem.

Connecting Prior knowledge

Supporting students to connect prior background knowledge with new learning strengthens their confidence in their learning, provides a level of relevance for them, and can support them in retaining new information. For example, before starting a unit on the physical world in science, students can review what they have learned about materials and energy in science, and measurements in maths, and bring in practical learning from their own experiences.

Student Access to Content and Materials

Having slides and materials available to students prior to the lesson scaffolds students' access, organisation, and learning. For the student who is anxious or likes to know the structure of a lesson, reviewing what is going to happen or finding the meaning of a new word means they feel prepared and ready for the class. It also means that a student can avail of a screen reader if required, or that they can turn on subtitles in a language of their choosing to help them focus or understand.

Multiple Means of Action and Expression

"Multiple means of action and expression" refers to designing options for interaction, expression and communication, and strategy development. This principle recognises that students vary significantly in how they navigate their learning environment and express their understanding of learning. As teachers, we must consider how students can best engage with their learning and demonstrate their knowledge, skills, and values. Rather than relying on a single, rigid approach, we should provide intentional options that allow students to achieve their goals. Some students may struggle to initiate tasks, express themselves clearly, or plan their actions. Others might have effective systems for planning and easily create essays, projects, or presentations. Additionally, some students may excel in written expression but may struggle with verbal communication, and vice versa. By offering multiple avenues for expression, we empower students to succeed and maintain their engagement. Below are some examples of multiple means of action and expression in practice. It is important to note that sometimes – for instance, mandatory standardised tests and state examinations – we as teachers have no choice but to give options, and therefore must include opportunities to prepare students to take these summative assessments.

Encourage Goal-Setting and Self-Monitoring

While we as teachers set the overarching goal for students to achieve, building students' capacity to set and monitor their own goals to achieve this develops their strategic development, regulation, resilience, and problem-solving skills. This involves making goals explicit and giving clear instructions on how to achieve these goals.

- Creating a rubric gives students that big picture in terms of the end goal, but breaks down the criteria or what they need to achieve into manageable steps with guidance on what the student will need to do in each step to gain the outcome or grade they are aiming for.
- Guiding students in setting their own personal learning goals to accomplish the task or assessment promotes independence and responsibility. This involves teaching students the skills to create checklists, roadmaps, or organisation apps to plan, reflect on, and monitor their progress in order to adapt, problem-solve, or ask for assistance if need be to move forward. For example, during reading week or World Book Week, students could set a goal to read or listen to a certain number of books, comics, etc., and use a reading log to track their progress and reflect on their achievement. For a technology project this would involve creating a project task plan with built-in reflection points or checkpoints that include consideration of knowledge and skills, decisions on the design, materials required, and steps to build the project. This could be done through a reflective journal or a visual workflow in digital or paper format.

Offer Multiple Ways to Demonstrate Knowledge and Understanding through Embedding Choice

Embedding choice into how students engage with and respond to learning gives them greater flexibility in the assessment space and allows for varied expression of learning. Allow students to choose from a variety of media to show their knowledge and understanding, whether this be in essay format, a presentation, dramatisation, creating an artefact, poster, or digital media. For example, in a language class, students might write a holiday postcard home, create a collage timeline of their holiday (on paper or digitally), create a vlog or blog of their holiday, create a reality TV-style video of their holiday, give a presentation on their holiday, or create a holiday highlights podcast.

Providing Clear Feedback

Providing clear feedback helps all students understand their progress and areas for improvement, boosting confidence and learning.

Give students specific feedback with clear guidance or examples of how to improve through the process and for final assignments and assessments. This can involve referring back to the assignment rubric and instructions or to the student's checklist as markers for progress. For example, after a student submits an assignment, highlight the strengths of the work. When highlighting areas for improvement, use the rubric and instructions to signpost steps to improve on the work. Where appropriate, refer to the strengths of the work as an example of how to improve an area.

Acknowledging and praising students for their efforts shows them their work is valued. This feedback should happen during the process as well as for the final product. For students who require extra scaffolds to complete a task or where feedback causes anxiety, this recognition helps build their confidence and motivation, encouraging them to continue working. For students who are doing well, acknowledging their effort sustains their motivation.

Key Takeaways

- UDL acknowledges and embraces the inherent variability of human cognition and emotion, recognising it as a fundamental facet of human existence and an asset that enriches the educational experience.
- UDL represents a crucial change in basic assumptions, moving away from the idea of teaching to an "average" student. Instead, it advocates for designing with intentional options that enhance the educational experiences of every student, acknowledging the diverse neurocognitive attributes present in any classroom.
- UDL is specifically designed to reduce inequities and remove barriers to learning that exist within systems, curriculums, and the environment, rather than viewing the student as the source of these barriers.
- Adopting a holistic UDL approach enhances the educational experiences of all students, promoting equity and access for everyone.

Strategies beneficial for specific cohorts often benefit many when offered as choices
- Implementing UDL involves providing multiple pathways (choice and flexibility) for students to engage with content, access information, and demonstrate their understanding. This includes using varied media and formats for representation, offering choices in how students express knowledge, and providing options for engagement.

Reflective Activities

Reflection can be useful when embedding a new approach like UDL into your practice. Moreover, individual and collective reflection is a key consideration in the UDL Guidelines (CAST, 2024). Perhaps the most useful place to start is to reflect on the barriers that currently exist for both your learners and also yourself as a practitioner.

Questions to guide reflection:
1. Think about your learners and their variability. What are the obvious barriers that come to mind? What are the less visible barriers present for your learners?
2. Consider any barriers you experienced as a learner in school. What helped to reduce these barriers? What were the results of these barriers being reduced for you?
3. In terms of the barriers identified in question 1, consider what opportunities are available to you to reduce these barriers?
4. What single action can you take in the short term to reduce a barrier in your classroom?
5. How will you know it is successful? How will you evaluate this change in practice?

This simple reflective activity aims to promote a successful and sustainable start to your journey as a UDL practitioner. Sustained reflective practice supports not only the UDL journey, but also wider inclusive practices.

Conclusion

Embedding UDL principles in a neurovariable classroom supports the unique way neurominority students learn while also creating learning experiences that ensure a more inclusive and effective learning environment for every student. By designing multiple means of engagement, representation, and action and expression, teachers can ensure that every student can participate, engage, and succeed in their learning. This UDL approach exemplifies the idea that what is necessary for some students often benefits many. This holistic approach not only accommodates neurominority students, but also enhances the overall educational experience, leading to a richer, more meaningful educational experience for the entire student body and promoting equity and access for everyone.

References

CAST. (2018). *Universal Design for Learning Guidelines*, Version 2.2. Retrieved from http://udlguidelines.cast.org

CAST. (2024). *Universal Design for Learning Guidelines,* Version 3.0. Retrieved from http://udlguidelines.cast.org

Chardin, M., & Novak, K. (2020). *Equity by design: Delivering on the power and promise of UDL.* USA: Sage Publications.

Meyer, A., Rose, D. H., & Gordon, D. (2014). *Universal design for learning: Theory and practice.* USA: CAST Professional Publishing.

Rose, T. (2017). *The end of average: Unlocking our potential by embracing what makes us different.* USA: Harper Collins Publisher.

Part III Introduction: Relationships in and around School
Edited by Rachael Davis

School can be an alienating environment for neurodivergent children, and is still often a place where conformity is valued over individuality. Many programs and initiatives aimed at supporting neurodivergent students continue to focus on "fixing" or "normalising" behaviours that are seen as different. Rather than embracing diversity, many of these approaches, either overtly or inadvertently, aim to make neurodivergent students conform to traditionally accepted norms. Often educators *want* to be inclusive, but by not critically engaging with these types of programmes used in schools, they can fail to recognise how biased and unhelpful such initiatives are to neurodivergent learners.

As a result, neurodivergent students' behaviours and communication styles are frequently misinterpreted, their needs go unnoticed, and their experiences are minimised. Interactions within the school environment are often misunderstood, and social, academic, and emotional experiences are not fully supported or valued. This is not just a problem for neurodivergent children – it is an issue that concerns and affects the entire school community. Moreover, everyone should better understand and embrace neurodiversity to ensure that all social, emotional, and educational needs can be met.

In this part we will explore how relationships – at different levels in and around the school – play a critical role in supporting neurodivergent children to be understood and listened to. We will talk about how different communities within school can contribute to creating environments where students feel truly safe, seen, and valued, and how intentions should be rooted in knowledge, reflection, and collaboration. Across four chapters, we will introduce how children can learn about neurodiversity in school, the experience of setting up peer support spaces for neurodivergent children, how non-teaching staff can act as curators of safety, and a framework that can be applied by multiple school stakeholders to make a school environment neurodiversity-affirmative. The authors will introduce aspects of their own lived experiences and evidence from research to offer practical insights into how to cultivate positive relationships in your own school community.

12

The Learning About Neurodiversity at School Programme in the Context of Neurodiversity-Affirmative Practice

Alyssa M. Alcorn, Amy Nic Thaidhg, and Alun Flynn

Introduction

Improving educational experiences and inclusion for neurodivergent children and young people has repeatedly been identified as a priority for families and neurodivergent communities, both in research literature and structured priority-setting exercises (e.g., recently in Ostaszewska & Harper, 2024). Poor knowledge of neurocognitive diversity, negative attitudes, and discriminatory behaviour have all been identified as problematic contributors to poor school experiences for this group. It may seem like an obvious strategy to address the issues above through direct teaching and training about neurodiversity with both professionals and pupils. However, there are a range of barriers to achieving this, from a current lack of neurodiversity-focused or neurodiversity-affirmative teaching materials to professional training constructed around single diagnostic labels (e.g., ADHD, dyslexia). At a structural level, professional or policy-based conceptualisations of diversity and inclusion rarely include neurodiversity.

Against this backdrop, the Learning About Neurodiversity at School (LEANS) research project began with a simple but thorny question: what would it mean to teach about neurodiversity in primary school? This project's answer is the multi-component **LEANS curriculum**: a teacher-delivered, whole-class programme for children aged 8–11, focusing on UK and Irish mainstream primary school contexts (i.e., school provision not specialised for disabled children). LEANS is freely downloadable for non-commercial use worldwide (Alcorn et al., 2022). It aims to increase pupil and teacher understanding of how differences in cognition, interaction, and sensory processing impact *everyone's* school experiences, and to promote inclusive actions and attitudes. Unlike psycho-education programmes designed for specific neurodivergent groups (e.g., Gordon et al., 2015) or professional training about individual diagnoses, LEANS is not an intervention for perceived deficits, but upskills all pupils and staff members through whole-class work focused on understanding and acceptance.

This chapter briefly describes LEANS, then discusses the ways in which it engages with concepts from the neurodiversity paradigm and emerging ideas around neurodiversity-affirmtive practice. A later section presents an edited conversation between the authors, who include the lead researcher/first author of the LEANS programme and evaluation (Alyssa) and two experienced practitioners (Amy, a primary teacher and LEANS design team member, and Alun, an educational psychologist and LEANS programme ambassador). They discuss experiences of LEANS in practice, and how neurodiversity teaching fits into a larger professional picture.

Background: The LEANS Programme

Development and Content

The LEANS programme was developed iteratively by a neurodiverse team of researchers (n = 7) and a participatory design team of educators representing professional and lived experience of neurodiversity (n = 8). Many research projects are closely specified ahead of time, but LEANS was effectively a "blank page" in terms of the type of educational resource that would be created. The design team developed and revised a plan for the content, format, and structure of the resource, as well as core definitions, key points (similar to learning objectives), and requirements for teacher guidance and activity content. An additional series of public online surveys solicited feedback on the planned resource content. These included a much larger group of neurodivergent adults, parents, educators, and members of the public (see Zahir et al., 2024). All materials, reporting, and further summary information, including the Teacher Handbook, are freely available online at https://salvesen-research.ed.ac.uk/leans.

The final LEANS programme has seven topic units:

1. Introducing neurodiversity
2. Classroom experiences, learning differences
3. Communication
4. Needs and wants, classroom supports
5. Fairness, equity
6. Friendships/relationships
7. Reflection and goal setting

Each unit uses a combination of content, including "explainer" videos that introduce key terms, hands-on activities, teacher-facilitated discussions, and stories about the tribulations and triumphs of a neurodiverse class. LEANS stories and examples stick closely to daily-life classroom situations and conflicts for this age group. For example, they tackle concerns about perceived unfairness of some pupils accessing specific supports not available to all.

Studying LEANS in Schools

Four mainstream Scottish primary schools hosted a **LEANS feasibility study** during August–December 2021 (two small rural schools, two larger urban schools), with teachers delivering the LEANS curriculum to their whole class and administering bespoke quizzes measuring knowledge of neurodiversity concepts, and children's attitudes and intended actions related to differences in their classrooms. In total, 139 children aged 8–11 years (average 9.8 years) participated in LEANS across seven classrooms; 62 of these children had parent/carer opt-in consent for their data to be used by LEANS researchers.

Broadly, findings suggested that after participating in LEANS, children could demonstrate knowledge of key concepts relating to neurodiversity and more often endorsed actions or interpretations of school situations that aligned with accepting or pro-diversity values. Pupils frequently enjoyed using the resources, and this led to concrete, actionable insights for some pupils – for example, that it can be "fair" if classmates receive differential treatment due to differing support needs (Alcorn et al., 2024).

The final iteration of the LEANS programme incorporated this pupil and teacher feedback and was released in June 2022, with 10,000-plus worldwide downloads after 26 months. Education professionals have been integral to LEANS' dissemination, locally promoting neurodiversity teaching as timely and relevant to existing priorities around inclusion, wellbeing, and diversity. Further data collection is planned to understand how and where the programme is being used in practice.

Neurodiversity Teaching as a Situated Undertaking

LEANS is *one* possible answer to the question of how we can teach about neurodiversity in primary school. It is a "situated and particular" answer, reflecting our team members' unique combination of goals and experiences, and developed in relation to schools, childhoods, and education practices as they existed in a specific time and place. For something to be situated and particular is the *opposite* of being "universal." Through the process of resource development, our team increasingly understood neurodiversity teaching and learning as *fundamentally* situated. In other words, it makes little sense to teach "general" neurodiversity content, for a "general" audience, because neurodiversity doesn't exist independently of people. While any group can be neurodiverse, that diversity (and its impact on group members) will *look different* across groups, places, and times. It is hard to go beyond dictionary definitions and convey what neurodiversity and neurodivergence are like without concrete examples that reference specific situations and groups. Teaching this situated content is, in turn, situated because learners/audiences also exist in a specific time and place (and age group!). LEANS fully embraced specificity in its narrative and interactive elements: it is about neurodiversity *within mainstream primary schools*, and its core audience is *mainstream primary pupils*. The goal is to facilitate learners' understanding of how neurodiversity is present and affects their lives *now* (whatever their neurotype), and to model possibilities for choices and changes. The essential point here for teachers is not to share neurodiversity vocabulary and then stop, because this will have very limited learning value on its own. Instead, work to engage your learners in how these new, high-level concepts apply to particular groups of people, in particular situations. What does neurodiversity *mean* for people's lives – and for them?

The Neurodiversity Paradigm in LEANS

LEANS presents the existence of human neurodiversity as a simple, non-negotiable fact. It moves on quickly to exploring *information processing* as the essential connection between biological neurodiversity and observable differences in people's learning and experiences. The programme's engagement with specific ideas from the neurodiversity paradigm (e.g., as discussed particularly in Walker, 2014) varies in overtness and degree. This was further shaped by an existing ecosystem of child-directed messaging around diversity and difference. The remainder of this section considers how the LEANS programme (teacher- and child-facing resources) engages with the following ideas:

1. Human neurodiversity occurs naturally in our population.
2. Neurodiversity is inherently valuable.
3. There is not a single "right" or "healthy" type of mind or neurocognitive processing style.
4. Neurodiversity shares social dynamics with other types of diversity.

Throughout this section, all discussion of resource items and key points is in reference to LEANS version 1.0 (Alcorn et al., 2022).

LEANS invokes the idea that **neurodiversity is "natural"** by using a woodland of mixed trees as an extended metaphor to introduce classroom neurodiversity (LEANS video 1.3). In this woodland, one group of trees forms the majority because the environment perfectly meets their needs for water, shade, etc. Other types of trees grow there, but they are minorities. Growing may be harder for them because the environment is less ideal for their needs. Neither neurotypicality nor neurodivergence should be seen as the "better," more desirable, or more useful category. To most people, trees lack strong value associations, and a willow tree is not inherently "better" or "worse" than a beech tree – they are only different, though both readily recognisable as trees. Discussing a *woodland,* rather than a park, garden, or orchard, was critical. The latter settings are planned and planted, with certain trees (i.e., types of people) deliberately selected as desirable or useful for that space, and others excluded. The woodland is an unplanned and "natural" environment where we *expect* variability and may find its absence unnerving. From the outset, LEANS encourages its users to think about human neurodiversity similarly: as something we should *expect* to encounter in our communities – it is ordinary and unsurprising.

LEANS does not directly state that **neurodiversity is inherently valuable**, though this was not a planned omission. Design team discussions focused on messaging regarding *individuals'* value, particularly the challenge of differentiating our content from generic messaging (e.g., in children's media or from schools) that all people are unique and important. This messaging isn't *bad*, but is unhelpful for engaging with nuanced, sometimes challenging information about neurodevelopment-related differences. The team also wanted to avoid narratives about valuing or celebrating neurodivergent people because they contribute "special" skills. The underlying message there is a transactional one, in which the value of "different" individuals is not inherent, but conditional on performing or contributing in socially valued ways (Venker & Lorang, 2024, unpick some of this messaging specifically in relation to children's books). Consequently, the LEANS stories deliberately avoid plots where a neurodivergent character miraculously saves the day or wins praise for an amazing talent.

Across units, LEANS spends considerable time on the concept that **there is no single "right" or "healthy" type of mind or neurocognitive processing style**. The Teacher Handbook gives very direct guidance on managing conversations where pupils or other adults equate neurodivergence with deficits, or with negative character traits, such as laziness:

> The thing to emphasise categorically here is that **there's nothing "wrong" with neurodivergent children**. They may appear different from classmates, perhaps *very* different—but being different isn't wrong or bad in itself. Neurodiversity can help us explain what we see in a way that *does not* blame individuals or ascribe negative traits, by pointing to information processing differences and differing needs.
>
> **(Teacher Handbook, p.230, emphasis in original)**

Children explore *"being different is not wrong"* messaging primarily through the LEANS stories and associated discussions. Several characters ask rude questions, call learning supports "cheating," and protest about neurodivergent classmates "getting out" of activities – *because children in the real classroom may have these questions and hear these views*. The teacher character carefully explains why these differences exist, but *are not* bad or wrong, further connecting them to concepts of support needs and equity as those units are introduced.

In development, the LEANS design team frequently explored the idea of "no single right mind" in terms of *multiple valid ways of being and doing* (e.g., communicating, solving problems). It was extremely important to neurodivergent team members that children and staff hear this message. The communication unit [#3] uses it most explicitly. For example: "different people may find it easier or harder to communicate in certain ways. All ways of communicating are useful and important, even if those ways might not be the same ones the people around me are using" (Key Point 10). The unit activities and stories seek to illustrate various communication strategies, and what it is like for these to be treated as in/valid by others.

As discussed in this book's Introduction and Walker (2014), **shared social dynamics across types of diversity** mean that neurodivergent people may face similar challenges to other minoritised or marginalised people in our society. LEANS directly talks about neurodivergent learners as a (sizeable!) minority group. The Teacher Handbook explicitly invokes a comparison with other minorities to emphasise why LEANS is a whole-class programme that particularly benefits from majority (neurotypical) participation, explaining:

> **Delivering neurodiversity teaching *only* to children with diagnoses or known support needs would be like teaching about cultural diversity *only* to children who are from minority groups in your community.** This is not to say that they would already know everything—but those lessons could effect far greater changes in perspective for children from majority groups, and be more likely to increase respect and acceptance in the classroom.
> **(Teacher Handbook, pp.20–21)**

Elsewhere, LEANS discusses school spaces and practices as the product of *deliberate choices* historically made in reference to the characteristics of a neurotypical majority. These may thus pose barriers to neurodivergent minorities, even to the point of being severely disabling or totally inaccessible. The stories highlight multiple issues of this type, particularly in relation to the sensory environment. Significantly, the stories also model examples of people *changing* environments and practices. This is the most important way LEANS engages with the "social dynamics" aspect of the neurodiversity paradigm: as the basis of **calling for change**.

LEANS and Neurodiversity-Affirmative Practice

The LEANS programme has three major goals: to change what people **know**, what they **think**, and what they **do** in the school environment. It does not, however, prescriptively tell educators how to "best" support their neurodivergent learners. It engages with neurodiversity-affirmative practice at a higher level by seeking to convince practitioners that **changes towards more affirming practice are possible and attainable** –and that knowledge and attitudes play a significant role in this transition.

Across its content, LEANS argues that **neurodiversity includes and concerns everyone.** *Every* classroom will be neurodiverse – thus, everyone has a stake in this topic, and everyone affects the environment through their knowledge, attitudes, and choices. The stories give many examples of this principle in practice. LEANS' final unit [#7] is structured around reflection and commitment to future change (e.g., revising classroom rules, goal setting). Throughout the programme, detailed teacher guidance also seeks to forestall the too common pattern in which minoritised people are implicitly or officially pressured to perform the labour of educating others, and/or to take responsibility for seeking change. For example, teacher guidance stresses a "no singling out" rule in which neurodivergent learners *should not* be called on to explain neurodivergence to classmates through disclosing their experiences (though they might volunteer to share). In scenario-discussion activities, neurodivergent pupils should not be painted as the sole problem – or solely responsible for solutions. *Everyone has a role.*

Accepting neurodiversity as everyone's concern barely scratches the surface of affirmative practice. The neurodiversity paradigm has truly radical implications because pathologisation of differences, ableism, and normalisation are deeply baked into education as we know it. Strongly neurodiversity-affirmative schools might look radically transformed. From the beginning, however, the LEANS programme has been unapologetically *un*-radical, and does not demand this kind of tear-it-all-down transformation. As a strategic choice, it seeks better school experiences within the current system. Why?

We view the best changes as being the ones that *actually happen*. Prioritising radical, systemic change may not (yet!) be helpful if it overwhelms people into inactivity. This is very possible given low baselines of neurodiversity understanding. **Right now, it *is* a meaningful change to get more schools talking about neurodiversity, and actively considering what these**

ideas mean for them. Even modest changes can meaningfully improve a neurodivergent learner's school day. A *need* for radical change doesn't preclude beneficial improvements now.

A Conversation on LEANS and Practice

In this section, chapter author and LEANS researcher Alyssa Alcorn speaks to her co-authors about their involvement with LEANS, and how neurodiversity teaching fits into their larger picture of professional practice. These conversations have been excerpted out of our wide-ranging discussions and edited for clarity and length.

Primary Teacher and LEANS Design Team Member Amy Nic Thaidhg

Amy is a mainstream primary teacher with a strong professional interest in additional support needs (ASN) and has over 15 years' experience teaching in Europe and the USA. Amy was in the original participatory design team that developed LEANS, and has delivered it in her classroom. She has also conducted original research on empathy development and LEANS.

> **Alyssa:** What was it like to use LEANS in class?
>
> **Amy:** I think the kids enjoyed it. I was teaching P5 [approximately age 9], and they were hitting the period where they were becoming a little bit more self-aware. There were kids who were *starting* to see that maybe they were a little bit different in some ways, but it wasn't yet a big thing. Therefore, you could have some really good conversations. Potentially if they were a little bit older, there maybe would have been a bit more awkwardness.
>
> I think they enjoyed the stories in particular. Every class would be able to identify with the stories in one way or the other. Once you had the stories as a basis, you could go off in multiple directions. Maybe that's just my teaching style, but the class tend to chat quite a bit and have the freedom to ask questions and discuss. So I felt LEANS was a good starter in that respect.
>
> **Alyssa:** It seems like the stories have succeeded in a fundamental way in terms of making ideas concrete for kids in this age group. I think that's a big challenge.

Amy: Sometimes I think they get the principle in a story, but actually making them connect it with themselves is the challenge. They can be very good at identifying right and wrong in a hypothetical sense, but assimilating that is another challenge. At least if they have the hypothetical awareness, it's a starting point.

Alyssa: Have you found any strategies that seemed helpful at supporting students to make those connections? Or is it just a long work-in-progress – and partly maturity?

Amy: Maturity plays an important part. Sometimes kids are at different points regarding understanding and awareness. You can have a couple of kids who are totally getting the underlying meaning and reflecting on it … and there will be others who are just seeing it as a story. They know the "right answer," but they're not seeing themselves in it. In my experience as a teacher, you have to accept that children will develop at their own pace.

Alyssa: How do you think that neurodiversity teaching, as a classroom topic, fits into the bigger picture of professional practice?

Amy: Since I started university, there's been more of an emphasis on minority rights and having respect and understanding for difference of *all* types. That can be religious differences, racial tolerance, sexual orientation, gender. Certainly, in primary school teaching, I think there was a time where you might have shied away from those topics with younger children, but with social media, children are becoming more aware of those things. You *are* having to address them. In general, the emphasis is very much on building that level of respect, acceptance, and understanding for every child, no matter who they are, and neurodiversity very much fits in with that.

Also, I think a lot of teachers are becoming more aware of what they have to do themselves. There is an understanding that there is less external support available, and so teachers are more likely to independently equip themselves to find solutions.

Alyssa: Yes, in another part of our conversation you described teachers' frontline responsibilities changing because resourcing and specialist support have changed over time. They have needed to "upskill" themselves around neurodivergence and other support needs. What do you think the impact of that has been?

Amy: People are actually seeing the bigger picture. There's huge health and wellbeing aspects to neurodiversity. It's no longer just about putting resources in place. For teachers, it's about understanding the condition itself, it's about making sure the pupil's self-esteem isn't affected by it, it's making sure that the class as a whole understands neurodivergence and they don't have any biases against it. It's part of the class, if that makes sense, as opposed to just an add-on. It becomes part of your ethos. In the same way, you could have had a child from another country and it would not be a point of discussion. These days, I think schools are more likely to go and celebrate that person's culture and make it a part of the class culture as well. Teachers will bring these differences in and make them a part of the community.

Educational Psychologist and LEANS Champion Dr Alun Flynn

Alun is an Educational Psychologist with over 40 years' experience, as well as a LEANS Champion (an official programme ambassador with specialised training, who offers support to other professionals). Here, he reflects on LEANS and neurodiversity-affirmative practice in relation to his role as Principal Educational Psychologist in Powys, Wales, UK, where he managed a team of educational psychologists working across ages and settings.

Alyssa: Why did you choose to be involved with the LEANS programme?

Alun: I've been part of improving schools' capacity to support autistic children. Fundamentally, I've tried to encourage schools to be as inclusive as possible for children who might be vulnerable. I think it's part of our role as educational psychologists to bridge between academia and practice in schools. That's what we're trained to do. We don't want to overwhelm schools with too much noise, and we want to really sustain any project work. We're selective in terms of identifying what we think will really make a difference.

I've been very thoroughly impressed by LEANS throughout, in terms of what was available publicly, and then through the Champions training. It is, of course, important to rely on work that has rigour in its research base, but also you think, "Well, what's really going to work with schools?" I saw the LEANS resource as something that was likely to be popular because it's a very practical resource that will appeal to children.

Alyssa: Do you think that there are any tensions between teaching about neurodiversity in the classroom and current professional practice or values?

Alun: No, I think it's very well aligned. We obviously have to work with what schools are expected – mandated – to deliver. They are instructed to teach about equity, diversity and the process of inclusion. A lot of the curriculum is playful and very accepting of diversity. The tension, I think, is about *expectation*. It's "Well, I've still got to get these children focused on their phonics and they've got to get to a certain level of reading by the end of Year 6," even though our Welsh curriculum is about stage rather than age.

Alyssa: I know that the LEANS Champions in Powys have been very successful at generating local interest in LEANS and neurodiversity. Do you think there are factors in your area that have contributed to people engaging?

Alun: We had backing from our senior managers, and we were fortuitous with some of the timing because of the introduction of the revised curriculum in Wales. There was a mandatory expectation of delivering this *sort* of resource. So, we emphasised that LEANS was going to be ...

Alyssa: A good investment, perhaps?

Alun: Yeah, that's right. Something that they were going to have to deliver anyway, and look! This is it. The work's been done for you, and you can just *use it*. It does take a little bit of bravery, I think, to get it going. We used our own credibility within the local authority to say, "Look, this is something that we recommend and we support."

We [Champions] ran a couple of workshops to support schools' introduction to it. It does require effort, and it's not a big effort. I think once you've got it, then you're OK and you can run with it. I think the big momentum came from the feedback from the children. I think that should drive people, really: this is something where children enjoyed participating. I think they liked the narrative style, the story aspect. They wanted to spend more time on it. They could see either something in themselves, or in children around them, or their siblings. I think it connects with quite a lot of children's lives.

Alyssa: What might be the longer-term outlook for neurodiversity teaching in Powys?

Alun: Sustainability is a big issue, and I think we've always tried to emphasise that this programme has some longevity and we're not going to suggest something new next week.

A lot of our schools are quite small, and they share quite a lot about what they're doing. I think there's nothing more successful than success. When they are saying "Actually, I've started delivering this, and this is the reaction I'm getting," that promotes momentum and a culture of acceptance. We hoped that as schools got the experience of running LEANS, they wouldn't necessarily need more workshops from us [Champions]. The schools are encouraged to work in clusters, so they could learn from each other. We would continue to support and encourage in whichever way we could, but I would hope that there would be a culture that could be maintained within each cluster.

Alyssa: That's an issue to work on – not only to get people interested in neurodiversity teaching the first time, but to make longer-term commitments.

Alun: I did think LEANS sort of hit the nail on the head. You think, "If not this, then what? If you're not doing this, then ... why not? And what else are you doing?" We try to be very supportive of schools, but I'll also try to challenge them from time to time: "So why aren't you doing this work?"

Conclusion

As noted earlier, the LEANS programme is *one* possible answer, or strategy, for teaching about neurodiversity in primary schools. The fact that the programme is being adopted following its public release suggests that the design team's choices have been successful in a fundamental way: LEANS is reaching schools and educators, who may now be engaging with neurodiversity concepts for the first time. The strategic choice to focus on improvement within the existing education system has also potentially been important in making this topic feasible and acceptable. Amy noted that LEANS being a ready-made package can be an important "safety net" for teachers new to the topic, or where it's perceived as contentious – like the way sex and relationships education might be packaged.

Feedback about children's personal connections to, and engagement with, the story content (from Amy, Alun, and others) has been an important endorsement of the situated teaching strategy. Many – though not all – participating children see neurodiversity as *about them and their class*. However, a downside of this situatedness is that it limits a given teaching programme's applicability – a problem when demand for resources is high and new development requires significant investment. Future design teams may face hard trade-offs between resource-specificity and audience size. A less specific, less situated neurodiversity resource runs the risk of not connecting with audience members (nor motivating them to change). As others pose future "answers" to what neurodiversity teaching can be like for different audiences, we would encourage them to continue LEANS' focus on action, not only improving knowledge. The goal remains to make education better for neurodivergent learners – and all learners.

Key Takeaways

Approach this task as *situated*. Neurocognitive diversity and its implications won't look the same for every group of people. Clearly identify your reference group – and your learners. Specificity can be a strength in connecting people to the content.

- Don't just tell your learners that neurodiversity includes them and that their actions impact others – work to *convince* them this is true, and illustrate what types of actions you are talking about.
- Be aware of how neurodiversity content might reinforce, contradict, or interact with existing messaging in your setting (e.g., about diversity, difference, disability, who or what is valuable).
- Linking neurodiversity to existing school-level and education policy goals can facilitate buy-in from leaders, staff, and the community.
- Consider long-term sustainability, and the role of shared professional cultures and practices in promoting neurodiversity-affirmative education.

Reflective Activities

Especially if you are new to integrating neurodiversity concepts into your professional practice, self-reflection can be an important tool in getting started. What are your relationships and decision making like now – and what do you aspire to change? Alun and Amy independently highlighted **staff-learner interactions** as central to neurodiversity-affirmative classrooms. Each author has offered a reflective question in this area.

Alyssa: LEANS guidance stresses that school staff are constantly modelling attitudes toward diversity – *and pupils are learning*. Are differences *really* accepted or valued, or do adults teach one thing while their actions signal something else?

What neurodiversity-related attitudes might I be modelling through my language and interactions with others, including interactions with other adults?

Amy: Everyone remembers the "good teacher" that they have. You have to try to *be* that good teacher, the person that your students remember fondly, that they remember believed in them. Everyone needs that.

How do I think my students will remember me, especially students with a different neurotype to mine? Why?

Alun: Professional training around special needs can often be labelled, rather than focusing on making classrooms inclusive. In education, we should try to be needs-focused as opposed to being "led by the label."

When I interact with a learner or make planning decisions in my setting, to what extent am I being led by diagnostic labels, versus knowledge of individuals' needs? Why?

References

Alcorn, A. M., Fletcher-Watson, S., McGeown, S., Murray, F., Aitken, D., Peacock, L. J. J., & Mandy, W. (2022). *Learning about neurodiversity at school: A resource pack for primary school teachers and pupils*. University of Edinburgh. https://salvesen-research.ed.ac.uk/leans

Alcorn, A. M., McGeown, S., Mandy, W., Aitken, D., & Fletcher-Watson, S. (2024). Learning about neurodiversity at school: A feasibility study of a new classroom programme for mainstream primary schools. *Neurodiversity, 2*. https://doi.org/10.1177/27546330241272186

Gordon, K., Murin, M., Baykaner, O., Roughan, L., Livermore-Hardy, V., Skuse, D., & Mandy, W. (2015). A randomised controlled trial of PEGASUS, a psychoeducational programme for young people with high-functioning autism spectrum disorder. *Journal of Child Psychology and Psychiatry, 56*(4), 468–476.

Ostaszewska, A., & Harper, G. (2024, March 24). *Top 10 priorities for research on neurodivergence*. Embracing Complexity. https://embracingcomplexity.org.uk/reports/top-10-research-priorities

Venker, C. E., & Lorang, E. (2024). A commentary on children's books about autism: What messages do they send about neurodiversity? *Autism Research, 17*(3), 452–458. https://doi.org/10.1002/aur.3081

Walker, N. (2014). *Neurodiversity: Some basis terms & definitions*. Neuroqueer. https://neuroqueer.com/neurodiversity-terms-and-definitions/

Zahir, R., Alcorn, A. M., McGeown, S., Mandy, W., Aitken, D., Murray, F., & Fletcher-Watson, S. (2024). Short report: Evaluation of wider community support for a neurodiversity teaching programme designed using participatory methods. *Autism, 28*(6), 1582–1590. https://doi.org/10.1177/13623613231211046

13

Empowering Neurodivergent Young People

Insights from a School-Based Peer Support Initiative

Francesca Fotheringham, Katie Barrowman, and Justine Young

Neurodivergent Young People in Mainstream Schools

Difficulties in School

While some neurodivergent young people (NdYP) have positive experiences attending mainstream school, many NdYP can find school tricky. Some commonly reported difficulties include building and maintaining peer relationships (Fink et al., 2015; Hoza, 2007) and feeling separate from the school community (Hebron, 2018). In turn, these experiences contribute to reduced feelings of wellbeing, self-efficacy, and self-confidence, and higher levels of social anxiety (Cooper et al., 2017; Cooper et al., 2023). When coupled with the social, emotional, physical, and hormonal changes experienced through adolescence, NdYP frequently find the school environment particularly challenging.

Masking and Camouflaging

"Masking" refers to the idea that some neurodivergent people hide or minimise traits they think might be seen as different to neurotypical norms. In a school setting, this can mean that a student may try to hide sensory sensitivities or suppress regulatory behaviours such as stimming. "Camouflaging," on the other hand, refers to the act of blending in to appear neurotypical. In a school setting, this can mean trying to imitate complex social cues that they don't fully understand, trying to mimic facial expressions, or rehearsing scripts for conversations. Masking and camouflaging are more than just shifting how you present in a different setting – it can be how someone appears all the time. In short, NdYP may appear to be coping well in school, but internally, due to the pressure of maintaining the facade, they may be struggling and need support.

When neurodivergent people mask and camouflage to avoid standing out, we know that there are many negative consequences for doing this, with research suggesting that continual masking and camouflaging can lead to increased stress and mental health difficulties, burnout, identity loss, and even suicidality (Radulski, 2022; Miller et al., 2021).

The Role of Identity

As educators, we work with many young people who want to avoid openly identifying as neurodivergent. One reason for this stems from a fear of "being found out," which can have a detrimental effect on anxiety and mental health among NdYP (Pearson & Rose, 2021; Samoilis, 2021). It can also make it difficult for NdYP to choose which social groups to identify with (or not). Dr Theresa Kidd (a researcher and clinical psychologist) recounts working alongside an NdYP who described having a "school self" and a "true self" – demonstrating the extent to which they were masking.

Additionally, a higher proportion of autistic young people identify as non-binary, non-heteronormative, and as part of the LGBTQ+ community (Dewinter et al., 2017), which can be an additional source of anxiety and social exclusion, potentially leading to further masking. However, this is not a cause of stress for everyone, as Kidd (2022) coined the term "Double Rainbow" to describe the support often derived from both communities (neurodivergent and LGBTQ+), acting as a positive protective factor and contributing to increased feelings of resilience.

Social challenges faced by NdYP can have a knock-on effect on academic experiences. The classroom and school can be a stressful and difficult environment for our neurodivergent learners, which can lead to higher absenteeism. Suggested factors contributing to this include higher incidences of somatic symptoms, school anxiety, mental health difficulties, and environmental stresses. Yet, under Scottish law, the 'Getting It Right For Every Child' policy (GIRFEC, 2012) sets legal precedence for educational equality. However, as indicated, the distinct ways neurodivergent learners perceive and react to school environments highlight the fact that we are not currently meeting the needs of every learner. Consequently, many parents/carers are bearing the burden of this gap for us.

Support for Neurodivergent Young People

The Deficit Model of Neurodiversity and Its Shortcomings

Historically, deficit-based narratives around NdYP suggested that they often struggle in school (and society) due to a lack of understanding of social skills. As a result, many well-meaning programmes and initiatives have tried to help NdYP to navigate their school experiences by attempting to "fix" or "normalise" the child, teaching NdYP to communicate and socialise in a neurotypical manner. This perpetuates the harmful misconception that neurodivergent people have a communication deficit, and in turn, assumes a lack of capacity for understanding communication (Milton, 2014).

This can leave NdYP feeling anxious, infantilised, and lonely. Yet as the Double Empathy Problem outlines (see Chapter 7), there is often a breakdown in communication between autistic people and neurotypical people due to their different experiences of navigating the world. This difficulty is *bidirectional* – meaning that difficulties are seen in both neurotypical and neurodivergent people, rather than a neurodivergent-specific communication deficit (e.g., Milton, 2023). As Milton argues, communication is a mutually negotiated construct embedded in context (Milton, 2014, Milton et al., 2022), and "participatory sense-making" would be a better framework for the neurodivergent experience than the deficit model, as it emphasises that social interaction is not individual, but joint sense-making (De Jaegher, 2023).

Overview of Traditional Supports and Efforts in Schools

As educators, we understand that schools are not only there to teach subject knowledge, but also to help young people to thrive on their terms and to provide relevant support for all students. Schools use a range of methods to support NdYP, such as flexible learning arrangements, Individualised Education Plans, pupil support assistants (also known as teaching assistants), sensory spaces, and specialised quiet areas. One of the authors' schools also provides social opportunities in the form of social groups for autistic students aged 11–12, to help with the transition into secondary school and as a way to meet other NdYP who may be experiencing similar challenges. In another of the authors' schools, staff strive to provide safe spaces for NdYP – for example, identifying pupils who were often excluded from school trips and organising alternative day trips with opportunities to build/strengthen relationships between peers.

Anecdotally, many NdYP in these spaces find their community in staff-led groups and clubs formed around shared interests, be that the chess club, LGBTQ+ groups, art clubs, role-playing or drama groups, and so on. Yet while these groups are excellent in terms of allowing young people to find each other and bond over shared interests, the focus is not explicitly around exploring their neurodivergence and what that means for them, so there is still a gap in the support offered for NdYP in school settings.

From the experiences of the authors, schools that *have* provided support groups for NdYP are predominantly run by staff who are not neurodivergent themselves and often have little to no input from NdYP in terms of the format of these sessions. Groups tend to focus on overcoming so-called "barriers" that neurodivergence presents and "coping" strategies that NdYP could use. While these groups are a step in the right direction, they often fail to offer opportunities for young people to have agency over their school experience that would allow them to thrive in school and be their authentic selves.

Shifting Towards Peer-Led, Student-Centred Models

The academic theory known as "collective self-esteem" suggests that identifying with a positively evaluated social group enhances feelings of social identity (Luhtanen & Crocker, 1991) and that the attributes of their social group influence an individual's self-concept. If NdYP were in a supportive friendship group that was also positively seen by other friendship groups, NdYP could see their neurodivergence as more positive, which helps promote self-acceptance and mitigate negative psychological outcomes (Cooper et al., 2017). This links to the NEST (NEurodivergent peer Support Toolkit) project, as it provides the space for NdYP to build friendships in a supportive and non-judgemental environment whilst having the scaffolding of a staff member for them to feel socially safe and secure. This links to the student-led nature of NEST, where the activity is "done with" rather than the traditional well-intentioned teacher-led supports which are "done to" NdYP.

In recent years, collective self-esteem has become more of an accessible protective factor for NdYP. One stereotype that was often associated with being NdYP is that they would be an outsider or loner, perhaps due to the differences in social understanding and interactions that often accompany neurodivergence. The idea of a support group may have seemed strange, as the understanding at the time was that these learners would not necessarily want or be able to take part in a group where social interaction and discussion were essential. However, as more young people were understood to be neurodivergent, what was once perceived as discomfort around social interaction was instead seen as a discomfort around the expectation that their social interaction should mirror that of their neurotypical peers.

Peer Support

Peer support is not a new concept, and has been used by many schools to help support various students (Houlston et al., 2009). Often this has functioned where a student from the "minority group" is "buddied" with a student from the "majority group." Therefore, within the context of neurodiversity, a neurodivergent student would be "buddied" with a neurotypical student (e.g., Carter et al., 2014, 2017; Hochman et al., 2015). However, this can often make NdYP feel that they need to learn how to mask and behave in a more neurotypical way. However, in a recent study where interviews were conducted with neurodivergent school leavers, many reported feeling better understood by other neurodivergent students (see Crompton et al., 2022). This directly contradicts previous ways of thinking, and highlights that NdYP have leadership and empathy skills to support other neurodivergent students.

Moreover, neurodivergent school leavers identified that opportunities for neurodivergent-specific peer support would have been highly beneficial in school (Crompton et al., 2022) and that the ideal school peer support would cater for all neurodivergent students rather than neuro-specific support. This deems the peer support intervention acceptable for NdYP as it values and gives weight to their voice and is considered an appropriate intervention by them, allowing for the intervention to be student-led (for further reading, see the UN Convention on the Rights of the Child, Assembly, 1989, Article 12; SEND Code of Practice, Department for Education & Department of Health, 2015).

Being given the space and opportunity for neurodivergent-specific peer support could help NdYP develop socially, emotionally, and academically, help combat social isolation, and build and maintain friendships with people who have common experiences and values (see Houlston et al., 2009). Peer support can be personalised to the group/community, is cost-effective, helps those attending to develop their identity, and increases academic self-efficacy, self-confidence, and feelings of belonging (Crompton et al., 2022).

Considering all the above, this is why the Neurodivergent Peer Support Toolkit, or NEST project, was created. From the onset, this project was intended to be a support created for and with NdYP. NdYP were there from the beginning, from the support being requested by NdYP to when NEST was being designed, and now, when various schools have piloted and evaluated NEST. The corresponding handbook is derived from the ideas and voice of the NdYP. Below is a brief explanation of how it was created and what's included.

The NEST Project

Designing the NEST Handbook

The NEST project used a co-design approach (for an overview of co-design, see Zamenopoulos & Alexiou, 2018; Brandsen & Honingh, 2018). In this case, input from NdYP and adults working with NdYP in the steering groups were equally valid to the researchers when designing the toolkit. This approach was used to ensure any design incorporated the views and perspectives of the NdYP community. Two co-design teams were recruited. The first was a young researcher group which comprised eight NdYP aged 13–15 years who had attended a mainstream high school in Scotland. The second was a team of nine adults who currently worked with NdYP. The group had a variety of professional backgrounds, including speech and language therapists, primary and secondary school teachers, and working for a charity that provided support and resources for NdYP and their families. Many of the members of this co-design team were also parents of NdYP, as well as being neurodivergent themselves. This meant that as the main researcher on the project, Francesca

Fotheringham could be confident that any peer support programme devised was firstly what the NdYP community wanted, and secondly could practically work in schools.

Francesca met each of the co-design teams six times over the summer of 2022. Whilst the meetings had a loose agenda, the researchers went into the project with no preconceptions as to what such an intervention "should" or "could" look like. She met the groups separately to minimise any feelings of hierarchy and inadequacy and to ensure that the voices and desires of the NdYP were maximised. To create cohesion between teams, ideas from discussions would be cross-pollinated between the teams. Interestingly, the young persons' team was more solution-focused in their discussions, while the adult team was more global and reflective. For example, when discussing safety in a peer support group, the adults spent a significant amount of time discussing the creation of a school environment where both the young people and staff felt emotionally safe and what this meant, whereas the young people set out a behaviour management plan they thought would be appropriate if any young person in the group broke confidentiality or hurt others (physically or emotionally). This allowed for the young persons' solution-focused ideas to be suggested to the adult team, and for reflective discussion points from the adult team to be presented to the young people. For example, the meetings discussed the practicalities of how to run a peer support group, such as when and where it should take place, how it should be organised, what would happen at the group, as well as how to build self-advocacy, wellbeing, school belonging, and identity. All of these have become sections in the NEST downloadable handbook (https://salvesen-research.ed.ac.uk/download-nest). Based on the discussions, the handbook was drafted and sent to the co-design groups for feedback before it was finalised and sent to four schools to be piloted. For further details on how the intervention came about and on the co-design teams, see Fotheringham et al., (2023).

What's Included in the NEST Handbook?

The NEST handbook is intended for readers with any level of understanding of neurodiversity to set up a peer support group in their school. It explains that the goal of the peer support group is not to teach neurotypical social norms, but to help foster a safe, supportive, and non-judgemental space for NdYP to support one another.

The NEST handbook outlines a weekly lunchtime or after-school club that any neurodivergent student could choose to attend. It was important to the young people not to have a mandatory list of neurodivergent students who were expected to attend. To cater to a diverse range of needs, the co-design teams suggested that schools alternate between an unscheduled "hang out" session and scheduled activities for the peer support group. The unscheduled sessions provide a safe space away from other groups and crowds and allow students breathing space to decompress, be on their phones, or build and maintain friendships without any judgement or pressure to socialise. The role of the adult facilitator, most likely a teacher or member of support staff, would be to organise access to the space where the sessions take place, guide the group when needed, and take their lead from the interests and needs of the group, rather than following their own pre-set agenda.

For the scheduled sessions, the co-design team suggested a variety of activities, which were grouped into four main topics in the downloadable handbook:

i. **Fun:** Activities such as watching movies, playing board or role-playing games, and designing logos.
ii. **Knowledge Building:** Activities like learning about neurodiversity, study tips for neurodivergent learners, and inviting speakers from within or outside the school.
iii. **School Community:** Activities include organising assemblies, raising money for charity, and advocating for a more neurodivergent-friendly school environment.
iv. **Policy:** Activities such as challenging school rules or codes of conduct to be more inclusive, lobbying MPs/MSPs, and discussing legislation relevant to NdYP.

Importantly, the NEST handbook encourages schools to create activities tailored to their unique community and the interests of the students attending the group.

An aspect that was important to the co-design teams (particularly to the young persons' team) was working with allies and neurotypical students. The handbook outlines that, when appropriate and by invitation only, neurotypical students should also learn about neurodivergence and how NdYP think, feel, and process the world, by attending sessions organised by the NdYP. This can be either within the peer support group time or at a separate session, like an assembly. This inclusion is crucial as everyone will eventually work with or befriend someone who is neurodivergent, and understanding neurodivergence and neurodiversity is essential so as not to widen the chasm between the groups. By inviting neurotypical students to learn about neurodivergence, this initiative could alleviate some of the challenges NdYP face in school, benefiting future generations.

Piloting the NEST Handbook

NEST was piloted in four schools across Scotland in the academic year 2022/3. The schools varied in rurality/urbanity, school size, and average Scottish Index of Multiple Deprivation (SIMD, 2020), and interventions already in place (such as some of the schools were already recognised Nurture Schools) to investigate how the toolbox package could work in different scenarios. The member of staff who would be facilitating the group was given the NEST package and asked to use it however they felt fit. This was so the research team could assess if NEST was interpreted as intended by school staff and evaluate how it could be adapted for a variety of different school settings. Below is a summary of how each of the four schools adapted NEST to suit their school setting.

School 1

School 1 approached the research team to participate in the NEST initiative after a student became aware of the project. The senior leadership team recognised the various challenges many of their NdYP experienced, and had invested effort in cultivating strong relationships with these young people. Therefore, they were keen to establish accessible support that would not overburden their staff, whilst providing researched benefits for their learners.

School 1 adopted an inclusive approach by extending the invitation to all NdYP across the entire school. Their underlying philosophy was to ensure that no student was excluded, and to accommodate those who identified as neurodivergent, with or without a formal diagnosis. This approach resulted in 20–30 students from across the school, attending each week. This was the group with the highest level of participation, presenting both challenges and advantages. For example, managing a larger group with diverse needs and personalities was more complex. However, it also facilitated opportunities for students to connect with peers from different parts of the school, reinforcing the notion that they were not alone. This inclusivity further demonstrated to the students that neurodiversity manifests in various forms.

School 2

Like many schools, School 2's empty classrooms were sought out by NdYP during breaktimes as a haven away from the bustling dining hall. Lunch clubs such as LGBTQ+, film, book, and the school magazine team were well attended by NdYP. However, solitary NdYP sitting in darkened rooms were still a familiar sight, indicating that there was still a gap in the support needed for NdYP. A young person at School 2 had taken part in the co-design of the NEST project and asked their pupil support department to take part in the pilot. School 2 chose to invite a group of 15 NdYP over a range of S1–S6 who had already accessed the pupil support department to set up and take part in the NEST Peer Support group. This decision was made due to negative dynamics between some students at the time. Opening the group to all initially could have discouraged quieter students, who would benefit from participating. It was anticipated that the group could potentially grow as the core pupils became more established and comfortable. Whilst some younger students already attended a social group with an autism outreach specialist, the NEST group was made up of NdYP from across all school years. The mix of age groups proved successful, with activities decided collectively, providing opportunities to build friendships. The group created their name and designed a logo, which was used as part of the school's Autism Awareness event. The most successful aspect of the NEST group was when older students shared with the younger ones their experiences of navigating transitions and finding the support they needed.

School 3

School 3 was keen to be involved as the young people had identified support for NdYP as a gap in the support offered across the school. Young people (including NdYP) were active in other areas of the equalities, including the Anti-Racist Society and the LGBTQ+ Club. Yet they expressed the need for a place where exploring and celebrating neurodiversity was the focus. The desire to add this to the school's "safer and braver spaces" meant that the opportunity for the school to take part in the project was both timely and necessary.

The lead staff member advertised the group in a range of ways, including:

- Posters around the school
- A PowerPoint slide on a big screen in the canteen area
- A short presentation delivered to all Personal and Social Education classes
- A text home to all parents

School 3 identified a room in a quiet corridor with dimmable lighting and soft furnishings, and the timing (Monday lunchtimes) was determined by staff availability. The uptake was modest, but the group remained stable throughout the school year. Through the NEST club, soon renamed by the members, NdYP were able to find a sense of community and belonging in a space that they felt ownership over, and with trusted adults supporting their aims. The feeling of being among peers who valued what they valued was greatly appreciated. The group decided to alternate each week between a play-based activity and raising awareness of neurodiversity, which worked well for engagement and kept the young people returning.

School 4

School 4 had invested considerable time and resources into developing supportive resources and spaces, and training staff for the benefit of their NdYP, who represented a disproportionate number of the enrolled students compared to other Scottish high schools. Their involvement in the NEST pilot was motivated by a commitment to incorporating the latest research to support all students effectively, as the school ethos is to utilise this research to best understand how to meet all students' needs.

Initially, School 4 took the approach of only inviting those who had previously engaged in the learning support department. Recognising the need for broader inclusion, the school later advertised the neurodiversity peer support group schoolwide. Unlike School 1, this approach did not result in a large turnout; however, this broad dissemination was highly beneficial, as it provided staff and students with a greater understanding of the neurodiversity paradigm and movement.

Challenges to Consider from the Pilot Schools

Overall, all the schools that participated in the NEST pilot encountered challenges during the year. Firstly, finding a suitable space for sessions was difficult as many schools are already space-poor. Several schools had existing safe spaces with adjustable lighting, various seating options, and areas where pupils would not be interrupted. Initially, some schools used these spaces for the peer support group, but this caused issues for students who needed the safe space but did not want to attend the group. Changing the space for the NEST group was problematic for many attending students, especially when schools needed to rearrange their spaces and classrooms.

Decisions on how to set up the peer support group presented further challenges. Staff had to choose whether to invite only those known to the department, invite those who would benefit most, or open it to all interested pupils. Staff deliberated the pros and cons of each option, such as excluding some pupils, missing those silently struggling or undiagnosed, or creating a large group with potentially conflicting personalities, overwhelming sensory stimuli, and overcrowding. The right setup and a consistent room were crucial to avoid conflicts between students and to ensure smooth operation. Some students struggled with the disconnect between their desired group dynamics and the code of conduct, and managing their own behaviours and emotions, thus finding the student-led nature of the group destabilising.

Another challenge was the natural rhythm of the school year. Key pressure periods, such as prelims and exam diets, and school strikes coincided with the pilot. This inconsistency affected students' perception of the peer support's reliability, leading to fluctuating attendance across all schools. This made it difficult and added workload to staff facilitators in planning and organising activities without knowing who would attend. Consequently, some senior leadership teams were concerned about the additional pressure on staff time, especially as facilitators often gave up their lunch breaks, impacting their wellbeing.

Finally, students had excellent ideas for activities, but these presented challenges for staff facilitators. The additional staff workload and students' difficulties in actualising their plans and providing necessary information hindered progress. For instance, one group wanted to produce a podcast but struggled to find time to plan and record episodes, while another wanted a cycle ride but struggled to provide information about their cycling experience. Time constraints were another barrier, with one school having only a 35-minute lunch break, making progress on their ideas slow, only meeting weekly. One of the authors leading their group pondered that dedicating more time, potentially from curricular time, would benefit not only the group members but all NdYP in the school, but this would bring its own challenges in terms of finding a suitable time to take young people out of lessons without impacting on learning progress, and adding pupil contact time to a staff member's day, which could impact time available to teaching lessons or planning and preparation.

Success Stories from the Pilot Schools

The pilot schools found the NEST project beneficial for their students and school community. Many staff facilitators and students noted key improvements in their wellbeing, such as building friendships, increasing self-confidence, and finding a safe space.

Students reported that the peer support group helped them feel less alone in their neurodivergent experience of school. By bonding over shared experiences, students formed relationships with other NdYP, sometimes for the first time. These friendships extended into other areas of school life, with staff facilitators enjoying observing students greeting each other in corridors and playing together during breaks. This social integration positively impacted their wellbeing and confidence. Students reported that their high school experience became more enjoyable compared to primary school, as they now had friends who understood them, enhancing their confidence through a supportive network where they could be themselves. One staff facilitator remarked on the pleasure of witnessing students becoming relaxed and playful. Older students enjoyed mentoring roles within the group, seeing their efforts as improving the school experience for future NdYP. Meanwhile, younger attendees benefited from observing older students' successes, learning from their experiences.

One of the groups found particular pleasure in being able to freely and openly talk about all the aspects of being NdYP. There was certainly discussion around the challenges that being neurodivergent brings to life, particularly school life, but refreshingly, the group spent more time discussing all the ways in which their neurodivergence enhanced their lives and brought them joy – the fact they recognised these feelings in each other added to the positivity and strengthened the bonds that were already forming between group members.

Students appreciated the peer support group for its student-led nature, feeling ownership and comfort in suggesting ideas. They valued being heard and not directed by adults, aligning with Article 12 of the UN Convention on the Rights of the Child (Assembly, 1989), which emphasises giving weight to students' views. The group provided a safe space away from neurotypical expectations, with understanding staff. This sense of ownership, inclusion, and being listened to made the group enjoyable and fun for many students, highlighting the importance of continuing the peer support group.

For further details on piloting NEST and to hear about experiences from staff and students, please see Crompton et al. (2024).

Key Takeaways

Although each group was unique, there were some key points on which the groups agreed when thinking about what would help make a successful group:

- Have a fixed location – predictability and consistency in this can help create a safer and braver space where young people can open up.
- Have a mix of ages to offer experiential support.
- Make sure the group has adequate time to meet and see through any ideas.
- Carefully balance selecting a smaller core group to avoid negative dynamics and overwhelming members, while advertising broadly to include any unidentified NdYP.
- Ask colleagues to promote the group, as this creates a shared sense of the importance of understanding neurodiversity – for example, having the group advertised by teachers in form classes or Personal and Social Education classes can help young people find their way to the groups and understand more about them before joining.
- Try to have a small team of staff (or responsible older pupils) involved, to share workload and to ensure the group can continue during staff absences.
- Consider having neurodivergent staff members as part of the facilitator team, as lived experience trumps any training.
- The group must, at its heart, be for and about the young people – you must be prepared to be led by them as far as possible.

Reflective Activities

- What support does your school offer for neurodivergent young people?
- What do you know about how your neurodivergent young people feel about the support they get in school?
- Do you think that a neurodivergent-specific peer support group like NEST could benefit your school community? And why?
- How could your neurodivergent young people have more of a voice within your school community?

Acknowledgements

The authors would like to express their sincere thanks to their collaborators on this project:

- All the staff and young people at the four schools who took part in the pilot of the NEST project
- Those who were in the adult co-design team: Harriet Axbey, Carrie Watts, Elliot Spaeth, Rose Bangs, Natalie, Victor, and three other team members
- The eight young people who were in the NdYP co-design team
- Others who were in the research team: Sue Fletcher-Watson, Katie Cebula, Sarah Foley, Charlotte Webber, Catherine Crompton
- The funders of the project: the Salvesen Mindroom Research Centre

References

Assembly, U. G. (1989). Convention on the rights of the child. *United Nations, Treaty Series, 1577*(3), 1–23.

Brandsen, T., & Honingh, M. (2018). Definitions of co-production and co-creation. In *Co-production and co-creation* (pp. 9–17). Routledge.

Carter, E. W., Asmus, J. M., & Moss, C. K. (2014). Peer support interventions to support inclusive schools. In R. L. Villa, J. S. Thousand, W. R. Stainback, & S. Stainback (Eds.), *Handbook of effective inclusive schools:* Research and practice (pp. 377–409). New York: Routledge.

Carter, E. W., Gustafson, J. R., Sreckovic, M. A., Dykstra Steinbrenner, J. R., Pierce, N. P., Bord, A., Stabel, A., Rogers, S., Czerw, A., & Mullins T. (2017). Efficacy of peer support interventions in general education classrooms for high school students with autism spectrum disorder. *Remedial and Special Education, 38*(4), 207–221. https://doi.org/10.1177/0741932516672067

Cooper, K., Smith, L. G., & Russell, A. (2017). Social identity, self-esteem, and mental health in autism. *European Journal of Social Psychology, 47*(7), 844–854. https://doi.org/10.1002/ejsp.2297

Cooper, K., Russell, A. J., Lei, J., & Smith, L. G. (2023). The impact of a positive autism identity and autistic community solidarity on social anxiety and mental health in autistic young people. *Autism, 27*(3), 848–857.

Crompton, C. J., Fotheringham, F., Cebula, K., Webber, C., Foley, S., & Fletcher-Watson, S. (2024). Neurodivergent-designed and neurodivergent-led peer support in school: A feasibility and acceptability study of the neurodivergent peer support toolkit (NEST). *Neurodiversity, 2*, 27546330241275248.

Crompton, C. J., Hallett, S., McAuliffe, C., Stanfield, A. C., & Fletcher-Watson, S. (2022). 'A group of fellow travellers who understand': Interviews with autistic people about post-diagnostic peer support in adulthood. *Frontiers in Psychology, 13*, 831628.

De Jaegher, H. (2023). Seeing and inviting participation in autistic interactions. *Transcultural Psychiatry, 60*(5), 852–865.

Department for Education, & Department of Health. (2015). Special educational needs and disability code of practice: 0 to 25 years. https://assets.publishing.service.gov.uk/government/uploads/system/uploads/attachment_data/file/398815/SEND_Code_of_Practice_January_2015.pdf

Dewinter, J., De Graaf, H., & Begeer, S. (2017). Sexual orientation, gender identity, and romantic relationships in adolescents and adults with autism spectrum disorder. *Journal of Autism and Developmental Disorders, 47*, 2927–2934.

Fink, E. et al., (2015). Assessing the bullying and victimisation experiences of children with special educational needs in mainstream schools: Development and validation of the bullying behaviour and experience scale. *Res Developmental Disabilities, 36*, 611–619.

Fotheringham, F., Cebula, K., Fletcher-Watson, S., Foley, S., & Crompton, C. J. (2023). Co-designing a neurodivergent student-led peer support programme for neurodivergent young people in mainstream high schools. *Neurodiversity, 1*, 27546330231205770.

GIRFEC, Scottish Government. A Guide to Getting It Right for Every Child. Edinburgh, United Kingdom: Scottish Government; 2012.

Hebron, J. S. (2018). School connectedness and the primary to secondary school transition for young people with autism spectrum conditions. *British Journal of Educational Psychology, 88*(3), 396–409

Hochman, J. M., Carter, E. W., Bottema-Beutel, K., Harvey, M. N., & Gustafson, J. R. (2015). Efficacy of peer networks to increase social connections among high school students with and without autism spectrum disorder. *Exceptional Children, 82*(1), 96–116. https://doi.org/10.1177/0014402915585482

Houlston C., Smith P. K., & Jessel J. (2009). Investigating the extent and use of peer support initiatives in English schools. *Educational Psychology, 29*(3), 325–344. https://doi.org/10.1080/01443410902926751

Hoza, B. (2007). Peer functioning in children with ADHD. *Journal of Pediatric Psychology, 32*(6), 655–663.

Kidd, T. (2022). *Helping autistic teens to manage their anxiety: Strategies and worksheets using CBT, DBT, and ACT skills*. London: Jessica Kingsley Publishers.

Luhtanen, R., & Crocker, J. (1991). Self-esteem and intergroup comparisons: Toward a theory of collective self-esteem. In J. Suls & T. A. Wills (Eds.), *Social comparison: Contemporary theory and research* (pp. 211–234). Hillsdale: Lawrence Erlbaum Associates, Inc.

Miller, D., Rees, J., & Pearson, A. (2021). 'Masking is life': Experiences of masking in autistic and nonautistic adults. *Autism in Adulthood, 3*(4), 330–338.

Milton, D. (2014). So what exactly are autism interventions intervening with?. *Good Autism Practice (GAP), 15*(2), 6–14.

Milton, D., Gurbuz, E., & López, B. (2022). The 'double empathy problem': Ten years on. *Autism, 26*(8), 1901–1903.

Milton, D., Waldock, K. E., & Keates, N. (2023). Autism and the 'double empathy problem'. In *Conversations on empathy: Interdisciplinary perspectives on empathy, imagination and othering* (pp. 78–97). Taylor and Francis.

Pearson, A., & Rose, K. (2021). A conceptual analysis of autistic masking: Understanding the narrative of stigma and the illusion of choice. *Autism in Adulthood, 3*(1), 52–60.

Radulski, E. M. (2022). Conceptualising autistic masking, camouflaging, and neurotypical privilege: Towards a minority group model of neurodiversity. *Human Development, 66*(2), 113–127.

Samoilis, G. (2021). 'It's like a disguise': Experiences of peer relationships and social camouflaging of autistic adolescent boys: An IPA analysis (Doctoral dissertation, London Metropolitan University).

Scottish Index of Multiple Deprivation. (2020). Scottish index of multiple deprivation 2020. Retrieved from https://simd.scot/#/simd2020/BTTTFTT/9/-4.0000/55.9000/

Zamenopoulos, T., & Alexiou, K. (2018). *Co-design as collaborative research*. Bristol University/AHRC Connected Communities Programme.

14

Islands of Safety
The Importance of Non-Teacher-Educators in Curating Felt Safety for Autistic Children and Young People

Kieran Rose

Into the Storm

The roar of the wind and the crash of the waves are deafening as the storm bears down upon me. I'm submerged in icy darkness, saltwater filling my mouth and nose. My limbs flail wildly as I struggle to the surface, tossed about like a rag doll by the relentless sea. Each wave crashes over me with brutal force, slamming high and low, turning around and around, spinning violently, unable to tell which way is up or down.

Panic claws at my throat.

The water is cold, numbing my fingers and toes as I fight to keep my head above the surface. My clothes cling to me, heavy and sodden, pulling me down with every frantic kick. It feels like cold hands are clawing and tugging at me, pulling me lower and lower.

The salt burns my eyes, the taste of the ocean bitter and unforgiving. The storm's fury is unrelenting, the sky an angry black, the sea a merciless, churning beast.

I gasp for air, each breath stolen by the next crashing wave, filling my lungs with more seawater than oxygen. My heart pounds in my chest, each beat a desperate plea for survival. My muscles scream in protest, exhaustion setting in as I struggle to stay afloat.

The waves, mocking my efforts, their sheer power overwhelming my small frame.

Time loses all meaning. Minutes, hours, they all blur together in a haze of fear and fatigue. My strength is waning, every kick and stroke weaker than the last. The relentless cold seeps into my bones, sapping what little energy I have left. The ocean's roar deafening, a cacophony of crashing waves and howling wind laughing at my helplessness.

With each passing moment, my movements grow slower, more lethargic and laboured. The fight is leaving me, replaced by a numbing acceptance. I can't keep this up much longer. The sea is too powerful, its depths too vast, its strength god-like. I'm just a tiny, insignificant speck in its midst. My fate is inevitable.

Just as I am about to surrender to the deep, I feel something solid beneath me. It takes a moment for my waterlogged mind to process the sensation, but then I realize: sand. I'm being thrown towards the shore. The waves push and pull at me as I scrabble for purchase. I'm yanked back and forth, tumbling, helpless for all their ferocity.

For a split second, it stops, time freezes along with the noise, the incessant force on me, and before me, in this eye of calm, is a hand. It reaches out to me, whoever is behind it hidden in a frozen fog of mist. I take an eternal second to muster a final reserve of strength and reach out to clasp it, slipping into warm darkness as I'm pulled upward onto the beach.

Drowning at Sea: Experiences of Autistic Children and Young People in School

Felt safety is the emotional and psychological experience found in the space between *knowing* you're safe and *feeling* safe. It's rooted in our interactions, environments, and internal dialogues. It's a sense of security and trust that goes beyond the absence of physical threats, encompassing emotional and psychological safety, and includes a feeling that your entire self, including your autonomic nervous system, is safe (Porter et al., 2021).

Why discuss safety in a chapter about autistic children and young people's experiences in schools, when schools are generally seen as safe places, filled with well-intentioned people focused on the wellbeing of the young people in their care? Felt safety is not a familiar sensation to many autistic young people generally, and specifically, many autistic young people do *not* currently feel safe in school.

Society consistently tells us that school is the safest place for a child, based on the long-held belief that a child can only learn and have a future if they are at school. For example:

> the best place to be is in school, surrounded by the support of their friends and teachers …. This is important not just for your child's learning, but also for their overall wellbeing, wider development and their mental health.
>
> **(Department for Education Education Hub Blog, UK Government)**

Yet increasing evidence, supported by years of anecdotal reports from autistic people and their parents, indicates that mainstream school practices, coupled with misinformation about autistic needs and ways of being, cause significant harm, and mean that school is *not always* the best place to be, *nor* does it always offer the best chance in life.

Young people spend a significant portion of their formative years within educational environments. While there isn't a measure for harm caused by educational settings, we can identify harm stemming from these settings by following through the elevated rates of poor mental health in autistic people (Autistica, 2019) extending into adulthood (Royal College of Psychiatry, 2022), high levels of exclusions (Autism Education Trust, 2022), increased non-attendance (Paulauskaite et al., 2022), and the number of parents forced into "elective" home education (Mullalley et al., 2024). Moreover, research remains limited when autistic learners are asked about their school experiences (e.g., Holmes, 2022; Cunningham, 2020; Henrich et al., 2010). What we do know is that anecdotally, what autistic young people and their parents are saying publicly, corroborates what is being expressed in the limited research: that their experiences within the school system are mostly often extremely negative, worsening from primary to secondary, and indicate a deep lack of understanding of need. Anecdotally, from a personal, and professional perspective, the experiences of myself, my own children, and tens of thousands of autistic parents, professionals, and young people also reflect this. In many fundamental ways, while generally we may have more awareness of "autism" as a concept, within education and societally, our ability and willingness to understand the nature and the experiences of autistic people and meet the needs of autistic people, specifically autistic young people, remain severely lacking. How can that not have an impact?

The idea of safety in educational environments is often framed around good intentions, but good intentions alone cannot create felt safety. However, such intentions *can* help when they are rooted in knowledge, reflection, and collaboration. Moreover, reflective practice requires considering the potential for causing harm, even unintentionally. This risk is heightened in a rigid educational system and when the needs of a misunderstood cohort, like autistic young people, are misperceived or contextualised through misunderstanding or misinformation.

To understand why autistic young people experience a significant lack of felt safety, we must move beyond our roles as educators and reflect deeply on the difference between what we know and what we think we know. As an autistic trainer and consultant, often in education settings, I find the lack of fundamental knowledge about modern autistic experiences in educational settings alarming. Educators receive insufficient training, and what they do receive is often superficial or outdated, lacking grounding in current theory and practice. We often describe autistic people as different, but do we truly understand what that means?

Offering a New Lens to Explore Difference

When the word "different" is used, it usually centres one group within a hierarchical power dynamic and "others" another. In psychological terms, in Western society, this dominant group is often classified as WEIRD (Western, Educated, Industrialized, Rich, Democratic) (Pearson & Rosie, 2023). Additionally, "White," "Cishet," and "predominantly male" could also be added to this list. "Different" often means *"different* from *'us,'"* with *"us"* being the neurotypical majority, instead of acknowledging that all groups are simply different from each other, in a non-hierarchical way.

Despite recent advancements in autism research, society and much of academia have held a fixed notion of autism for the past 30–40 years, focusing mainly on White boys who exhibit certain stress-exacerbated behaviours, and not accounting for intersectional experiences across a variety of domains, from co-occurring conditions through to gender, race, and ethnicity. Instead, autistic people are often viewed through a lens of normativity:

they are seen as "more autistic" if their needs are different from the norm, and "less autistic" if their needs are less clear. Our understanding of the differences between autistic and non-autistic young people is shaped by opinion, prejudice, and bias. The "knowledge" we hold about autism comes from various sources: academic texts, training, personal experiences, media, and fiction. We rarely question the accuracy of these sources, often accepting them without examining whether they are the truth.

This model lacks insight. Looking is not the same as *seeing*, just as thinking you know is not the same as *knowing* – especially when the model has historically excluded internal experiences. What if needs aren't *less* different, but just *appear* that way? If we don't identify something, does it mean it doesn't exist? Of course not. Yet this flawed notion persists in the autism narrative, *especially* in education. The dominant narrative "they are fine in school" really means "they appear fine." This translates to "they are minimally disruptive and meet school's expectations," effectively saying that the child is meeting the school's needs, and we will ignore that their own needs may be unmet, because they are not as important.

Since around 2015, the academic understanding of autism has shifted significantly. Progressive psychology and sociology now prioritise collaboration, co-production, and participation as best practice, and research has started to focus on recognising autistic people as competent witnesses of their own experiences. Around that time, a sort of tipping point was reached, whereby the previous advocacy of autistic people was platformed by a growing wave of autistic advocates utilising the growth of the internet and the relatively new widespread reach of social media. Suddenly, conversations that had previously happened on a small and local scale, or which had been historically restricted to those with internet access, were being held on very public platforms with worldwide reach. Alongside this, more autistic people had access to research, and were able to openly reflect and critique that research publicly, which in turn led to more openly autistic people accessing academia, and autistic people already within academia feeling safer to come out. In a very short space of time we have had the development of new fields of research and debate within psychology, philosophy, and sociology, with critical autism studies and critical neurodiversity studies now strongly recognised areas of interest. This has had the byproduct of other fields questioning their professional practice, and more and more autistic professionals feeling safer to come out and speak to their own experiences as autistic people within those fields. These new areas of research have centred and valued

Islands of Safety

co-production and a collaborative approach which prioritises the needs and desires of autistic adults and young people. We've learned that many earlier theories about autism were wrong, stigmatising, and harmful (Murray et al., 2005; Rose, 2018), and that this has had a huge and negative knock-on effect towards the way professional fields and services, like education, have viewed, understood, and treated autistic young people, and that services accessed by autistic young people, upon reflection with this new information, might not be as safe as we have previously assumed them to be.

What Does This Mean for Autistic Young People in School?

It means that misunderstanding autism as a disorder, or as something that should be overcome, is harmful. Autistic young people in unsafe environments are at risk, facing an existential threat to their identity.

As an autistic person, nearly every domain of your being as a human is potentially up for pathologisation, correction, and stigmatisation. This is illustrated in Figure 14.1.

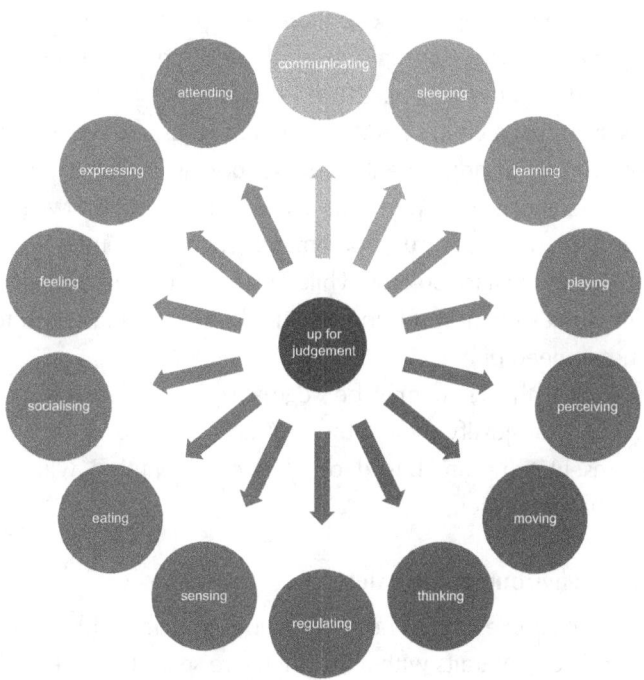

Figure 14.1 Examples of Pathologication in Daily Life

When people do not recognise someone as autistic, they still perceive differences and respond, often in an unintentionally stigmatising way, based on their normative ideals of how people should behave. Even without knowing someone is autistic, their actions may be judged as "wrong" according to these standards.

Significant differences may lead to the child being labelled as "disordered." For example, for young people with more visible needs, interventions aimed at making them conform to normative standards – such as social skills training, joint attention training, behavioural programmes, and emotional regulation training – are often used (Sandbank et al., 2023, 2024).

These programmes, despite being well-intentioned, are habitually based on outdated theories, and in that well-intentioned way, aim to normalise autistic young people to fit the centred group's ideals. Another issue is that often these interventions are considered "gold standard," having been formulated without reflecting on or taking account of the problematic historical state of autism research which has omitted autistic experiences and considered that what we think we know, and what we actually know are not the same thing. Effectively, so much has changed in our understanding of autistic experiences, within a framework of there being a wide variety of different human experiences, that the majority of these interventions don't consider (Milton et al., 2022; Dwyer et al., 2024; Pearson & Rose, 2021, 2023).

Conversely, when a child's needs are less obvious, mainstream education often applies minimal adjustments, and support is sometimes forgotten. A quiet child who consistently performs academically and follows instructions is often considered "fine" or unproblematic. Their differences go unnoticed unless one knows what to look for, while what might be perceived as less significant differences might result in the child being considered more acceptable and not in need of help.

In both cases, the child may be stigmatised with labels like "odd" or "quirky," which can justify their "othering" and overlooking genuine needs. Differing presentations are based on different identities, with one more acceptable than the other.

This is not an environment of safety.

The following examples might help the reader understand how the interaction of neurodivergent traits with a less inclusive school culture and environment leads to feeling unsafe:

- What if I told you that autistic young people's attentional styles differ significantly from non-autistic young people's (Mahler & Rose, 2024a; Price, 2023)? Autistic young people often require a deep focus driven by interest and intrinsic motivation, and transitioning between focus states can be jarring or painful.

This understanding could affect how the school day is structured.

- What if I told you that autistic young people's communication styles and use of language are fundamentally different from the neurotypical norm (Reframing Autism, 2019)? Autistic interpretation and use of language, and the ability to connect with the spoken word are different to what is considered typical.

This realisation might affect how you teach and interact with autistic young people.

- What if I told you that autistic young people's social motivations and ways of socialising are rich and meaningful, but distinct from those of non-Autistic young people (Mahler & Rose, 2024)?

This could challenge assumptions about friendships, teamwork, and the effectiveness of social skills interventions, which might inadvertently invalidate autistic authenticity.

- What if I told you that autistic young people's emotional experiences are not disordered, but misinterpreted due to assumptions around emotions? Autistic emotional communication is often misinterpreted and misunderstood to the point that many autistic young people are essentially gaslit out of their emotional insight and responses, and either lose or never develop a connection with their internal selves (Shackleton, 2021).

This could challenge assumptions about the narrative around emotional regulation for autistic young people.

To summarise, if we were to use words and phrases that hold meaning for and are integral to autistic experience from a framework of insight, rather than observation, they would include: monotropism, gestalt language processing, masking, safety in predictability, Double Empathy, intersectionality, sensory trauma, hermeneutical injustice, poly-victimisation, minority stress, stigma, fawning, burnout, stimming, alexithymia, interoception, diversity in social intelligence, hyper-empathy, stress and distress, trauma, ableism, and many, many more.

How many of these terms do you know? The irony is that autistic young people are "infovores," eaters of information, and lovers of learning, yet exist within educational settings that fail that love of learning because the school environment is unsafe.

None of this is an indictment against educators. I recognise that educators have their own personal context and this interacts with a system that does not always accommodate or support what is needed by both the educator and learner. What I think *is* missing is the explicit acknowledgement that a key function of a robust system is to support all actors – in this context, both the educator and the learner. If we desire to change and improve the experiences of autistic young people within educational settings, supporting them towards felt safety by providing an Island of Safety, this misperception and harm must be reflected upon and addressed, even if that reflection is deeply uncomfortable and challenging.

A Temporary Life Preserver: What Is an Island of Safety?

The notion of an Island of Safety for autistic young people is a simple one. It is a temporary way of offering respite within an environment which is causing harm. Education must evolve to embrace diverse learning methodologies and recognise that the vast amount of information available today surpasses traditional educational purposes. Schools need to adapt to guide students in navigating this information rather than competing against it. The education system must acknowledge its historical focus on uniform academic achievement, which inherently leads to marginalisation. The typical response to that marginalisation is SEND. The whole notion of "special educational needs" only highlights baked-in exclusion by centring the needs of one group of people.

Whilst stakeholders can (and should) continue to argue and advocate for seismic changes in the system, we still need to find ways of working effectively in a flawed system that continues to cater for the mythical middle/imagined typical learner.

Currently, adjustments in schools can be compared to handing half-pumped-up armbands to a child drowning in the storm. For example, environments can be altered: ear defenders might be worn, and time-out cards might be used, along with forms of adjustments. These can be constructive steps towards accessibility in an inaccessible environment. But ultimately, you are still being mandated to be in a space where the way that you are taught (and expected to carry out your day) does not meet your processing, transitional, and communicative needs. Making meaningful and lasting changes is a long-term process, an evolution that is hopefully in progress. In the mean time, education needs to offer something beyond some basic reasonable adjustments: It *has* to feel *safe*.

This does not mean an area in school or an after-school group (a bubble, a base, a sensory room, etc.); while a geographical space *may* form part of an Island of Safety, it is so much more. An Island of Safety leans hard into felt safety. It is somewhere to breathe, to gain sustenance and strength, knowing that the person in need of it will have to return to the storm-ravaged water.

An Island of Safety looks to identify that space between knowing you are safe and actually feeling safe. An Island of Safety is non-prescribed; it is a person, it is a room, it is a feeling, a connection, a haven, a place of exploration, somewhere to play, a place of healing, of therapy without therapeutic intervention, a place without any academic agenda, of co-regulation, of understanding, of empathy. It is a place of honesty and trust. An Island of Safety is somewhere to just *be*.

Sometimes All a Member of Staff Can Be Is an Island of Safety

The interactions educators have with a child will echo throughout their lives. Anyone with this degree of a persistent lack of felt safety will remember the people who made a difference because of the joy, the love, and the safety that was curated. Marginalised people remember being *seen*.

Considering the short-, medium-, and long-term consequences of negative life outcomes experienced by Autistic people – from fragmented identity development to internalised shame, stigma, and ableism, sometimes being *seen* can be the difference between a young person growing up and ageing into adulthood, and them not being here at all. It may seem dramatic to say so, but the more Islands of Safety that can be provided (being *seen* by someone, having a temporary island to crawl up onto out of the tempestuous sea somebody is drowning in), the greater the likelihood that the child does not drown.

In a seemingly unchanging system, repeated rescue efforts might appear futile – but they are never in vain. If an educator can create a safe space where an autistic child is seen as a unique individual and met with trust and honesty, this will be remembered. Despite ongoing harm and persistent struggles, the sense of felt safety will endure, resonating.

The impact of creating a safe space may positively influence their life outcomes, even if its effects are not immediately visible. The Island of Safety not witnessing this success does not equate to failure; the impact made on the future version of the young person you curated felt safe for – no matter how fleeting your time together and maybe unseen to you but still significant.

With enough Islands of Safety, even in a world focused on neuro-normative ideals, autistic people *can* thrive. If autistic people are supported to have tools of connection, acceptance (self-understanding and self-advocacy), agency (understanding choices beyond what you are informed are your choices), autonomy (acting on those choices), and authenticity (being more yourself by recognising and meeting need, not suppressing, having felt-safety), our life outcomes can look very different. To truly thrive, autistic people need the tools and the modelling to swim against the tide and swim towards Islands of Safety of their own making.

For educators, it may be against their remit to encourage students to swim against the tide, but simply giving them time to breathe in their childhood days might be the reminder autistic young people need in their adult lives, that there are people who can act as Islands of Safety, and model for them that autistic people can be Islands of Safety too, by building them for other autistic people.

Swimming against the Tide: Becoming and Curating an Island of Safety

There is a reason this chapter is focused on non-teaching educators as providers of an Island of Safety, and that is simply because non-teaching staff within educational settings often exist in the spaces between, the same spaces where felt safety can be found: the relational space, the emotional space, the non-academic, holistic environmental space. Teaching staff often do not have the opportunity to curate Islands of Safety, but that does not mean that they cannot support, listen to, facilitate, and platform those who might have the opportunity to.

Creating an Island of Safety requires profound reflective practice. This means examining oneself critically, considering not just one's actions, but also the underlying personal beliefs and biases that influence them. Reflective practice should challenge these deeply ingrained aspects, prompting educators to confront uncomfortable and difficult questions about their assumptions and practices.

There are several practical ways to answer these questions and move forward constructively and productively, for example:

Having context:

- Understanding autistic experiences is key to shifting towards becoming safe. This doesn't mean going on "autism awareness training," but means embedding oneself in the narrative, Seeking out autistic voices, and leaning into shared experiences.
- Source training produced and delivered by professional autistic people that reflects intersectional narratives, and picks apart the autism narrative, looking into research that is created collaboratively and through co-production reading about the history of autism, and comparing that to these new sources of information, and being critical of everything one comes across.

Recognising and understanding identity, masking, and marginalisation:

- Recognising being autistic as an identity and seeking to understand autistic identity while moving away from the diagnostic and deficit model of autism is key to curating safety. Masking is at the heart of autistic experience. Autistic people develop fragmented and stigmatised identities based on the negative experiences we have. Frustratingly, educators often see masking as only a superficial social narrative, whereby an autistic person dons a "neurotypical" mask around "neurotypical" people. Masking is an incredibly complex topic and action, grounded in stigma, trauma, and a lack of felt safety (Pearson & Rose, 2021; 2023), and the professional world is seriously misinformed about those complexities. If I got a penny for every educator who has said "I know autism when I see it," "nobody can mask for that long," "everybody masks," "they are fine in school," "young people that young can't mask," "someone with ADHD can't mask" without understanding the complex experiences that are being dismissed and undermined by these statements – I would be rich.

Seeking context and understanding of experiences requires and curates empathy:

- Empathy differs from sympathy in that it involves genuinely understanding and *feeling* another person's perspective. When you haven't shared similar experiences, an empathy gap emerges, creating challenges for both parties. Addressing this Double Empathy Problem (Milton, 2012) and bridging the gap is crucial for creating an Island of Safety.

Compare the fleeting moments of fear experienced by a non-autistic child who loves school with the daily, consistent fear faced by an autistic student whose needs are unmet. This child may fear school even before arriving, and may relive it at home, struggling to articulate their overwhelming, unnameable fear. This isn't about resilience. Marginalised groups, including autistic young people, exhibit remarkable resilience. However, resilience is often discussed from a privileged perspective, overlooking the trauma that educational settings can inflict.

Consider the trauma of living in constant fear, where the predictability of that fear, sought by autistic people in a confusing and invalidating world, becomes a twisted form of safety, something to cling onto, but interpreted as "They love the structure that school gives them." This fear is not irrational, but rooted in continuous invalidation and stigmatisation from a system and people in power who we are assured are trustworthy, in an environment we are assured is "safe."

An Island of Safety is not a room. To create felt safety, an educator must connect with an autistic child emotionally. It can eventually involve practical steps, like following their passions, supporting their understanding and exploration of their autistic identity, providing opportunities for community connectedness, and using a validation-based approach rather than one focused on change. First, though, building a trusting relationship is essential. Moving forward, this will allow the educator to advocate effectively from a place of understanding, not assumption.

An Island of Safety is a reminder that educators work with people, not exam results, not "future workers," not young mathematicians, or young scientists. Educators work with human beings, not current or future productivity.

Ultimately, though, an Island of Safety is likely to be brief, transient, a moment where safety is felt and known. But ultimately it must end, as the child is thrown back into the storm.

Returning to the Storm

> *"You can't stay here."*
> *I nod, knowing; recognising the sadness in their voice.*
> *I look out at the mile high waves, the ripping and roaring explosion of storm spoiled sea. Taunting me.*
> *Disconnect*
> *Confusion*
> *Uncertainty*
> *Isolation*
> *Unbelonging*
> *Unsafe.*
> *The water is black, dark, and terrifying.*
> *For a moment I had respite and peace. For a moment I felt validated and seen.*
> *An Island of Safety, yet so fleeting a moment in time.*
> *Hopeful of another moment soon, another opportunity to draw breath, a chance to feel safe.*
> *With the resignation of one condemned, I walk out into the waves,*
> *And back to the ocean.*

Key Takeaways

- The concept of "difference" often centres on neurotypical norms. A non-hierarchical, identity-based understanding of difference is needed to validate all experiences.
- Schools often misjudge or overlook Autistic needs – labeling visibly different children as disordered, which can result in systemic harm and unmet needs.
- Staff must engage in deep, critical reflection to dismantle biases, understand masking and identity, bridge empathy gaps, and support autistic students in feeling safe and understood in a historically invalidating system.

Reflective Activities

The following are a series of reflective questions to support you in your journey to becoming an Island of Safety:

What qualities do you embody that help you be an Island of Safety?

- How do you reflect? Do your reflections inform your practice?
- How can you hold space for an autistic young person?
- How embedded are you in the autistic narrative?
- What is your understanding of autistic identity and understanding?
- What sources have informed your understanding of autistic identity and ways of being?

Have you ever been an Island of Safety before?

- When? How? *Why* was it needed?
- What did you do?
- How did you feel? Is this sustainable?
- Was it true human support, felt safety, trust, and co-regulation?

Are you alone, or are there other potential Islands of Safety within your school?

- Are there educators within school some autistic young people might gravitate towards?
- Are there potential collaborators who can challenge you reflectively?
- How much agency do you have for change?

How could your school help your autistic students avoid trauma, and to find joy in their school experience?

- How might your school change to mean an Island of Safety is not needed?
- How can you facilitate change within your educational setting?

Practical Resources

Provided below is an additional list of practical resources to support your reflective journey and to support curating an Island of Safety (please note these are not series of tools to make a prescriptive toolbox; a reflective practitioner will recognise these as basic first steps to a deeper understanding):

1 **An Autistic Education**

An article exploring a generational personal experience of the school system: https://theautisticadvocate.com/an-autistic-education/

2 **"An introduction to the Double Empathy Problem" and "An introduction to Monotropism"**

Accessible, free short animations briefly introducing you to the Double Empathy Problem and monotropism: https://www.youtube.com/watch?v=qpXwYD9bGyU; https://youtu.be/qUFDAevkd3E?si=1vOsMWEerdqJBsdW

3 **Autistic Masking: Understanding Identity Management and the Role of Stigma**

A book that draws together the most up-to-date research about autistic masking, moving beyond the social narrative and incorporating intersectionality, combining psychological and social theory, with lived experience: https://www.amazon.co.uk/Autistic-Masking-Understanding-Identity-Management/dp/1803882115

4 **Neurobears**

A licensed course aimed at autistic young people, to help them and a safe adult explore their autistic identity. This is the only course of its kind in the world with an academic evidence base (Mullalley et al., 2024): https://theautisticadvocate.com/neurobears/

References

Autism Education Trust & University of Birmingham. (2022). *Investigation of the causes and implications of exclusion for autistic CYPand young people in England*. Retrieved from https://www.autismeducationtrust.org.uk/sites/default/files/2022-01/exclusion-research-report_final.pdf

Cunningham, M. (2020). 'This school is 100% not autistic friendly!' Listening to the voices of primary-aged autistic CYP people to understand what an autistic-friendly primary school should be like. *International Journal of Inclusive Education, 26*(12), 1211–1225. https://doi.org/10.1080/13603116.2020.1789767

Dwyer, P., Williams, Z. J., Lawson, W. B., & Rivera, S. M. (2024). A transdiagnostic investigation of attention, hyper-focus, and monotropism in autism, attention dysregulation hyperactivity development, and the general population. *Neurodiversity, 2*. https://doi.org/10.1177/27546330241237883

Henrich, J., Heine, S. J., & Norenzayan, A. (2010). The weirdest people in the world? *Behavioral and Brain Sciences, 33*(2–3), 61–83. https://doi.org/10.1017/S0140525X0999152X

Holmes, S. C. (2022). Inclusion, autism spectrum, students' experiences. *International Journal of Developmental Disabilities, 70*(1), 59–73. https://doi.org/10.1080/20473869.2022.2056403

Mahler, K., & Rose, K. (2024a). *Interoception and monotropism: Paying attention to autistic and ADHD experiences*. Retrieved from https://www.kelly-mahler.com/product/on-demand-course-interoception-and-monotropism/

Mahler, K., & Rose, K. (2024b). *Interoception and autistic masking: Lost connections*. Retrieved from https://www.kelly-mahler.com/product/lost-connections/

Milton, D. E. M. (2012). On the ontological status of autism: The 'double empathy problem.' *Disability & Society, 27*(6), 883–887. https://doi.org/10.1080/09687599.2012.710008

Milton, D., Gurbuz, E., & López, B. (2022). The 'double empathy problem': Ten years on. *Autism, 26*(8), 1901–1903. https://doi.org/10.1177/13623613221129123

Mullally, S. L., Wood, A. E., Edwards, C. C., Connolly, S. E., Constable, H., Watson, S., Rodgers, J., Rose, K., & King, N. (2024). 'I like being autistic': Assessing the benefit of autistic-led psychoeducation for autistic CYP. *medRxiv*. https://doi.org/10.1101/2024.07.12.24310317

Murray, D., Lesser, M., & Lawson, W. (2005). Attention, monotropism and the diagnostic criteria for autism. *Autism, 9*(2), 139–156. https://doi.org/10.1177/1362361305051398

Paulauskaite, L., Timmerman, A., Kouroupa, A., Allard, A., Gray, K. M., Hastings, R. P., ... & Totsika, V. (2022). Elective home education of children with neurodevelopmental conditions before and after the COVID-19 pandemic started. *Frontiers in Psychology, 13*, 995217.

Pearson, A., & Rose, K. (2023). *Autistic masking: Understanding identity management and the role of stigma*. Retrieved from https://www.autisticslt.com/communicationfeatures

Pearson, A., & Rose, K. (2021). A conceptual analysis of autistic masking: Understanding the narrative of stigma and the illusion of choice. *Autism Adulthood, 3*(1), 52–60. https://doi.org/10.1089/aut.2020.0043

Porter, J., McDermott, T., Daniels, H., & Ingram, J. (2021). Feeling part of the school and feeling safe: Further development of a tool for investigating school belonging. *Educational Studies, 50*(3), 382–398.

Price, E. (2023). *Autistic communication & interaction styles: Diversity in communication methods*. Retrieved from https://www.autisticslt.com/communicationfeatures

Reframing Autism. (2019). *Autistic social motivation: A summary of Jaswal and Akhtar for non-academics*. Retrieved from https://reframingautism.org.au/autistic-social-motivation-a-summary-of-jaswal-and-akhtar-for-non-academics/

Royal College of Psychiatry. (2022). *Suicide and autism, a national crisis*. Retrieved from https://www.rcpsych.ac.uk/docs/default-source/improving-care/nccmh/suicide-prevention/workshops-(wave-4)/wave-4-workshop-2/suicide-and-autism---slides.pdf?sfvrsn=bf3e0113_2

Rose, K. (2018). *The inside of autism: Session one: The history of autism*. Retrieved from https://theautisticadvocate.com/ioamembership/

Sandbank, M., Bottema-Beutel, K., Syu, Y.-C., Caldwell, N., Feldman, J. I., & Woynaroski, T. (2024). Evidence-b(i)ased practice: Selective and inadequate reporting in early childhood autism intervention research. *Autism, 28*(8), 1889–1901. https://doi.org/10.1177/13623613241231624

Sandbank, M., Bottema-Beutel, K., LaPoint, S. C., Feldman, J. I., Barrett, D. J., Caldwell, N., ... & Woynaroski, T. (2023). Autism intervention meta-analysis of early childhood studies (Project AIM): Updated systematic review and secondary analysis. *BMJ, 383*, Article e071757.

Shackleton, H. (2021). *The world of work is changing, it's time our education system did too*. Retrieved from https://www.inflect.co.uk/future-work-rethink-education/

UK Government. (2024, January 3). How to improve your child's school attendance and where to get support. Education Hub. Updated February 29, 2024. https://educationhub.blog.gov.uk/2024/01/improving-school-attendance/

15

The LISTEN Framework
Fostering a Values-Led Neurodiversity-Affirmative Climate in Schools
Paula Prendeville

What Is the LISTEN Meta-Framework, and Who Is It For?

As a meta-framework, LISTEN provides a clear and consistent framework for all interested parties in schools (including students, their families, teaching assistants, teachers, school leadership, and wider school communities) to speak a common language to meet the needs of all in their community. This framework targets the disjointness that currently exists in school communities to meet the needs of neuro-minorities by focusing on building positive relationships in schools, and facilitates the nurturing of relationships to foster a greater understanding of lived experiences and implementing these voices into practice.

This framework signposts you to where all areas of change could happen in your school. Below, where each section is explained in detail, there will be examples of change that different school partners could implement.

This framework can be useful for everyone who interacts with school systems, including educational psychologists, other allied health professionals, and policy makers, by providing a collective and unified approach to supporting all students, and most importantly, it places the voice of neurodiverse learners at the centre. This framework can be adopted and adapted to meet the specific local needs of a school while also applying a holistic neurodiversity-affirmative approach, informed and guided by the principles of Universal Design for Learning (UDL), which are discussed elsewhere in this book.

The LISTEN meta-framework is inspired by the phrase "nothing about me, without me," emulating Article 12 of the United Nations Convention on the Rights of a Child (UNCRC), which gives a child the right to express their views freely, be listened to, and for their opinions to be taken seriously. This framework is an appeal to "listen" to the voices of neurodivergent students to guide the implementation of equity, diversity, and inclusive practices that cultivate neurodiversity-affirmative climates in schools. The LISTEN framework is intended to provide a progressive vision for neurodiversity-affirmative practices in schools. It can also support entire school communities to have a greater awareness and understanding of the experiences of neuro-minorities. Practitioners who want to do these things can use the LISTEN meta-framework as a helpful start in promoting empathic and nurturing school environments that are attuned to all members.

This framework is guided by the following key factors:

- L – Leadership and Language
- I – Integrity and Intersectionality
- S – Systems, Space, and Sensory Sensitivities
- T – Trauma-Informed Practice, Transitions, Trust, and Time
- E – Empathy, Equity, and Ethical Practice
- N – neurodiversity-affirmative Needs-Based Planning

Below, each factor is explored and reflective statements are presented from multiple viewpoints to demonstrate how the LISTEN framework could promote neurodiversity-affirmative practices in schools. You will find reflective activities at the end of each sub-section.

L: Leadership and Language

Leadership

The LISTEN meta-framework promotes authentic and empathic leadership. This is where school leaders recognise the needs of neurodivergent students by cultivating a school climate where all students feel psychologically safe, enabling them to thrive. LISTEN encourages leaders to reflect on this framework to promote a neurodivergent learning community that values fairness and respect in all interactions. This includes an acknowledgement that supporting a neurodiversity-affirmative school community is inclusive of its neurodivergent students, neurodivergent staff, and the wider community, including family members and professionals who may also be neurodivergent.

This approach enables schools, as organisations, to implement a shared vision with meaningful goals that harnesses leadership at all levels. It is important that agreed neurodiversity-affirmative practices are monitored by schools, and that students' views on these are shared and reviewed on an ongoing basis. It is recommended that leaders recognise the importance of building capacity within school communities to increase the knowledge, skills, and understanding of the lived experiences of neuro-minorities to promote neurodiversity-affirmative attitudes and values, including the promotion of empathic, respectful, and meaningful interactions.

The following reflective activities you can find in each section are presented as ways that communities of each perspective (students, parents, school staff, and school leadership) can reflect on how leadership in their school appropriately promotes neurodiversity-affirmative practices.

Reflective Activity: Focusing on the Role of School Leadership

Student perspective	Parent/guardian perspective	School staff perspective	School leadership perspective
I feel safe in school. Supporting adults ask me what works best for me when I am in school. I know the supporting adult(s) I can go to if and when I need help.	School leadership understands the specific needs of my child. I feel listened to as a parent/guardian. My child is safe in school.	As a school, we are supported by leadership to meet the neurodivergent needs of our students. We are provided with adequate training opportunities to support neurodivergent students. All staff promote an inclusive leadership approach. There is a culture of collaboration in our school. UDL approaches are promoted. Student diversity is promoted and celebrated in our school.	I have a clear vision of an inclusive approach that is shared among everyone in my school community. I promote the values of inclusive practice outlined in the LISTEN framework. I recognise the importance of promoting neurodivergent approaches that support all members of my school community.

Language

A reframing of language is required to foster a values-led, positive neurodiversity-affirmative school culture. There are tensions in the use of the terms "neurotypical" and "neurodivergent" due to lack of understanding of a person's needs. School communities need to be consulted on their preferences with respect to neurodiversity-affirmative, inclusive, and respectful language used, which may include a person-first approach, identity-first approach, or the use of "neurodivergent" as a preferred term ascribed to a sense of identity for a person. The LISTEN framework advocates for the positive use of language in all communications that accepts and celebrates diversity. While the proliferation in knowledge and understanding of the needs of autistic learners has increased considerably in recent years, there continues to be a dearth in awareness and understanding of other neurodivergent students' experiences and the barriers they encounter on a regular basis. These experiences impact on students' quality of life and their active participation in schools and communities.

As an example, some students face barriers arising from the lived experiences of a rare disease or brain injury. Some of these conditions may remain hidden, and a lack of understanding and acknowledgement of the additional barriers these students can often experience influences their participation in school. For example, the impact of physical and cognitive fatigue can vary for students, and this can have a bearing on their sense of safety.

Strategies for Inclusion: (1) Promoting Total Communication

- Schools are encouraged to promote total communication approaches that include neurodiversity-affirmative verbal, paraverbal, and non-verbal approaches, informed by UDL.
- Discussions on preferred modes of communication when engaging with families are also recommended. This includes supporting families where language can act as an additional communicative barrier, which may hinder neurodivergent students from thriving in school.
- To promote a values-based approach, it is necessary that respectful and empathic interactions are emulated in all communications relayed throughout schools. This includes supports to reduce communication barriers experienced by families from minority backgrounds which can encumber them from advocating for their child.

Reflective Activity: Thinking about Use of Language

Student perspective	Parent/guardian perspective	School staff perspective	School leadership perspective
I experience neurodiversity-affirmative use of language in my school. My wishes and preferences for the language I use to identify my neurodivergent strengths and needs are honoured. I observe my peers using respectful neurodiversity-affirmative language when referencing diversity. My preferred mode of communication is facilitated and honoured.	My child's school demonstrates a positive neurodiversity-affirmative and respectful use of language when engaging in any form of communications about my child. The school demonstrates an awareness and understanding of the diversity of my child's needs. My child's communication preferences are respected and promoted in school.	We promote a positive neurodiversity-affirmative use of language in our school. We have sought the views of our neurodivergent school members on their language preferences. We are open to learning how we can promote inclusive, safe, and neurodiversity-affirmative use of language attributed to diversity.	As school leaders, we promote neurodiversity-affirmative use of language. We regularly engage with our neurodivergent school community to seek their wishes and preferences on the language that is attributed to differences in learning needs. We promote a values-based use of language that is respectful to the needs of our diverse school community.

I: Integrity and Intersectionality

Integrity

This factor promotes fairness, honesty, and unbiased approaches to decision making in schools. Predictability and consistency in all interactions, processes, and procedures are essential to imbue a sense of security for neurodivergent students.

Strategies for Inclusion: (2) Facilitating Shared Decision Making

- This factor recommends shared decision making practices to support meaningful participation of all its members, including neuro-minorities, to build positive relationships.
- It is important to recognise the impact of cognitive biases on decisions that are made, particularly when school decisions have historically not always been in the best interests of members.
- Facilitating shared decision making practices, informed by UDL, fosters a partnership approach and promotes integrity in school communities which mitigates the impact of bias.
- With greater proliferation of technology to support neuro-minorities, particularly with the rapid increase in the use of generative artificial intelligence (AI) to promote inclusive approaches, it will be important for schools to promote integrity by increasing awareness of the impact of bias to safeguard against the risk of harm in all decisions that are made, and also with any AI applications that are promoted in schools.

Reflective Activity: Acting with Integrity

Student perspective	Parent/guardian perspective	School staff perspective	School leadership perspective
I am treated fairly in school. My views, wishes, and preferences are sought for any decisions that affect me. My school is responsive to my communication needs and uses UDL approaches to obtain my views. My decisions are honoured.	The school treats my child fairly. They make adequate and reasonable adjustments to enable my child to make their views, wishes, and preferences known. They use neurodiversity-affirmative communication approaches to support my child. I believe the school acts with integrity when interacting with me and my child.	As a school, we treat all our students fairly. We make unbiased decisions that positively affect their school experience. We are clear and transparent in our communications with our neurodivergent community and recognise and honour their preferences when making decisions. This may include giving them time to consider a decision and using UDL approaches when seeking their views, wishes, and preferences.	As school leaders, we promote fairness, integrity, and honesty in all our interactions. We recognise the neurodivergent needs of our school community and seek their views on decisions that affect them. We promote neurodiversity-affirmative total communication approaches that recognise the need to make adequate and reasonable adjustments to support a person.

Intersectionality

Intersectionality refers to the ways in which minority identities, incorporating protected characteristics of gender, ethnicity, socio-economic status, disability, etc., intersect and impact negatively on people, resulting in experiences of oppression, discrimination, and imbalance in power dynamics. The LISTEN framework advocates for schools to adopt an intersectional approach to acknowledge how a person's participation in school life can be affected, and to consider this factor when implementing inclusive practices in schools. Adopting the LISTEN framework promotes an intersectional approach that enables school systems to integrate their planning to address systems of oppression and discrimination. This will assist schools to alleviate the impact of poverty and disability along with other intersecting inequalities experienced by minority members of a school community.

Reflective Activity: Raising Awareness of Intersectional Needs

Student perspective	Parent/guardian perspective	School staff perspective	School leadership perspective
My school recognises, understands, and supports my intersectional needs and provides me with extra support.	My child's school recognises the additional challenges that my child can experience, and sensitively supports them with additional assistance to mitigate the potential impact of their minority status and intersectional needs. The school understands the challenges I experience as a parent of a neurodivergent child who is also navigating the school system as a member of a minority group.	As a school, we acknowledge, plan, and support for the additional intersectional needs experienced by members of our neurodivergent school community.	As school leaders, we implement a flexible, creative, and respectful approach to support our neurodivergent school community who have additional challenges due to their minority status. As a school, we address intersectional needs by promoting the inclusive values of the LISTEN meta-framework.

S: Systems, Space, and Sensory Sensitivities

Systems

The LISTEN meta-framework is a systems approach to guide the implementation of cultural change by fostering positive and neurodiversity-affirmative practices at all levels in schools. Promoting a systems approach requires everyone in school communities to "listen" to each other and to work in partnership towards the common goal of embedding values-based inclusive practices that celebrate the diversity of all members. This is inclusive of the views of students, teaching assistants, teachers, school leadership, and the wider school community around ways in which neurodiversity-affirmative practices can be embedded in all aspects of school life. This will require regular and meaningful engagements with all stakeholders, facilitated by open, trusting, and transparent communicative processes.

Reflective Activity: Promoting a Positive School System

Student perspective	Parent/guardian perspective	School staff perspective	School leadership perspective
My learning experiences in school are positive. I feel supported by everyone around me.	My child's school is positive about supporting the diverse needs of its learners that include communications I receive, and my interactions with all its staff.	As a school, we raise awareness of the needs of our neurodivergent students and promote positive neurodiversity-affirmative practices across our school community.	As school leaders, we support the needs of our neurodivergent community at all school levels.

Space

The social model of disability recognises the impact of the environment as a barrier to full participation of individuals with disabilities. I worked with a young man who, when expressing his preference for a change in his environment, stated "my universe is having a problem" as an alternative to asking people for help. This phrase inspires the Space factor in the LISTEN meta-framework to recommend that schools audit the following types of environments to modify school spaces to support the regulation needs of its members.

Strategies for Inclusion: (3) Examining Environmental Influences

The seven different types of environments presented below should be considered by schools to have a greater understanding of how these environments can support, or perhaps impact negatively on, students' lived experiences of school life.

Physical Environment

This includes the physical space in which a person is situated and the range of physical factors that can impact on them, including layout, sensory factors (sound, light, smells, etc.), or social factors (people and what they are doing). The physical environment may also include postural or seating systems a person is using (i.e., a type of seating or wheelchair). For example, it is important for wheelchair users to have the opportunity to use activity chairs to support their participation. Some people concentrate better having access to sensory cushions, beanbags, yoga balls, etc. to meet their sensory needs.

Processing Environment

This encompasses how the processing environment supports individuals to respond to the world around them in different ways and at different speeds. This may vary depending on a range of factors, including a person's working memory, cognitive ability, executive functioning skills, and response to sensory stimuli. A neurodivergent student once relayed to me, "I can look at you, I can listen to you, or I can talk to you, but I am unable to do all these things together." This means that just because a student does not look like they are engaging in a classroom does not mean that they lack concentration, motivation, or interest to do so. It could mean that they are trying to process their environment in a modality that is most comfortable for them at that moment in time.

Emotional Environment

Neuro-minorities can be hyper-attuned to their emotional environment, and may experience acute sensitivities in how they regulate their emotions or attune to emotional expression in others. Due to black-and-white thinking styles, this can sometimes lead to catastrophic thinking patterns, resulting in stressful experiences of emotional distress and overwhelm. It is important for school communities to be aware of this, particularly in discussions that may trigger an intense response for neuro-minorities. It is important to promote psychologically safe emotional environments for students in schools by promoting wellbeing, thus enabling them to thrive.

Sensory Environment

This refers to how a person's sensory system can impact on their sense of security in positive or negative ways. This is discussed in further detail in the "Sensory Sensitivities" sub-section below.

Social Environment

This environment encompasses the impact of the social world. Seeking information on neuro-minorities' experiences of their social environment is required to promote psychologically safe learning environments. Some social environments can be triggers for overwhelm that some students may experience in busy environments. In addition, rule-bound thinking patterns may support or hinder participation in their social environments. Some neuro-minorities may have a preference to participate in learning on a one-to-one basis or in small or large groups at varying times.

Communication Environment

Schools can promote positive and neurodiversity-affirmative communication environments by considering the various pragmatic uses of language. Promoting a UDL approach to the communication environment, and seeking the communication preferences of its members, should be creatively explored by schools. This includes supplementing communication approaches that integrate verbal, paraverbal, and non-verbal approaches. This may include promoting sign language, augmented and alternative communication systems, core boards, intensive interaction, and other modes of communication, and the preferences of some neuro-minorities to communicate via technology using robots.

Internal Environment

The internal environment can have an impact on a person's ability to fully engage in school life, and this is dependent on how they feel. For example, if someone is ruminating or replaying an event internally, this can impact on their capacity to be fully present. Levels of fatigue, hunger, etc. can also be affected by a person's internal environment.

Reflective Activity: Promoting Positive Use of Space

Student perspective	Parent/guardian perspective	School staff perspective	School leadership perspective
People who support me recognise my needs in all aspects of my environment and make adaptations that make me feel safe.	My child's school, recognises that my child can respond in different ways to aspects of their environment. We work together to identify adaptations in these environments to enable my child to thrive in school.	As a school, we regularly discuss ways that we can make positive neurodiversity-affirmative adaptations to school spaces to support our neurodiverse community.	As school leaders, we foster neurodiversity-affirmative spaces and seek regular consultation around ways that spaces can be improved.

Sensory Sensitivities

LISTEN recommends that school communities build their capacity to increase awareness and understanding of sensory sensitivities, and the impact of these sensitivities on their members. Individuals have a range of sensory systems through which they process their sensory world. These include smell, vision, touch (tactile), sound, balance (vestibular) and their body awareness in space (proprioception). In recent times, there has been increasing awareness of the impact of the interoception sense, which refers to how individuals process internal sensations such as heart rate, feeling hungry, body temperature, pain, and their emotional system. Sensory systems are unique to everyone, and some individuals can experience hypo-sensitivities (under-recognition) or hyper-sensitivities (over-recognition) that impact on them. Some individuals have the capacity to regulate their sensory systems; others, particularly neuro-minorities, can have experiences of struggling to regulate, hindering their ability to engage with the world around them.

Neuro-minorities can experience hyper-focus in their sensory system, which means that they focus their attention on one specific thing to the exclusion of everything else in their environment. For example, if a student has a heightened auditory sensitivity to a particular sound occurring in their immediate environment, or perhaps in another space, their focus is on this sound over anything else, which may impact on their inability to fully participate. Others may experience hypo-focus on some aspects of their sensory systems, which can elevate their potential risk of harm in school environments. For example, individuals can under-register heat and thus increase their potential risk of burns.

Strategies for Inclusion: (4) Creating a Calming Sensory Environment

Students can experience a bombardment of their sensory systems that may be further compounded by the impact of space factors outlined above. For example, many schools advocate for the use of team teaching as an inclusive pedagogical approach. It is important to recognise the overwhelm that students may experience from team teaching.

It is recommended that the views of students are sought, and that schools consider student preferences and creatively explore alternative approaches. The inadvertent harm that may be perpetuated from a lack of understanding of the sensory bombardment experienced by students on a daily basis can be significant, as reoccurring experiences of overwhelm are traumatic. Raising awareness of the impact of sensory bombardment is essential to promote psychologically and sensorially safe environments to mitigate the impact of burnout, which can in some significant instances lead to school refusal. Schools have a duty to safeguard against harm. Promoting sensory regulation strategies in Low Arousal environments is recommended. All students benefit from access to sensory and movement breaks to support their proprioception, vestibular, and interoception needs. Raising awareness and understanding of sensory sensitivities benefits everyone.

Reflective Activity: Raising Awareness of Sensory Sensitivities

Student perspective	Parent/guardian perspective	School staff perspective	School leadership perspective
My school asks me about my sensory needs. My school honours my sensory preferences and supports me to feel sensorially safe in school. I have access to regular sensory breaks that help me to regulate.	My child's school recognises the impact of my child's sensory needs. The school facilitates sensorially safe environments to meet my child's sensory needs.	As a school, we have the knowledge and understanding of the impact of the sensory world on our neurodivergent community. We regularly seek the views of our community around their preferences for neurodiversity-affirmative sensory practices to meet their sensory needs.	As school leaders, we use creative approaches to promote flexible approaches to support all members of our school community to feel sensorially safe and to thrive.

T: Trauma-Informed Practice, Transitions, Trust, and Time

Trauma-Informed Practice*

Studies have shown that a high percentage of students with disabilities are exposed to adverse childhood experiences risk compared to their neurotypical peers. Neurodivergent adults speak of the trauma they experienced in schools due to their exposure to environments which lacked understanding of their sensory needs. Neurodivergent students can experience intense pain from heightened sensitivities. During these periods, they may engage in fright, flight, freeze, flop, or fawn responses which can distort their sense of safety in the moment. Individuals who have extended exposure to traumatising events in their environments can develop chronic trauma. They startle easily and experience overwhelm that is perceived by others as an emotional outburst. The lack of understanding of students' regulation needs, categorised in schools as "challenging behaviours," can fail to recognise the impact of sensory needs and the duty of schools to promote psychologically safe environments.

Bullying, social exclusion, and a general lack of understanding of a person's needs can impact significantly on neurodivergent individuals. These experiences, defined as microaggressions, are often compounded over time and develop into trauma responses. The psychological ramifications of a lack of understanding of the lived experiences that students with chronic conditions encounter in school environments are considerable, and the impact they have on the wider family is immense. It is important for schools to recognise that the emotional responses they observe could be as a result of reliving a trauma experience, impacting on a student's ability to feel safe, to engage in learning, and to participate meaningfully in school life. This may also be compounded by the impact of other types of traumas that may include cultural trauma and/or intergenerational trauma. It is essential that schools attune to the needs of their students who have an increased risk of experiencing trauma in schools. Promoting empathetic, collaborative partnerships based on trust is essential to facilitate positive outcomes for students. To implement this, it is recommended that schools adopt a neurodiversity-affirmative, trauma-informed response by promoting the factors outlined in the LISTEN framework.

Reflective Activity: Fostering Trauma-Informed Practices

Student perspective	Parent/guardian perspective	School staff perspective	School leadership perspective
I feel safe in school. My school regularly checks in with me to see if I feel safe in school.	My child's school is trauma-informed and is attuned to their needs. The school promotes psychologically safe environments. The school communicates with me regularly to discuss ways in which my child's environment can be adapted if they experience overwhelm and become dysregulated.	We are a trauma-informed school. We regularly engage in reflective practice to determine ways that we can promote a neurodiversity-affirmative and safe environment for everyone in our community.	As school leaders, we recognise the impact of trauma on our community. We promote empathetic, collaborative partnerships and psychologically safe environments that are trauma informed. We seek the support of external experts when required.

Transitions

To promote psychologically safe environments in schools, it is essential that structure and predictability are promoted, with flexible, agile and creative approaches applied when needed. This requires schools to take the time to identify students' transition needs and to implement a consistent approach. This includes supporting students with transitions that occur on a daily, weekly, termly, and yearly basis, and to ensure that any changes are communicated with them in advance. It is recommended that schools act in students' best interests and, where possible, seek students' wishes and preferences, which are honoured and promoted using neurodiversity-affirmative and practice-informed approaches.

Strategies for Inclusion: (5) Understanding and Promoting Transitions

Due to variations in a person's response to their environment and their sensory needs, including the potential impact of prior dysregulating experiences, it is essential that regular check-ins with students are facilitated to determine if any adaptations are required. For example, some students may experience overwhelm when entering a school in the morning due to the sensory bombardment they experience, compounded by additional environmental factors outlined in the Space factor above. This experience at the start of a school day can result in cognitive and sensory saturation for a person, where energy levels are depleted, impacting on their capacity to participate meaningfully in school life.

- By tweaking a timetable to facilitate a later school start time, when entrances and corridors are quieter, a neurodivergent student is supported to transition to a Lower Arousal environment of the classroom with familiar and established routines.
- It is essential that the wishes and preferences of students are sought for transitions.
- Advanced planning for all transitions is recommended.
- It is also advised to consider using total communication and UDL approaches if required and appropriate.

The expectation of engaging in normative transitions with neurotypical peers can often cause anxiety and, in some instances, significant stress for neurodivergent students without their views been sought or adequate advanced preparations and flexibility in approaches.

Reflective Activity: Planning and Supporting Transitions

Student perspective	Parent/guardian perspective	School staff perspective	School leadership perspective
I am supported in all transitions in school. My school always prepares me in advance for any changes that occur.	Structure and predictability are promoted in my child's school. The school acts in my child's best interests when planning and facilitating transitions for my child.	We promote structure and predictability in our school to the best of our ability. We recognise the importance of having well-planned and managed transition support for everyone in the school community.	As school leaders, we recognise the importance of promoting neurodiversity-affirmative-informed transition planning. We are creative, agile and flexible to meet the transition needs of our students.

Trust

The LISTEN framework recommends that this factor is given explicit attention when implementing neurodiversity-affirmative approaches. Schools that meaningfully engage and actively promote a partnership approach in seeking the views of all interested parties, and listening and promoting those views, will develop trust among their communities and foster psychological safety for all their members. Establishing and promoting trusting engagements embeds values-based practices that support neuro-minorities in schools.

Reflective Activity: Fostering an Environment of Trust

Student perspective	Parent/ guardian perspective	School staff perspective	School leadership perspective
My school seeks my views and follows through on plans they make with me. This makes me feel safe in school.	I trust my child's school to support my child and to act in their best interests.	We listen to the views of our neurodivergent members. We act in their best interests and honour their wishes and preferences.	We foster trusting environments that are responsive to the needs of our neurodivergent community by embedding the LISTEN meta-framework in our school.

Time

Time is also a consideration for schools in fostering a neurodiversity-affirmative climate. It is important to acknowledge that implementing the LISTEN framework, as a cultural change process in schools, will take time. This factor encompasses how schools support neurodiversity-affirmative management of students' time, how the changing neurodivergent needs of students across their lifespan in schools are supported, and recognising how needs vary depending on students' contexts and interactions. This may include promoting students' skills for life or reflecting on how schools support students with neurodegenerative conditions, particularly if they have a life-limiting condition, and how schools can support them to participate meaningfully in school life for as long as possible. This factor also acknowledges the rapid changes that have taken place in education in recent times, particularly with the impact of technology and the risks and benefits of advancements in AI to promote higher levels of participation and independence for neurodivergent students. This is particularly important in the context of facilitating reasonable adjustments for students to facilitate positive learning environments. In addition, it is important for schools to be vigilant in any applications that are being considered and to reflect on their potential longer-term impact over a student's lifespan in school and beyond.

Reflective Activity: Considering the Impact of Time on Change Processes

Student perspective	Parent/guardian perspective	School staff perspective	School leadership perspective
My school asks me how I feel and what I need support with, and understands that my needs are likely to change over time.	My child's school seeks my views on implementing neurodiversity-affirmative practices in my child's school. My child's school has discussed and planned for my child's learning trajectory through their school years. My school has discussed how my child will develop skills for life to increase their independence and participation skills as they develop.	As a school community, we recognise that it will take time to build our capacity to implement all the factors of the LISTEN meta-framework in our school. We promote skills for life among all our students.	As school leaders, we prioritise cultural change practices in our school community and will take the time to implement them in a meaningful and positive way. We collaborate with all community members and seek their views on the barriers to and facilitators of positive cultural change neurodiversity-affirmative practices over time. We promote skills for life among all our students.

E: Empathy, Equity, and Ethical Practice

Empathy

The LISTEN meta-framework promotes empathetic and attuned approaches to meet the needs of all members in a school community. Neuro-minorities may attune to empathic responses in various ways. Attunement means being attentive to others and engaging with them using their preferred mode of communication. Attuning to others, and navigating the social world, can be a challenge for neuro-minorities due to balancing external factors in their environment along with internal factors in how they process their sensory world. This can be overwhelming and exhausting, and may result in individuals withdrawing from engaging with others. It is recommended that schools promote empathy by raising awareness of the experiences of their neurodivergent members in navigating school life due to a lack of access to neurodiversity-affirmative environments.

Alexithymia is a condition where some neurodivergent individuals experience challenges in identifying, recognising, and describing their own emotions and ascribing emotions in others. This includes physical sensations in their internal environment that can be attached to certain emotions. Individuals with alexithymia experience elevated anxiety levels due to their experience of confusion at their inability to recognise emotions in others, or from emotions they observe that can be misinterpreted – for example, interpreting someone who is crying as sad, where these tears could be expressions of happiness. This condition is estimated to affect one in ten people; however, a significant number of autistic individuals are affected by it. There is a gradual recognition of the impact of alexithymia as it can elevate an individual's experiences of anxiety in the social world. In partnership with professionals and neurodivergent students, it is recommended that schools promote empathetic engagements and wellbeing initiatives to educate school communities on neurodivergent emotional understanding and expression.

Reflective Activity: Promoting Empathetic Engagements

Student perspective	Parent/guardian perspective	School staff perspective	School leadership perspective
My circles of support in school are attuned to my neurodivergent ways of interacting with the world around me. I have opportunities to regulate safely in school and have access to Low Arousal environments when I need them.	My child's school recognises my child's emotional regulation and expression and honours these in a safe and neurodiversity-affirmative way.	We promote empathetic, neurodiversity-affirmative interactions in our school community which recognise, attune and respond appropriately and safely to diversity in emotional expression among our neurodiverse community.	We are attuned to various forms of emotional expression and have created safe environments to enable our neurodivergent community to regulate safely.

Equity

The LISTEN meta-framework advocates for the promotion of equity in all school engagements. This may include seeking the views of students, where meaningful and appropriate to do so. Equity is also promoted by facilitating shared decision making processes – for example, how finite school resources are used fairly and equitability. This factor also advises schools to consider the impact of their implicit bias on decisions that are made that may inadvertently impact on others. The concepts of fairness and equity are important to promote trust, and are particularly important for autistic students. It is recommended that schools exercise an appropriate degree of transparency in plans, and that decisions are clear, consistent, and made in students' best interests.

Reflective Activity: Advancing Equitable Practices

Student perspective	Parent/guardian perspective	School staff perspective	School leadership perspective
I am treated fairly. My rights as a neurodivergent learner are honoured.	My child's school takes a rights-based, neurodiversity-affirmative approach to supporting them in school.	All students are treated equally and their views are sought on decisions that affect them. The independence and participation of all students are promoted in our school.	We promote fairness and equity in our school community. We speak openly about the impact of bias and promote transparency in in our decision making. The best interests of our students are central to our decision making at all times.

Ethical Practice

Schools require a commitment to ethical practice to promote the LISTEN meta-framework effectively. This includes implementing ethically informed, neurodiversity-affirmative practices guided by a rights-based, social justice approach to values and human flourishing. The realities of school life can be a challenge to navigate at times, and may include the potential for ethical drift in professional decision making due to organisational and wider systemic demands. To promote neurodiversity-affirmative practices, it is incumbent upon schools to reflect on their ethical practices explicitly as part of their review processes. It is recommended that schools attune to context-specific ethical approaches that validate and support neuro-minorities in their communities. This requires a heightened awareness and respect for diversity – for example, cultural variations in parenting practices. Additionally, there is an increase in ethical challenges emerging as a result of the risks and benefits of social media and AI usage in school communities.

Access to technology has greatly enhanced the participation of neurominorities in school life. It is essential that any decisions to promote or remove technology from schools is given careful ethical deliberation particularly in balancing safety and positive risk-taking that is developmentally appropriate, promoting independence to enable students to access the curriculum and to use technology appropriately. The LISTEN framework advocates for the promotion of student autonomy. Specifically, this may include school processes that seek students' views on decisions, exercise appropriate informed assent and informed consent procedures, safeguard students' confidential information, and take reasonable steps to respect the developing autonomy of teenagers as they progress through their school life.

Reflective Activity: Committing to Ethical Practices

School staff perspective	School leadership perspective
We are committed to ethical practice and reflect on our practice on an ongoing basis. We discuss ethical dilemmas. We have awareness and respect for diversity.	Ethical leadership is promoted in our school community by ensuring the best use of school resources to support our neurodivergent students.

N: Neurodiversity-Affirmative Needs-Based Planning

Frameworks that identify the needs of students are not new in education. Since the mid-1950s, Maslow's hierarchy of needs has been used to delineate a person's needs in the following five categories, physiological, safety, love, esteem, and self-actualisation. Scott Barry Kaufmann's (2021) transcendence model is a more contemporary approach that promotes needs according to a person's security needs and growth needs. He advises that it is necessary to have both needs met so that individuals can realise their full potential.

This model is particularly applicable to informing planning for neurodivergent students as it promotes the importance of psychological safety to enable a student to thrive in school. To promote basic security needs, he advises that individuals require access to safety, connection, and self-esteem. In the context of a neurodivergent lens, individuals need to feel psychologically safe and have control of their environment. To achieve emotional safety, it is essential that neuro-minorities feel safe with the people around them who are attuned to their needs. For growth needs, an individual requires exploration, love, and purpose. To have fulfilling and enriching school experiences, it is important that neurodivergent students continue to develop to enable them to reach their potential and thrive in school.

Key Takeaways

This chapter outlines the LISTEN meta-framework to foster a values-led neurodiversity-affirmative climate in schools. Its aim was to promote a common language that all members of school communities can use to nurture positive relationships in and around schools to enable everyone to thrive. Key recommendations to consider include the following:

- Engage with community members to seek their views on the LISTEN framework as a shared vision to foster a neurodiversity-affirmative climate in your school community.
- Make an implementation plan using the factors of LISTEN that are adapted specifically to the needs of your school community.
- Use reflective activities to develop and guide the promotion of a shared approach.
- Seek the views of neurodivergent members of your school community on ways the school environment can be adapted to create neurodiversity-affirmative-friendly spaces.

Reference

Kaufmann, S. (2021). *Transcend: The new science of self-actualization*. New York: Penguin Random House.

16

Conclusion
A Shared Journey Forward

Navigating the Path: Acknowledging Challenges and Embracing Possibilities

In this final chapter we want to acknowledge your commitment to joining us on this important journey – exploring the profound potential of the neurodiversity paradigm for not only our learners, but for everyone involved in education. As a reader, you now stand poised to become a vital agent of change, empowered by this new understanding. For the neurodiversity paradigm to embed in education, we need passionate practitioners like you to bring its powerful insights from theory and research into the practical reality of the classroom.

The idea of potential future changes in neurodiversity-affirmative practice is truly inspiring. However, we also want to be honest and acknowledge that deeply engaging with the ideas in this book – whether as a reader, chapter author, or editor – requires significant intellectual effort and a willingness to grapple with new perspectives. This book hasn't offered a superficial overview of neurodiversity; it is not a simple "how-to" manual or a series of quick checklists. Instead, the diverse chapters have presented theoretically complex and sometimes challenging ideas.

Moreover, we recognise the significant systemic changes needed to cultivate authentic inclusion and neurodiversity-affirmative practices. You may feel you are tinkering at the edges, you may or may not have support from your school leaders, you may have to work hard to identify what "neurodiversity-affirmative" means in your day-to-day practice.

To help you, in this chapter we address some of these challenges by offering a clear synthesis of key themes and core understandings, followed by practical, actionable steps to assist you in translating the content of this book into meaningful actions at the individual practitioner, school-wide, and even beyond-school levels.

While it is impossible for one book to encompass every context and address every crucial issue, we look forward with genuine anticipation to witnessing readers using insights from the chapters in transforming individual settings, contexts, and daily practice!

Core Understandings That Support Neurodiversity-Affirmative Practice

Let's take a moment to highlight some of the central understandings underpinning the discussions in this book:

1. **Embracing a New Lens:** Each chapter has been thoughtfully informed by the neurodiversity paradigm. We understand that adopting this relatively new paradigm can sometimes feel like navigating unfamiliar territory, bringing with it challenging ideas, evolving terminology, and possibly a process of unlearning ingrained perspectives.
2. **Bridging the Knowledge Gap:** This book contributes to the field of knowledge and understanding needed by practitioners needed to further embed the neurodiversity paradigm within education.
3. **Shifting Towards Radical Inclusion:** The chapters collectively encourage a fundamental shift away from the ideas of fixing perceived deficits in individuals and a misplaced drive for normalcy, towards equitable and inclusive approaches where all learners are truly valued and included.
4. **Centring Neurodivergent Voices:** This book actively promotes epistemic justice by prioritising learning from the lived experiences and expertise of neurodivergent individuals. All chapters have intentionally included neurodivergent perspectives, and neurodivergent-led theories. For example, Milton's Double Empathy theory and the concept of monotropism have significantly informed the chapters.
5. **Deepening our Understanding:** Although the chapters are varied in tone, author background, and content, collectively they foster a nuanced understanding of the role of the neurodiversity paradigm in education that moves beyond a superficial "neurodiversity-lite" approach. This deeper engagement equips you to critically evaluate approaches and thoughtfully select appropriate teaching resources and methodologies.

6. **Shared Values:** Throughout the book, several core understandings recur. Some concepts that resonate throughout the chapters include belonging, collaboration, intersectionality, relational approaches, person-centred support, environmentally responsive practices, and learner autonomy.
7. **Transforming Educational Experiences:** Ultimately, each chapter contributes to a fundamental shift in focus – moving away from misguided attempts to "fix" the individual learner and instead towards actively improving educational experiences for everyone by:

    - Fostering strong relationships that cultivate a deep sense of belonging
    - Actively recognising and dismantling inequities while providing tailored support for individual challenges
    - Creating flexible and responsive learning environments that offer every individual an equitable opportunity to flourish and thrive
    - Drawing upon insightful neurodivergent-led theories like Double Empathy and monotropism to design creative and truly neurodiversity-affirmative learning experiences

Charting Your Course: Practical Steps for Embracing Change

As you consider how to integrate the neurodiversity paradigm into your practice, here are some practical actions we encourage you to consider:

Embrace Reflection and Growth: Throughout this book, the chapter authors have consistently encouraged you to reflect on your own practice and cultivate a mindset of continuous learning and adaptation. The most impactful teachers are those who embrace reflective practice, constantly learning and refining their approaches based on the unique needs of their learners.

Acknowledge and Navigate Challenges: Reflection involves honestly identifying and acknowledging the challenges you might encounter. We are keenly aware of the significant demands on your time and energy as teachers, including the realities of introducing new approaches. These reflective questions are offered to support you in identifying and navigating potential hurdles:

- Do I feel supported in my environment to experiment with new approaches and view mistakes as learning opportunities?
- How might I proactively address potential resistance from colleagues and/or school leadership?
- How can I realistically integrate these ideas amidst the everyday demands of busy classrooms, numerous initiatives, and competing priorities?

Focus on Positive Impact: We recognise that engaging with the content of these chapters requires effort and commitment. However, we also want to underscore the powerful potential for the positive outcomes that embracing a neurodiversity-informed approach can bring. For instance, Chapter 5 highlighted how creating sensory-friendly environments can lead to increased engagement for many learners, while Chapter 7 explored the power of embracing a compassionate pedagogy to enhance learner engagement and motivation. As you revisit the chapters, we encourage you to reconnect with the many examples of positive change and consider how a similar approach may be impactful in your setting.

Ultimately, making a shift towards the neurodiversity paradigm that is built on values of equity, respect, and acknowledging diversity opens up possibilities for increased learner engagement, improved wellbeing for all, and a richer, more responsive learning environment. While the journey may present some obstacles, the profound positive impact of creating a learning space where every learner feels a deep sense of belonging through experiences of being truly seen, valued, and empowered is immeasurable!

Engage in Gradual and Sustainable Implementation: Remember that change doesn't need to happen all at once. Taking a step-by-step, sustainable approach is key. The "plus one" approach can be a helpful strategy for planning and achieving meaningful change. Some plus one approaches include:

1. To begin, identify just one small, actionable takeaway you can implement in your practice. This could be as simple as using one of the reflective sections from a chapter or experimenting with one of the practical suggestions provided within the chapters. For example, offering a "walk and talk" approach with a learner (see Chapter 8) or using a strong interest of one of your learners as a lesson starter.

Conclusion: A Shared Journey Forward

2. Choose one chapter topic that resonates with you or is relevant to your setting. This could be focusing on introducing one Universal Design for Learning principle in your methods or assessment practices.
3. Select one topic that, although relevant, is challenging. Seek out relevant professional development opportunities – for example, training workshops, podcasts, videos and articles to deepen your understanding.

Cultivate Collaboration: Working together can significantly support the shift towards a more holistic, school-wide approach to the neurodiversity paradigm. Here are some ideas for collaborative practice:

1. Share a brief summary of a chapter that particularly resonated with you with your colleagues during a staff meeting to spark discussion and shared learning.
2. Partner with some colleagues to collaboratively implement one small change in your respective practices and then share your experiences. This could be through informal conversations or a more structured approach like Lesson Study.
3. Organise a book study group with school colleagues, your professional learning network, or community of practice to discuss the ideas in a specific chapter.
4. Explore models and resources outlined in the book like the LISTEN framework, LEANS resources or the Saturation Model collaboratively to evaluate your school's current neurodiversity-related knowledge and practices and identify areas for growth.

Engage in Knowledge Exchange: The transformative potential of the ideas within this book will be amplified as you, our readers, share your examples and experiences of good practice through knowledge exchange. This multiplier effect can be realised through active participation in communities of practice, teach meets, and by engaging in and disseminating action research projects.

A Final Invitation

Regardless of where you are on your journey as a reader and practitioner, your willingness to engage with the neurodiversity paradigm is a truly significant and commendable step. By embracing this paradigm, you are doing so much more than just meeting the needs of neurodivergent learners; you are actively enriching the educational experience for everyone in your classroom and beyond. Neurodiversity-informed practitioners like you are instrumental in fostering future generations that deeply understand, genuinely value, and celebrate the diversity of human minds. This is not just effective teaching; it is truly transformative practice. We warmly welcome you on this vital journey towards a more inclusive, hopeful, and equitable future for all!

Index

ableism 103–104, 190
activity/ies: group 112; "Headteacher for the day" 45; participatory 130; *see also* reflective activities/practice
ADHD 103, 136; breaktimes and 23; diagnosis 137–138; working memory and 136
agency 25, 27–28
anxiety 76–77, 143, 254; -based nonattendance 128; thought loops 95–96; *see also* stress
artificial intelligence 140, 142
assessment: needs 141–142; neurodivergence 138–139; *see also* diagnosis
assistive technology 140, 142
attendance: *can't not won't* 89–90; unaddressed needs and 26, 92, 103, 128, 218
attention 141, 223
Attention, Monotropism, and the Diagnostic Criteria for Autism 86–87
autism/autistic 23, 72, 103; critical studies 220; differences 219–220; identity 227–228; inertia 87; interventions 222; masking 227–228; pathologisation 221–222; research 220; self-esteem and 88; stigma 221, 227–228
autonomy 25, 27–28, 105; group 111; structure and 26; student 168; teacher 109

"behaviour" 76–77
Belonging in School 107; *see also* sense of belongingbias 138, 164; implicit 103–104; negative 104
breaktimes 1, 169–170; ADHD and 23; green spaces 22; neurodivergent children 23–26; restricting as punishment 22, 25; staff roles during 29–30; structure 25–26
bullying 1, 22–26, 37, 78, 248
burnout 91–92, 136

calm environment, creating 246–247
camouflaging 120, 199–200
Casson, Devin 57; on SPaRKs 59–63
chair committee 40–41
Chapple, Elly, "flipping the narrative" 81
Character Strengths 151–153, 156; -based language 154–157; and inclusive education 156–157; interventions 154
Child Q 139
choosing, playground equipment 8–11
Churchill Fellowship 38
classroom: flexible seating 40–41; neuro-inclusive 112
collaboration/collaborative 40, 45, 49, 54; cultivating 263; learning 110–112; music 62; teacher-student 74
collective self-esteem 202–203
communication 189; in autistic young people 223; hesitation 122; listening 108, 141; multiple means of action and expression 173; non-verbal 130–131; polytropic 87; strengths-based language 154–157; style 122–123; teacher discourse 155; total 237; voice 121–125
community, building 167–168
competence 105; neurodivergent learner 120–121; staff 149–150
consistency: constant 80; in teaching 73–75
coping mechanisms 76–77, 124
co-production 74, 81, 220–221, 227

265

Index

creativity 62–63, 141
curriculum: inclusive 77–78

demand avoidance 87, 90–91
developmental language disorder, play initiation 24–25
diagnosis: ADHD 137–138; neurodivergence 37
disability: competency-based models 150; discrimination 23–26, 37; environment and 4; in films 78; medical model approach 155; rights 21
discrimination 138, 183; disability 23–26, 37; marginalised groups 103–105, 229
diversity: -lite approaches 149–150; play 23
Double Empathy Problem (DEP) 90, 120, 201
draw and talk approach 129–130
dyslexia 137, 141, 171
dysregulation 75–76, 81

education: autism-friendly 72; home 28; inclusive 27, 36–37, 143–145, 154, 156–157; positive 149–150; rights-based 107; variability 165; youth-led approach 64
emotions/emotional: alienation 26; contagion 109; environment 244; fear 229; loneliness 24; safety 108–109
empathy 72, 120, 228; reflective practice 255
engagement: access to content and materials 173; connecting prior knowledge 172–173; embed predictable routines and clear expectations 169–170; embedding choice 174; foster belonging and community 167–168; goal-setting and self-monitoring 174; media and format options 170–171; multiple means of action and expression 173; multiple means of representation 170; optimise choice and autonomy 168; optimise relevance and value 168–169; visual cues and systems 171–172
environment: calm, creating 246–247; communication 244–245; emotional 244; internal 245; physical 243; processing 243–244; sensory 244; social 244
expressive language skills 140–141

feedback: student 175
felt safety 217–219, 228
fidgeting/stimming 23, 36, 88, 95, 124, 129–130
Fisher, N. 88, 90
flexible seating 38–39, 49–50; chair committee 40–41; leadership buy-in 43–44; pupil voice 45–46; research 43–44; staff voice 47–48; whole-school approach 41–43
flow 112, 152
following instructions 141, 143
forest school 27–28

goal/s: -setting 174
green spaces: breaktimes 22; playground 7, 14

health and safety *see* safety
home education 28, 218
hyper-focus 88, 246

identity 165; autistic 227–228
implicit bias 103–104
inclusion/inclusive: creating a calming sensory environment 246–247; curriculum 77–78; design 29–30; differentiation 23; education 27, 36–37, 143–145, 154, 156–157; environmental influences 243–245; groups 110; language 153–154; learning 71; 78; 103; play 29–30; playground design 3; playground equipment 8–9; radical 90–92; shared decision making 239; total communication approaches 237; understanding and promoting transitions 250
"Incubator Sessions" 58
interoception 77–78, 246
intersectionality 107, 219; "Double Rainbow" 200
intersubjectivity 111–112
interventions 78; autism 222; medical model 104; Positive Psychology 149–150; wellbeing 154
intrinsic motivation 90, 92–93
It Takes All Kinds of Minds conference 67, 138

Kaufmann, Barry, transcendence model 257–258
Kilpatrick, R. 120–121

knock-on effect 142, 201, 221
knowledge 71; exchange 263; Knightsmith on 72

language: inclusive 153–154; reflective activity 238; strengths-based 154–157; *see also* communication
leadership: buy-in, flexible seating 43–44
learning/learners: collaborative 110–112; embedding choice 174; feedback 175; goal-setting and self-monitoring 174; inclusive 71; intersectional 139–140; love of 224; Low Arousal approach 75–76; 96nature-based 28; niche construction 149; polytropic 97; variability 165; visual systems 171–172; *see also* engagement
Low Arousal approach 75–76, 246–247
Low Arousal Supports Educational Resilience (LASER) *see* LASER Approach
Lundy Model 120–121, 123; audience 127; influence 127–129; space 126; voice 124–126

Mahler, Kelly 77–78
masking 37, 74, 87, 109, 199–200, 227–228
Maslow's hierarchy of needs 257
mentoring 63–64
Milton, Damian 72, 93, 120, 201
questionnaire 87–88, 96; movement breaks 169–170
multiple means of representation 170
Murray, Dinah 86
Music with Erin 52

nature-based learning 28
needs: assessment 141–142; autistic children 220; intersectional student 241; Maslow's hierarchy of 257; security 257–258
neuroconstructivism 21, 23–24
non-verbal communication 130–131

"othering" 155–156, 169, 220
outdoor play 3; policy 11–15; weather and 13; *see also* playground
overstimulation, reducing 9

parallel play 91
passion 89

pedagogy 149; inclusive 67–68, 78, 103; play-based 27; reflective practice 109
peer: interactions 111; modeling 24–25; support 203–204
play 1, 141; -based pedagogy 27; diversity in 23; fidget toys 36; fixed 22; free 25–26; group 111–112; inclusive 29–30; initiation 24–25; loose parts 10–11, 22; parallel 91; policy 11–15; prompts and cues 9; recuperative function 20; soft 27; solitary 24; spaces, for adolescents 14–15; structure 25–26; wellbeing and 20; *see also* breaktimes
playground: accessibility choosing play equipment 8–11. *See also* equipment, playground; equipment 10–11; green spaces 7, 14; inclusive design 3; inclusive equipment 8–9; layout and design 5; markings 9; orientation path 6; post-primary 13–14; transitional spaces 6; Universal Design (UD) 4, 7–8; zoning 5–6
"plus one" approach 262–263
policy 77; 'Getting It Right For Every Child' 201; open-door 41; play 11–15; and practice 74–75
polytropic learners 87, 97
Positive Education 149–150; inclusive language 153–154
Positive Psychology 148–150
post-primary play spaces 13–14
practice: -informed research 38; policy and 74–75
privilege, neurotypical 105–106
proprioception 9, 246–247
psychology, positive *see* Positive Psychology
punishment, restricted breaktime 22, 25

radical inclusion 90–92
recess *see* breaktimes; playground
reflective activities/practice 16, 31, 49, 66, 83, 98, 109, 113, 131, 158–159, 176, 190, 225–228; acting with integrity 240; advancing equitable practices 256; committing to ethical practices 257; fostering an environment of trust 252; fostering trauma-informed practices 249; impact of time on change processes 253; planning and supporting transitions 251; promoting a positive

Index

school system 242; promoting empathetic engagements 255; promoting positive use of space 245; raising awareness of intersectional needs 241; raising awareness of sensory sensitivities 247; school leadership 236; thinking about use of language 238
research: assistants 45; autism 220; flexible seating 43–44; pupil voice 45–46; rights-informed 120–121
resilience 81, 229
rights: -based education 107; of disabled children 21; -informed research 120–121
risk assessment: forest school 28; outdoor play 13
routines 9, 25, 80–81, 95; flexible 96; forest school 28; predictable 169–170 emotional 108–109; outdoor play 13; risk assessment 13; Saturation Model 79–80

scaffolding 143, 173, 175
school/s: breaktimes 22; distress 90; forest 28; inclusive culture 143–144; 212safety. *See* safety; stakeholders 12; vision for outdoor play 12–13
Scotland, 'Getting It Right For Every Child' policy 201
security needs 257–258
self-esteem: autism and 88; collective 202–203
self-regulation 21, 73, 77–78
Seligman, M. E. 149, 152; PERMA model 150
sense of belonging 74–75, 94, 144, 167–168
sensory: environment 244; overload 26–27; profiles 11, 26–27, **36**rooms 36; support 36–37; systems 246
situated content, teaching 186, 196
social, emotional, and mental health (SEMH) 135, 140
Social Determination Theory (SDT) 104–105
social groups 202; collective self-esteem 202–203; peer support 203–204
social skills 111–112
special education needs and disabilities (SEND) 37–38, 155–156, 224

speech and language therapy 141–142
staff 13; cultural competency 149–150; mentoring 63–64; roles and responsibilities during breaktime 29–30; training 26; views on flexible seating 47–48
stakeholders, school 12
stammering 106
stigma 37, 104, 138; autism 221, 227–228
stimming *see* fidgeting/stimming
strengths-based language 154–157
stress 26, 76–77; burnout 136; reduction 81–82; teacher 102
structure: autonomy and 26; forest school routines 28; play 25–26

teachers and teaching: autonomy 109; consistency 73–75; discourse 155; instructional inadequacy 109; Islands of Safety 225–228; Low Arousal approach 75–76. *See also* quality 67; situated content 186, 196; stress 102; support 156
"them and us" mentality 104–105
therapy: occupational 38; speech and language 141–142
"think sensory" 26–27
training: autism awareness 227; staff 26–27
transcendence model 257–258
transitions/transitional: planning and supporting 251; spaces, playgrounds 6; understanding and promoting 250
trauma 76–77; -informed practice 248
trust 94; fostering an environment of 252

UN Convention on the Rights of the Child 204; Article 12 12, 123, 234–235; Article 23 21; Article 31 11, 21
Universal Design for Learning (UDL) 164, 175–177; multiple means of engagement 167; variability 165–166; *see also* engagement
Universal Design (UD) 29–30; playgrounds 4–5, 7. *See also* playground

values 107, 113, 173, 204; in action 152; -based education 234–238, 242, 252
visual learning 171–172

walk and talk approach 129, 262–263
WEIRD (Western, Educated, Industrialized, Rich, Democratic) 219
wellbeing 3, 104–105, 149; interventions 154; play and 20; resource 124–126; and social connectedness 150
whole-school approach 94, 128; flexible seating 41–43; LASER Approach 81–82; Saturation Model 79–80; to sensory support 36–37
working memory 136, 140; neurodivergence and 142–143

For Product Safety Concerns and Information please contact our EU representative GPSR@taylorandfrancis.com
Taylor & Francis Verlag GmbH, Kaufingerstraße 24, 80331 München, Germany

www.ingramcontent.com/pod-product-compliance
Lightning Source LLC
Chambersburg PA
CBHW071813230426
43670CB00013B/2445